Steps to Good Grammar

169 Lessons, Exercises, and Tests

by Genevieve Walberg Schaefer

J. WESTON
WALCH
PUBLISHER
PORTLAND, MAINE

User's Guide
to
Walch Reproducible Books

As part of our general effort to provide educational materials which are as practical and economical as possible, we have designated this publication a "reproducible book." The designation means that purchase of the book includes purchase of the right to limited reproduction of all pages on which this symbol appears:

Here is the basic Walch policy: We grant to individual purchasers of this book the right to make sufficient copies of reproducible pages for use by all students of a single teacher. This permission is limited to a single teacher, and does not apply to entire schools or school systems, so institutions purchasing the book should pass the permission on to a single teacher. Copying of the book or its parts for resale is prohibited.

Any questions regarding this policy or requests to purchase further reproduction rights should be addressed to:

Permissions Editor
J. Weston Walch, Publisher
321 Valley Street • P. O. Box 658
Portland, Maine 04104-0658

1   2   3   4   5   6   7   8   9   10

ISBN 0-8251-2876-5

Copyright © 1988, 1997
J. Weston Walch, Publisher
P.O. Box 658 • Portland, Maine 04104-0658

Printed in the United States of America

CONTENTS

INTRODUCTION

Steps to Good Grammar, a sequential series of worksheets for duplication with accompanying teaching guide pages, is an analytical, systematic, repetitive, and cumulative method of helping students to understand the basic unit of communication, the sentence. It covers the grammar included in most seventh-grade English books. The manner of development is compatible with the mental maturity of adolescents and satisfies their need to experience success.

Students in this age group enjoy analytical learning. In *Steps to Good Grammar* they are given instruction in analyzing simply worded definitions, rules, and the relationships that exist among the various sentence parts. They are easily led to understand all the parts of sentences in whatever patterns the sentences are arranged.

Each sentence part is explained in a separate unit. It is defined in simplified traditional terms, it is given a graphic symbol of identification, and it is used in sample sentences which are then presented in diagram form. Finally, it is included for analytical recognition in the practice sentences, along with all the previously learned elements.

This repetitious, cumulative method assures the students' retention of understandings they assimilate as they progress through the study.

Students of all ability levels enjoy learning by this simple, explicit method which presents a single small goal in each unit. Many who have become convinced that they cannot achieve discover that by expending just enough effort to complete the first assignment, they too can earn scores of 100. Having easily reached the first small goal, they anticipate being and are, in fact, successful in reaching each additional small goal.

Students who have been accustomed to being successful respond enthusiastically to the obvious, pure logic of a system that enables them to understand the English sentence as clearly as they understand various principles of mathematics.

The study progresses from the most rudimentary sentence, the simple subject-verb form, to sentences containing sophisticated word arrangements with a variety of complements and modifiers. This developmental approach helps students to gain control over their sentences and to increase their ability to communicate grammatically and meaningfully.

By understanding sentence parts, students are able to apply, both in speaking and writing, the principles of correct usage that pertain to them. They have the basis for utilizing more advanced forms of sentence structure.

Students who understand sentence parts share a "language" that their teacher may use to make specific suggestions to the students for improving their original writings. Students, themselves, acquire the knowledge they need to proofread or edit their own writings and those of others.

Studies strongly indicate that students who understand the composition of sentences read with greater comprehension.

Knowing how to use their tools is an absolute prerequisite for shop students in producing superior projects. Similarly, knowing how to form effective, grammatical sentences is an absolute prerequisite for academic-course students in producing creative, expressive writings.

USING THE MATERIALS

Steps to Good Grammar contains facing pairs of pages. Each reproducible student page is accompanied by a Teacher's Guide page that contains teaching suggestions, explanatory notes, supplemental information, proposed grading scales where appropriate, and an answer key for the exercises on the student page.

Many pages for duplication in *Steps to Good Grammar* serve a dual purpose. One page may include two copies of one half-page drill; another, two separate half-page drills; another, a half-page final drill and a half-page unit test. Check all pages to be sure that only the number you need are duplicated.

For each reproducible student page with two copies of one half-page drill, the Teacher's Guide page carries this notice:

> This reproducible page contains two copies of one half-page drill/test. Cut each duplicated page in half; give each student one half-page.

You will notice that some time-honored definitions and terms usually applied to the study of grammar are not used here. Among the many are transitive and intransitive verbs, abstract and concrete nouns, noun adjuncts, adjectivals, and intensifiers. Distinguishing among classes of the different parts of speech is not essential to students' understanding of sentences.

The term "predicate" is not used, since it refers to nothing specific and may contain a great variety of different individual parts. Instead, the students are led to a firm understanding of the verb and of all sentence parts that affect or are affected by the verb.

"The verb is the word that tells what is being done in the sentence and/or is one of the twenty-three helping verbs."

Every student is required to memorize the list of helping verbs. In the definition, the concept of "what is being done" or the term "doing" is preferred to "action," since students easily recognize a verb as being something *they can do.*

"The pyramids have been standing for thousands of years."

(Not much "action" there! But what have they been *doing?*)

The concept of "doing" is especially helpful to students in identifying adjectives following linking verbs and adverbs following doing verbs:

"Mom was tired." (Can you *do* tired?)

"Joe ran quickly." (Can you *do* quickly?")

A "say and ask" system enables students to recognize and understand sentence parts related to the verb. Say the verb and ask "Who?" or "What?" before it. The word that answers the question is the subject. Say the subject and verb and ask "What object?" The word that answers the question is the direct object. Say the subject, the verb, and the direct object and ask, "Who got it?" The word that answers the question is the indirect object. Thus students recognize nouns and pronouns according to their relationship to the verb in the sentence.

Nominative and objective personal pronouns are almost always misused only when more than one are used in any sentence part. Therefore, immediately after students have studied the use of nouns in a particular sentence part, they are instructed in the use of two or more pronouns in that position.

Students learn that adjectives and prepositional phrases used as adjectives tell *which one, what kind, how many,* and *whose* about the nouns they modify. By analyzing the added meaning adjectives and adjective phrases give to nouns, students easily recognize them and begin to use them correctly and expressively.

Adverbs give added meanings of *how, when, and where* to verbs and of *how much* to adjectives and adverbs. Adverbial phrases give a fourth meaning of *why* to verbs. With these understandings, students use adverbs correctly and interestingly.

Following the units that contain sentences with "doing" verbs, students are given instruction in the use of linking verbs. Since the term "predicate" has not been used, "linking verb complement-noun" or "linking verb complement-adjective" is used. These lengthy labels are abbreviated LVC-N and LVC-A. Complement is defined as "completer." It *completes* the meaning of the sentence.

Once students fully comprehend the parts of speech and parts of sentences, they are in a position to apply understandingly the principles of correctness. The use of nominative and objective pronouns is reviewed completely on pages 176-185. The remainder of *Steps to Good Grammar* is devoted to a thorough coverage of correct usage applied to all sentence parts.

* * * *

It is important that you allot some class time every day to sentence study in order to keep the procedures and the acquired learnings fresh in your students' minds.

Particularly when introducing each new element, you should instruct your students to verbalize every step in analyzing the practice sentences. Suppose the new element is the *appositive* and the sentence is:

"Yesterday, my uncle gave my little brother Joey a new skateboard."

Each student should say:

1. Gave is the verb; draw two lines under it.
2. Uncle is the subject; draw one line under it.
3. Uncle gave what object? Skateboard is the direct object; write **D.O.** above it.

4. Who got it? Brother is the indirect object; write **I.O.** above it.
5. Joey is the appositive that identifies brother; write **Appos.** above it.
6. Yesterday is an adverb that tells "when" about the verb; put brackets around it.
7. My, my, little, a, and new are adjectives; draw circles around them.

This takes time! But, as one student is reading aloud and identifying the sentence parts, the others are listening, reading silently, and thinking and writing their own identification symbols. Finally, as you read the sentence and approve the correct identification of the sentence parts, all students are able to correct any mistakes they may have made.

We know that the study of grammar as a separate entity does little to improve students' ability to write and speak well. Therefore, students need to realize that the main benefit from such study is the acquisition of understandings that will enable them to speak and write effectively and expressively. Their learnings are tools for them to use.

The over-all objective of *Steps to Good Grammar,* with its repetitious procedures, is that grammatical, effective use of their language will become a natural, almost intuitive part of students' thinking, speaking, and writing.

Steps to GOOD GRAMMAR

169 LESSONS, EXERCISES, and TESTS

PRETEST: RECOGNIZING VERBS

> This reproducible page contains two copies of one half-page drill/test. Cut each duplicated page in half; give each student one half-page.

A pretest is an important exploratory device for determining how firm a background each student has on the material being covered. Some may have an excellent understanding; others may have very little knowledge.

In announcing this pretest, explain to students that the scores they receive on it in no way affect their report card grades. The results will merely indicate what they understand and what they need to learn about recognizing verbs.

While handing out the papers, *give absolutely no instruction as to what a verb is.* In response to possible questions, simply say that students should remember what they have learned in the past and should draw two lines under all verb words. Assure them that after a few days of study they will have no trouble at all in recognizing verbs.

You can give a two-part score. One part reflects the student's ability to recognize actual verb words. Since there are 26 verb words, each one has an approximate value of 4%. If 5 were not underlined, the score would be 80%.

The second part of the score takes into account underlining of words that are not verbs. Give each of these words a 2% value. If 6 nonverbs were underlined, the 12% reflecting that lack of understanding should be subtracted from the 80%.

The two-part score would be 80%/68%. When returning the papers, explain the scores so that each student can concentrate on clearing up any confusion he or she may have had.

1. These flowers were grown in Hawaii.
2. Did those boots fit you?
3. Ted must really have worked hard for that prize.
4. Had Dad changed his mind?
5. The students should have checked their work.
6. Mary will be leaving soon.
7. The sun suddenly disappeared behind a cloud.
8. The man baked a chocolate cake.
9. Why didn't you answer?
10. The little girl walked into the house and called her mother.
11. Can this set of shelves be moved?
12. Sue had not gone to school.

VERBS

PRETEST: Recognizing Verbs

Instructions: Draw two lines under each *verb* word.

1. These flowers were grown in Hawaii.
2. Did those boots fit you?
3. Ted must really have worked hard for that prize.
4. Had Dad changed his mind?
5. The students should have checked their work.
6. Mary will be leaving soon.
7. The sun suddenly disappeared behind a cloud.
8. The man baked a chocolate cake.
9. Why didn't you answer?
10. The little girl walked into the house and called her mother.
11. Can this set of shelves be moved?
12. Sue had not gone to school.

NAME _____ DATE _____ 3

VERBS

PRETEST: Recognizing Verbs

Instructions: Draw two lines under each *verb* word.

1. These flowers were grown in Hawaii.
2. Did those boots fit you?
3. Ted must really have worked hard for that prize.
4. Had Dad changed his mind?
5. The students should have checked their work.
6. Mary will be leaving soon.
7. The sun suddenly disappeared behind a cloud.
8. The man baked a chocolate cake.
9. Why didn't you answer?
10. The little girl walked into the house and called her mother.
11. Can this set of shelves be moved?
12. Sue had not gone to school.

© 1988, 1997 J. Weston Walch, Publisher

Steps to Good Grammar

RECOGNIZING VERBS

1. Read aloud, as students read silently, all the material up to Practice.

2. Instruct students to memorize the définition of a verb and, in order, the list of twenty-three helping verbs.

3. Remind students, if there is resistance to memorizing the list in the order given, that they have memorized many things in order during their years in school:

   (a) They can all say the twenty-six letters of the alphabet in order.
   (b) They can all count in order from 1 to 100, and beyond.
   (c) Of course they can memorize the twenty-three helping verbs in order.

4. Inform students that they will be asked to write the list perfectly the next day at the beginning of class, and also on the next two days. Perfect writing on three successive days firmly implants the words in their minds.

5. A grade incentive can be successful.

   (a) Give each student who writes the list perfectly the first day 100% or *A+*. For perfect writing the second day, add a check: 100% ✓. For perfect writing the third day, the 100% becomes an important test grade.

   (b) Students who make a mistake the first day but write the list perfectly the second day earn 90% or *A−*. Perfect writing the second time receives a 90% ✓; for the third perfect writing, 90% becomes a permanent test grade.

   (c) Students who write perfectly for the first time on the third day can earn 85% or *B* and must write the list perfectly two more times to earn a permanent *B*.

   (d) All students should be required to memorize and write, or say, the list perfectly three times. After-school sessions may be necessary. The lowest grade recorded for completing the assignment should be 75% or *C*. Knowing that they can earn at least a *C* could help the few resistant students to do the memorizing.

6. Guide students in completing the Practice exercises to establish their understanding of the information given about verbs, which will be used throughout *Steps to Good Grammar.*

   - Sentence 1: Point out that *very, fast,* and *around* are not verb words because you can't *do* them, and they are not on the list of helping verbs.

   - Sentence 2: Point out that many questions begin with a helping verb.

7. Collect and check papers, record scores, and return papers to students the next day.

1. Joe <u><u>had run</u></u> very fast around the track.
   a. The helping verb is: *had*   b. The doing verb is: *run*
   c. The complete verb is: *had run*

2. <u><u>Did</u></u> anyone <u>run</u> faster than Joe?
   a. The helping verb is: *Did*   b. The doing verb is: *run*
   c. The complete verb is: *Did run*
   d. Why is *faster* not a verb word? *You can't do "faster" and it's not in the list of helping verbs.*

3. Joe's record <u><u>was</u></u> not <u>broken</u> by anyone.
   a. The helping verb is: *was*   b. The doing verb is: *broken*
   c. The complete verb is: *was broken*
   d. Why is *not* not a verb word? *You can't do "not," and it's not in the list of helping verbs.*

VERBS

Recognizing Verbs

In sentence study, the first word to recognize and understand is the *verb*.

DEFINITION: The **verb** is the word that *tells what is being done* in the sentence, and/or is *one of the twenty-three helping verbs.*

DOING VERBS are words that *can be done* — you can do them.
You can *go, stand, believe, refuse, nominate, give, jump.*

HELPING VERBS are often *used with doing verbs* to give exact meaning:

Sue <u>tries</u>.   Sue <u>was trying</u>.   Sue <u>will try</u>.   Sue <u>had tried</u>.

Sue <u>could be trying</u>.   Sue <u>should have tried</u>.

In all six sentences, <u>try</u> is the doing verb; the subject is <u>Sue</u>. The helping verbs give the sentences very different meanings.

1. **Memorize,** *in order,* this list of twenty-three helping verbs:

   is, am, are, was, were, be, being, been; has, have, had; do, does, did; shall, will, should, would; may, might, must; can, could

   Recognize them as easily as you do the letter *A* or the number 1.

2. Some of these verbs may be the only verb words in the sentence:

   He <u>has had</u> many successes.   She always <u>does</u> her homework.

PRACTICE: In each sentence below, look for "helping verbs" that you memorized; look for "doing verbs" that can be done; draw two lines under the verb words; write answers in the blank spaces.

1. Joe had run very fast around the track.

   a. The helping verb is: _____   b. The doing verb is: _____

   c. The complete verb is: _____   _____

2. Did anyone run faster than Joe?

   a. The helping verb is: _____   b. The doing verb is: _____

   c. The complete verb is: _____   _____

   d. Why is *faster* not a verb word? _____

   _____

3. Joe's record was not broken by anyone.

   a. The helping verb is: _____   b. The doing verb is: _____

   c. The complete verb is: _____   _____

   d. Why is *not* not a verb word? _____

   _____

© 1988, 1997 J. Weston Walch, Publisher

Steps to Good Grammar

SUBSTANTIATION!

> This reproducible page contains 5 copies of a one-fifth page list of verbs. Cut each duplicated page in fifths and give each student one fifth-page.

Memorizing the list of helping verbs in order is a valid first assignment. Here's why:

1. It is a sufficiently challenging task.

2. All students can memorize the list without too much difficulty.

3. Successful memorization gives students a real feeling of successful accomplishment.

4. Instant recall of the words provides a firm base for future understanding.

5. Successful recognition of the complete verb in every sentence becomes an easy task.

6. All students can earn a high grade on the unit test.

7. Students develop an expectancy of being successful.

8. Past successes are the strongest motivators for achievement.

9. Most sentences in *Steps to Good Grammar* contain verbs with "helpers"; understanding verbs and their helpers is a prerequisite for sentence study.

    (a) All other sentence parts hinge around the verb.

    (b) A firm base for understanding the relationship among all sentence parts is established.

    (c) Students develop a knowledge of good sentence structure.

    (d) The quality of their original writings improves.

    (e) Improved reading comprehension is a natural concomitant to understanding sentence structure.

*** Of Interest ***

Each helping verb is used to convey a variety of meanings. Consider the word *would*. According to the *Funk and Wagnalls Standard College Dictionary*, *would* was originally used as the past tense of *will*.

Currently, we use *would* as a true past to express habit or custom:

"In those days, I would ride my horse every day."

In certain verb phrases we use *would* as past tense: *would have, would have had, would have been*:

"I would have volunteered if I had known he needed help."

Other meanings expressed by *would*:

1. Intention: I said I would go.

2. Desire: He would like to go.

3. Condition: I would go if I could.

4. Determination: I decided I would not go.

5. Request: Would you give me a call tomorrow?

6. Preference: I would rather see you elected than Joe.

7. Probability: His leaving would have serious consequences.

8. Possibility: It would seem that I was wrong.

9. Futurity: He was looking for something that would please his wife.

HELPING VERBS

Memorize this list *in order* so that you can write the verbs perfectly.

IS	BE	HAS	DO	SHALL	MAY	CAN
AM	BEING	HAVE	DOES	WILL	MIGHT	COULD
ARE	BEEN	HAD	DID	SHOULD	MUST	
WAS				WOULD		
WERE						

HELPING VERBS

Memorize this list *in order* so that you can write the verbs perfectly.

IS	BE	HAS	DO	SHALL	MAY	CAN
AM	BEING	HAVE	DOES	WILL	MIGHT	COULD
ARE	BEEN	HAD	DID	SHOULD	MUST	
WAS				WOULD		
WERE						

HELPING VERBS

Memorize this list *in order* so that you can write the verbs perfectly.

IS	BE	HAS	DO	SHALL	MAY	CAN
AM	BEING	HAVE	DOES	WILL	MIGHT	COULD
ARE	BEEN	HAD	DID	SHOULD	MUST	
WAS				WOULD		
WERE						

HELPING VERBS

Memorize this list *in order* so that you can write the verbs perfectly.

IS	BE	HAS	DO	SHALL	MAY	CAN
AM	BEING	HAVE	DOES	WILL	MIGHT	COULD
ARE	BEEN	HAD	DID	SHOULD	MUST	
WAS				WOULD		
WERE						

HELPING VERBS

Memorize this list *in order* so that you can write the verbs perfectly.

IS	BE	HAS	DO	SHALL	MAY	CAN
AM	BEING	HAVE	DOES	WILL	MIGHT	COULD
ARE	BEEN	HAD	DID	SHOULD	MUST	
WAS				WOULD		
WERE						

Steps to Good Grammar

DRILL 1

Suggestions:

1. Completing drill and practice work:

   (a) Direct class in analyzing half of the sentences.

   (b) Students then complete the exercise silently on their own.

   (c) Volunteers read sentences and describe their markings.

2. Students may correct in class:

   (a) Students keep their own papers, changing any errors they may have made and writing correct forms.

   (b) Students handing in completely correct papers earn 100%.

   (c) Each error not corrected lowers recorded grade by 5%.

   Understanding this system of rewards and penalties induces students to listen and stay on task. Correcting your own errors is an important phase of learning.

3. Teacher may correct:

   (a) Students want papers corrected and returned promptly.

   (b) Paper-correcting can become a monumental task.

   (c) Justified simplification:

   i. Select and check each student's work on one section.

   ii. Select and check each student's work on certain sentences most indicative of students' understanding: Part I—2, 5; Part II — 1, 3, 4, 9, 10, 12, 13, and 14.

   (d) Make clear to students the section or sentences checked.

   (e) The grade recorded for the selected items is fairly representative of the student's work on the entire page.

4. Homework:

   (a) Students gain confidence and experience the greatest success by completing the papers in class under teacher supervision.

   (b) Occasionally you may assign a paper begun in class for completion as homework; correct as above.

Procedure:

1. First writing of list of helping verbs.

2. Call special attention to Reminder items.

3. Reinforce concepts introduced on page 6.

---

1. Just then my sister screamed.
2. My horse walked slowly along.
3. Don usually mows the lawn.
4. Hailstones bounced off the roof.
5. That man installs swimming pools.
6. For once Bill came early.
7. Dad shook his head at me.
8. A sports car roared past us.
9. The squirrel chattered noisily.
10. Tom finished his homework.

---

1. Roger has won the election for student body president.
2. This bill must be paid within thirty days.
3. Plans are already being made for the class trip.
4. Our ship will be sailing early in the morning.
5. Mom is planting all the gladiolus bulbs.
6. Our neighbor had held that job for twenty-five years.
7. Stan may have a good idea for campus improvement.
8. Sonya usually does have her pen. →
9. Have your cousins arrived from Sweden?
10. Why shouldn't Jill tell me the reason? →
11. Gary usually doesn't drive very fast. →
12. Could he have gone with us to the beach?
13. Did Mrs. Spade tell you about her travels in South America?
14. The little boy was being teased by his big brother.
15. Do you recognize verb words now?

VERBS

DRILL 1: Locating Verbs in Sentences

Part I. Instructions: *Think* what is being done in each sentence. Draw two lines under the *verb* words that tell *what is being done*.

1. Just then my sister screamed.
2. My horse walked slowly along.
3. Don usually mows the lawn.
4. Hailstones bounced off the roof.
5. That man installs swimming pools.
6. For once Bill came early.
7. Dad shook his head at me.
8. A sports car roared past us.
9. The squirrel chattered noisily.
10. Tom finished his homework.

HELPING VERBS

Be sure you have memorized these!

is	be	has	do	shall	may	can
am	being	have	does	will	might	could
are	been	had	did	should	must	
was				would		
were						

Part II. Instructions: Draw two lines under each *helping verb* and under each *verb* word that tells *what is being done*.

1. Roger has won the election for student body president.
2. This bill must be paid within thirty days.
3. Plans are already being made for the class trip.
4. Our ship will be sailing early in the morning.
5. Mom is planting all the gladiolus bulbs.
6. Our neighbor had held that job for twenty-five years.
7. Stan may have a good idea for campus improvement.
8. Sonya usually does have her pen. →

    > **Reminder:** Sometimes the complete verb is made up of verbs you memorized.

9. Have your cousins arrived from Sweden?
10. Why shouldn't Jill tell me the reason? →

    > **Reminder:** *n't* should not be underlined; *n't* is a contraction of *not*.

11. Gary usually doesn't drive very fast. →
12. Could he have gone with us to the beach?
13. Did Mrs. Spade tell you about her travels in South America?
14. The little boy was being teased by his big brother.
15. Do you recognize verb words now?

> **Reminder:** Every sentence ends with a mark of punctuation!

Steps to Good Grammar

DRILLS 2 & 3

This reproducible page contains two different half-page drills/tests. You may cut each duplicated page in half and give each student one half-page at a time, or you may distribute the entire duplicated page and work one drill/test at a time.

Remember: Have students write the list of helping verbs.

Drill 2

Sentence 10: If students suggest that *lurch* is a verb, point out the true verb: *had startled* is what was *done*. The thing that *had startled* us was the lurch.

Drill 3

Reinforce the fact that nonverbs should *never* be underlined because they can't be done, and they're not in the list of helping verbs.

Sentence 12: Someone may question *as he*; actually, *he* is the subject of an understood verb — as he (*can run*). Elliptical clauses will be taken up much later in this book.

Sentence 20: Yes, people can *do* the word *work*. However, here *work* is the *thing* you *might check*.

Possibly Drill 3 could be assigned for homework after working Drill 2 in class.

1. John slid quickly down the pole.   2. Possibly she believed the gossip.

3. Was that your sister?   4. Dr. Jones introduced us to her husband.

5. Who was that?   6. The dog jumped over the fence.

7. My sister and I walk to school.   8. Pete sneaked quietly from the room.

9. Martha might have finished the project.   10. The sudden lurch of the bus had startled us.

11. Pedro will ask her.   12. Dad does drive Mom's car.

13. Joan will have left by now.   14. The conductor must have found it.

15. Has Lisa finished her homework?   16. Couldn't you do the math problems?

17. When will he return the tickets?   18. Have you ever answered her letter?

19. Bryan must not have known about the parade.   20. This ends the drill!

---

1. Where was your book?   2. My brothers played football all morning.

3. Dad told us a strange story.   4. The United States flag waves in the breeze.

5. Why did Juanita come home early today?   6. An old woman was seen on the corner.

7. Betty will be leaving soon.   8. Sasha could have lost her ring on the bus.

9. Must you do your homework now?   10. You should have been helping me with the dishes.

11. Did Carl hit the ball over the fence?   12. Can you run as fast as he?

13. Has Jared ever tried that before?   14. Matt is playing the part of Scrooge.

15. The costumes have not yet arrived.   16. Does that dog whine all the time?

17. Something must have happened to Uncle Don.   18. He has never done that before.

19. I may be going to Hawaii next summer.   20. You might check your work!

VERBS

DRILL 2: Locating Verbs in Sentences

Instructions: Draw two lines under the verb words.

1. John slid quickly down the pole.   2.   Possibly she believed the gossip.

3. Was that your sister?   4.   Dr. Jones introduced us to her husband.

5. Who was that?   6.   The dog jumped over the fence.

7. My sister and I walk to school.   8.   Pete sneaked quietly from the room.

9. Martha might have finished the project.   10.   The sudden lurch of the bus had startled us.

11. Pedro will ask her.   12.   Dad does drive Mom's car.

13. Joan will have left by now.   14.   The conductor must have found it.

15. Has Lisa finished her homework?   16.   Couldn't you do the math problems?

17. When will he return the tickets?   18.   Have you ever answered her letter?

19. Bryan must not have known about the parade.   20.   This ends the drill!

VERBS

DRILL 3: Locating Verbs in Sentences

Instructions: Draw two lines under the verb words.

1. Where was your book?   2.   My brothers played football all morning.

3. Dad told us a strange story.   4.   The United States flag waves in the breeze.

5. Why did Juanita come home early today?   6.   An old woman was seen on the corner.

7. Betty will be leaving soon.   8.   Sasha could have lost her ring on the bus.

9. Must you do your homework now?   10.   You should have been helping me with the dishes.

11. Did Carl hit the ball over the fence?   12.   Can you run as fast as he?

13. Has Jared ever tried that before?   14.   Matt is playing the part of Scrooge.

15. The costumes have not yet arrived.   16.   Does that dog whine all the time?

17. Something must have happened to Uncle Don.   18.   He has never done that before.

19. I may be going to Hawaii next summer.   20.   You might check your work!

Steps to Good Grammar

FINAL DRILL

This reproducible page contains two copies of one half-page drill/test. Cut each duplicated page in half; give each student one half-page.

Remember: Have students write the list of helping verbs.

Longer, somewhat more complicated sentences are presented here. The emphasis is on recognizing complete verbs separated by the subject.

Before reading the instructions to the class, ask students for the definition of a verb.

This exercise, completed perfectly in class, could be sent home as a study sheet for the test scheduled the next day.

Announce that the test on recognizing or locating verbs in sentences is scheduled for tomorrow.

1. Will Dad go to the soccer game with us?   2. That boy could have worked harder.

3. The girls are already experimenting with their chemistry set.

4. The box of books may have arrived today.   5. Did David return his book?

6. The men should have finished the job by now.   7. Would you like a piece of pie?

8. Were you and she playing tennis today?   9. Dan hurriedly left the room.

10. You and I can finish the project tonight.

11. The little boy was being helped by his teacher.   12. I shall write my report tonight.

13. Everyone should do the first ten problems.   14. Might Dad have left his office already?

15. Why aren't you going home?

VERBS

FINAL DRILL: Locating Verbs in Sentences

Instructions: Draw two lines under each verb word. (Remember: A word is a verb if it tells what is being done in the sentence and/or if it is in the list of twenty-three helping verbs.)

1. Will Dad go to the soccer game with us?   2. That boy could have worked harder.

3. The girls are already experimenting with their chemistry set.

4. The box of books may have arrived today.   5. Did David return his book?

6. The men should have finished the job by now.   7. Would you like a piece of pie?

8. Were you and she playing tennis today?   9. Dan hurriedly left the room.

10. You and I can finish the project tonight.

11. The little boy was being helped by his teacher.   12. I shall write my report tonight.

13. Everyone should do the first ten problems.   14. Might Dad have left his office already?

15. Why aren't you going home?

VERBS

FINAL DRILL: Locating Verbs in Sentences

Instructions: Draw two lines under each verb word. (Remember: A word is a verb if it tells what is being done in the sentence and/or if it is in the list of twenty-three helping verbs.)

1. Will Dad go to the soccer game with us?   2. That boy could have worked harder.

3. The girls are already experimenting with their chemistry set.

4. The box of books may have arrived today.   5. Did David return his book?

6. The men should have finished the job by now.   7. Would you like a piece of pie?

8. Were you and she playing tennis today?   9. Dan hurriedly left the room.

10. You and I can finish the project tonight.

11. The little boy was being helped by his teacher.   12. I shall write my report tonight.

13. Everyone should do the first ten problems.   14. Might Dad have left his office already?

15. Why aren't you going home?

Steps to Good Grammar

TEST

This reproducible page contains two copies of one half-page drill/test. Cut each duplicated page in half; give each student one half-page.

The purpose of the test is to check students' ability to recognize or locate complete verbs.

Suggested grading:

1. Each of the 20 complete verbs has a value of 5%.

2. Example: Sentence 13

<u>Could be going</u> is the complete verb;

<u>going</u>, the doing verb, expresses half of the meaning = 2½%.

<u>Could be</u>, the helping verbs, express half of the meaning = 2½%.

If *could* and *be* are not underlined, or if even one of them is not underlined, the helping verb meaning is not complete, resulting in a 2½% deduction.

3. Deduct 2% for each nonverb word underlined.

1. Mom <u>is making</u> arrangements for our vacation.

2. That strange man <u>was seen</u> near the scene of the crime.

3. The frightened children <u>screamed</u> loudly.

4. John certainly <u>must have had</u> a lot of fun.

5. Will <u>arrived</u> early for school.

6. Healy <u>might have borrowed</u> the book.

7. My horse <u>galloped</u> across the field.

8. Max <u>should have brought</u> his pencil.

9. Joe <u>will</u> probably <u>win</u> the election.

10. Elaine <u>may help</u> in the library.

11. I <u>am writing</u> my book report.

12. The little boy <u>was being punished</u>.

13. <u>Could</u> Mimi <u>be going</u> home now?

14. Your letter <u>has</u> just <u>arrived</u>.

15. <u>Does</u> Gary <u>drive</u> too fast?

16. Linda <u>cannot go</u> with us.

17. <u>Were</u> you <u>driving</u> your dad's car?

18. <u>Do</u> you really <u>like</u> that rock group?

19. Every day we <u>would walk</u> home.

20. <u>May</u> we <u>stop</u> now?

VERBS

TEST: Locating Verbs in Sentences

Instructions: Draw two lines under each verb word.

1. Mom is making arrangements for our vacation.

2. That strange man was seen near the scene of the crime.

3. The frightened children screamed loudly.

4. John certainly must have had a lot of fun.

5. Will arrived early for school.

6. Healy might have borrowed the book.

7. My horse galloped across the field.

8. Max should have brought his pencil.

9. Joe will probably win the election.

10. Elaine may help in the library.

11. I am writing my book report.

12. The little boy was being punished.

13. Could Mimi be going home now?

14. Your letter has just arrived.

15. Does Gary drive too fast?

16. Linda cannot go with us.

17. Were you driving your dad's car?

18. Do you really like that rock group?

19. Every day we would walk home.

20. May we stop now?

NAME _____ DATE _____ 15

VERBS

TEST: Locating Verbs in Sentences

Instructions: Draw two lines under each verb word.

1. Mom is making arrangements for our vacation.

2. That strange man was seen near the scene of the crime.

3. The frightened children screamed loudly.

4. John certainly must have had a lot of fun.

5. Will arrived early for school.

6. Healy might have borrowed the book.

7. My horse galloped across the field.

8. Max should have brought his pencil.

9. Joe will probably win the election.

10. Elaine may help in the library.

11. I am writing my book report.

12. The little boy was being punished.

13. Could Mimi be going home now?

14. Your letter has just arrived.

15. Does Gary drive too fast?

16. Linda cannot go with us.

17. Were you driving your dad's car?

18. Do you really like that rock group?

19. Every day we would walk home.

20. May we stop now?

Steps to Good Grammar

PRETEST: RECOGNIZING NOUNS

This reproducible page contains two copies of one half-page drill/test. Cut each duplicated page in half; give each student one half-page.

Remind students that pretest scores have no effect on their report card grades. This pretest merely indicates how well they are able to recognize nouns.

Do not give students the definition of a noun. They should recall what they know about nouns and underline the ones they recognize.

Explain errors the students have made when the pretest is returned to them:

1. Some may have underlined *river bank*. *Bank* is, of course, the noun; *river*, an adjective, tells "what kind" of bank.

2. Having just memorized *might* in the list of helping verbs, some students might not have recognized it here as a noun, meaning "strength."

3. In *at last, last* may be difficult to recognize as being a noun. Relate it to *at midnight* or *at noon.*

Suggested grading: 29 nouns

-1, 96	-6, 79	-11, 61
-2, 93	-7, 75	-12, 57
-3, 89	-8, 71	-13, 54
-4, 86	-9, 68	-14, 50
-5, 82	-10, 64	-15, 46

Deduct 1 point for each non-noun word underlined.

Bob was not a good swimmer. One hot day in August, at a picnic on the river bank, he swam out too far into the swiftly moving water. When Bob let his feet down, he could not touch bottom! He became panicky. His friends were shouting excitedly. On the shore the picnickers, who did not know that Bob was in trouble, laughed as they ran up and down. Bob shouted, "Help!" He shouted again. His friends paid no attention because they did not hear him. Bob was really tired now. He decided he must save his strength. He caught his breath and paddled slowly for a few minutes. Then he pulled toward the shore with all his might across the current. Finally, he put his feet down again. At last he could feel the bottom! Bob had helped himself.

NOUNS

PRETEST: Recognizing Nouns

Instructions: Draw a single line under each noun in this story.

Bob was not a good swimmer. One hot day in August, at a picnic on the river bank, he swam out too far into the swiftly moving water. When Bob let his feet down, he could not touch bottom! He became panicky. His friends were shouting excitedly. On the shore the picnickers, who did not know that Bob was in trouble, laughed as they ran up and down. Bob shouted, "Help!" He shouted again. His friends paid no attention because they did not hear him. Bob was really tired now. He decided he must save his strength. He caught his breath and paddled slowly for a few minutes. Then he pulled toward the shore with all his might across the current. Finally, he put his feet down again. At last he could feel the bottom! Bob had helped himself.

NAME _____ DATE _____ 17

NOUNS

PRETEST: Recognizing Nouns

Instructions: Draw a single line under each noun in this story.

Bob was not a good swimmer. One hot day in August, at a picnic on the river bank, he swam out too far into the swiftly moving water. When Bob let his feet down, he could not touch bottom! He became panicky. His friends were shouting excitedly. On the shore the picnickers, who did not know that Bob was in trouble, laughed as they ran up and down. Bob shouted, "Help!" He shouted again. His friends paid no attention because they did not hear him. Bob was really tired now. He decided he must save his strength. He caught his breath and paddled slowly for a few minutes. Then he pulled toward the shore with all his might across the current. Finally, he put his feet down again. At last he could feel the bottom! Bob had helped himself.

© 1988, 1997 J. Weston Walch, Publisher

Steps to Good Grammar

RECOGNIZING NOUNS

Students should know the definition of a noun: A noun is a name word for a person, place, thing, quality, or idea.

This exercise includes many "quality" or "idea" nouns.

1. Jack has a very good idea.
2. The parade will go down this street to the marina.
3. Honesty is the best policy.
4. Mark never changes his mind.
5. Many books have been stacked on the tables in the library.
6. The new church is in a beautiful setting overlooking the bay.
7. The list of winners of the writing contest will be printed in the newspaper.
8. Some nouns that are names of qualities are honesty and integrity.
9. Three books have disappeared mysteriously from my locker.
10. Al has bought a new football and a catcher's mask.
11. John Nolan brought the two new students with him to the meeting.
12. My father and my aunt studied physics at Northwestern University.
13. The restaurant on the corner makes a delicious taco salad.
14. Cathie bought a gold chain with her birthday money.
15. Our family went to Canada last summer.
16. Cheerfulness can become a habit.
17. The class has been discussing intolerance and prejudice.
18. My father and his friend play golf every Saturday.
19. The girl in the designer jeans has the lead in the play.
20. Remember, adjectives and determiners may come before a noun.

NOUNS

Recognizing Nouns

DEFINITION: A **noun** is a "name" word. It is the *name* we can use to talk or write about:

> a person (Paul, teacher, woman, lawyer);
>
> a place (St. Louis, school, marina, Mt. Diablo);
>
> a thing (pencil, orange, homework, spider);
>
> a quality or idea (happiness, danger, justice).

FACTS:

1. Nouns have many different uses in sentences. You will study each use in great detail.

2. Adjectives, including articles — *a, an, the,* and determiners such as *this, which, your, two* — may come before a noun.

PRACTICE: Draw a single line under each noun in the following sentences.

1. Jack has a very good idea.

2. The parade will go down this street to the marina.

3. Honesty is the best policy.

4. Mark never changes his mind.

5. Many books have been stacked on the tables in the library.

6. The new church is in a beautiful setting overlooking the bay.

7. The list of winners of the writing contest will be printed in the newspaper.

8. Some nouns that are names of qualities are honesty and integrity.

9. Three books have disappeared mysteriously from my locker.

10. Al has bought a new football and a catcher's mask.

11. John Nolan brought the two new students with him to the meeting.

12. My father and my aunt studied physics at Northwestern University.

13. The restaurant on the corner makes a delicious taco salad.

14. Cathie bought a gold chain with her birthday money.

15. Our family went to Canada last summer.

16. Cheerfulness can become a habit.

17. The class has been discussing intolerance and prejudice.

18. My father and his friend play golf every Saturday.

19. The girl in the designer jeans has the lead in the play.

20. Remember, adjectives and determiners may come before a noun.

Steps to Good Grammar

USING NOUNS — PRACTICE

Encourage students to write unusual nouns as they complete this page individually. It offers them the opportunity to practice their creative thinking, which they can share orally when all have finished the writing.

Answers will vary.

NOUNS

Using Nouns — Practice

REMEMBER: A **noun** is a "name" word we can use to talk or write about a person, place, thing, or quality/idea.

Part I: Instructions: After each article or determiner, write a different noun of your choice.

1. the _____

2. a _____

3. an _____

4. this _____

5. that_____

6. these _____

7. those _____

8. which _____

9. many _____

10. most_____

11. few _____

12. some _____

13. several _____

14. both _____

15. three _____

16. nineteen _____

17. my _____

18. his _____

19. her _____

20. your _____

21. our _____

22. their _____

Part II: Instructions: Write four nouns for each of the following:

1. Names of qualities:

_____ _____

_____ _____

2. Names of things:

_____ _____

_____ _____

3. Names of places:

_____ _____

_____ _____

4. Names of persons:

_____ _____

_____ _____

Steps to Good Grammar

FINAL DRILL AND TEST 1

This reproducible page contains two different half-page drills/tests. You may cut each duplicated page in half and give each student one half-page at a time, or you may distribute the entire duplicated page and work one drill/test at a time.

(39 nouns)

-1, 97	-5, 87	-9, 77	-13, 67
-2, 95	-6, 85	-10, 74	-14, 64
-3, 92	-7, 82	-11, 72	-15, 62
-4, 90	-8, 80	-12, 69	

Final Drill

This final drill may be used as a self-test. Instruct students to complete it as though they were taking a test. Students correct their own papers and grade themselves according to this scale:

Test

This test is somewhat more challenging than the following one. Give your students the one that is most appropriate for them.

Grading scale for 45 nouns:

-1, 98	-5, 89	-9, 79	-13, 69
-2, 96	-6, 87	-10, 76	-14, 66
-3, 93	-7, 84	-11, 73	-15, 64
-4, 91	-8, 82	-12, 71	-16, 62

1. Grandmother has the key for this lock.
2. When she and Grandfather came to the United States from Germany, they had six children in their family.
3. People from many other countries are becoming citizens of our country.
4. Jealousy and hatred are nouns that name qualities or ideas.
5. Many sunken ships lie on the ocean floor.
6. Marlene bought her dress, the one with the striped jacket, at Hilson's.
7. Four barking dogs, followed by a crowd of laughing children, ran out of the yard, across the street, and down to the school.
8. The mechanic may have put new tires on the car.
9. Apples, oranges, and seedless grapes are in the refrigerator.
10. The thirsty boys drank a quart of milk.

1. In health class, we watched a film about the effects of drug abuse.
2. The Boy Scout was carrying a heavy bundle of old newspapers.
3. Dad called on our new neighbors, who are from South Korea.
4. Sitting on the fence were two birds, a robin and a sparrow.
5. The members of the committee have gone in the elevator to the fifteenth floor, where the meeting is being held.
6. On our vacation, we are going to visit some national parks — Yosemite, Grand Canyon, Zion, and Bryce.
7. Honesty and sincerity are qualities admired by many people.
8. Sharon said that her mom and dad were born in Concord, California.
9. On Wednesday, a famous mountain climber talked to our class about her experiences in the Himalayas.
10. Tom sent Juan a detailed letter about his activities at summer camp on the lake.

NOUNS

FINAL DRILL: Locating Nouns in Sentences

Instructions: Draw a single line under each noun in these sentences.

1. Grandmother has the key for this lock.
2. When she and Grandfather came to the United States from Germany, they had six children in their family.
3. People from many other countries are becoming citizens of our country.
4. Jealousy and hatred are nouns that name qualities or ideas.
5. Many sunken ships lie on the ocean floor.
6. Marlene bought her dress, the one with the striped jacket, at Hilson's.
7. Four barking dogs, followed by a crowd of laughing children, ran out of the yard, across the street, and down to the school.
8. The mechanic may have put new tires on the car.
9. Apples, oranges, and seedless grapes are in the refrigerator.
10. The thirsty boys drank a quart of milk.

NAME _____ DATE _____ 23

NOUNS

TEST 1: Locating Nouns in Sentences

Instructions: Draw a single line under each noun in these sentences.

1. In health class, we watched a film about the effects of drug abuse.
2. The Boy Scout was carrying a heavy bundle of old newspapers.
3. Dad called on our new neighbors, who are from South Korea.
4. Sitting on the fence were two birds, a robin and a sparrow.
5. The members of the committee have gone in the elevator to the fifteenth floor, where the meeting is being held.
6. On our vacation, we are going to visit some national parks — Yosemite, Grand Canyon, Zion, and Bryce.
7. Honesty and sincerity are qualities admired by many people.
8. Sharon said that her mom and dad were born in Concord, California.
9. On Wednesday, a famous mountain climber talked to our class about her experiences in the Himalayas.
10. Tom sent Juan a detailed letter about his activities at summer camp on the lake.

© 1988, 1997 J. Weston Walch, Publisher

Steps to Good Grammar

TEST 2

Grading scale for 35 nouns:

-1, 97	-4, 89	-7, 80	-10, 71	-13, 63
-2, 94	-5, 86	-8, 77	-11, 69	-14, 60
-3, 91	-6, 83	-9, 74	-12, 66	-15, 57

1. Is there another shirt this size in a different color?

2. The miners rode on a cart into the mine shaft.

3. Dad bought a new jacket at the Sports Chalet.

4. The books on this shelf are mysteries.

5. Our little neighbor and her dog were sitting on the curb, watching cars go by.

6. The kittens climbed out of the basket and followed their mother to the back door of the house.

7. On Fridays, that teacher never gives his students any homework.

8. Sharon said that her mom and dad were born in Concord, California.

9. The mechanic has put new tires on the car.

10. Mark never changes his mind.

NOUNS

TEST 2: Locating Nouns in Sentences

Instructions: Draw a single line under each noun in these sentences.

1. Is there another shirt this size in a different color?

2. The miners rode on a cart into the mine shaft.

3. Dad bought a new jacket at the Sports Chalet.

4. The books on this shelf are mysteries.

5. Our little neighbor and her dog were sitting on the curb, watching cars go by.

6. The kittens climbed out of the basket and followed their mother to the back door of the house.

7. On Fridays, that teacher never gives his students any homework.

8. Sharon said that her mom and dad were born in Concord, California.

9. The mechanic has put new tires on the car.

10. Mark never changes his mind.

NAME _____ DATE _____ 25

NOUNS

TEST 2: Locating Nouns in Sentences

Instructions: Draw a single line under each noun in these sentences.

1. Is there another shirt this size in a different color?

2. The miners rode on a cart into the mine shaft.

3. Dad bought a new jacket at the Sports Chalet.

4. The books on this shelf are mysteries.

5. Our little neighbor and her dog were sitting on the curb, watching cars go by.

6. The kittens climbed out of the basket and followed their mother to the back door of the house.

7. On Fridays, that teacher never gives his students any homework.

8. Sharon said that her mom and dad were born in Concord, California.

9. The mechanic has put new tires on the car.

10. Mark never changes his mind.

Steps to Good Grammar

REVIEW QUIZ

This review quiz provides a refresher exercise in recognizing verbs and maintains noun recognition.

1. My best friend lives in the white house across the street.

2. I bought a new program for my computer at the bookstore.

3. Lisa, Karen, and Sue are good friends.

4. Did Jon tell Dad about the accident?

5. The salesman brought out several pairs of shoes.

6. The team and the cheerleaders rode in the school bus to the game.

7. Has your brother shown his award to your parents?

8. A large book with a red cover was lying on the desk.

9. Our neighbor has been a mail carrier for several years.

10. Last Wednesday, the teacher took our class to the museum.

REVIEW QUIZ: RECOGNIZING VERBS AND NOUNS

Instructions: Draw two lines under each verb word; draw a single line under each noun.

1. My best friend lives in the white house across the street.

2. I bought a new program for my computer at the bookstore.

3. Lisa, Karen, and Sue are good friends.

4. Did Jon tell Dad about the accident?

5. The salesman brought out several pairs of shoes.

6. The team and the cheerleaders rode in the school bus to the game.

7. Has your brother shown his award to your parents?

8. A large book with a red cover was lying on the desk.

9. Our neighbor has been a mail carrier for several years.

10. Last Wednesday, the teacher took our class to the museum.

NAME _____ DATE _____ 27

REVIEW QUIZ: RECOGNIZING VERBS AND NOUNS

Instructions: Draw two lines under each verb word; draw a single line under each noun.

1. My best friend lives in the white house across the street.

2. I bought a new program for my computer at the bookstore.

3. Lisa, Karen, and Sue are good friends.

4. Did Jon tell Dad about the accident?

5. The salesman brought out several pairs of shoes.

6. The team and the cheerleaders rode in the school bus to the game.

7. Has your brother shown his award to your parents?

8. A large book with a red cover was lying on the desk.

9. Our neighbor has been a mail carrier for several years.

10. Last Wednesday, the teacher took our class to the museum.

© 1988, 1997 J. Weston Walch, Publisher

Steps to Good Grammar

SIMPLE SENTENCES

Teachers, of course, have developed their own methods of helping their students to understand, retain, and use the concepts they present. You could use the following procedure for the accompanying student page to emphasize the importance of covering each element, again and again.

1. Read aloud, as students read silently, instructive items 1, 2, and 3.

2. Question students to fix the concepts in their minds:

    (a) What is a simple sentence?
    (b) What are three "must" requirements in a sentence?
    (c) Complete this statement: "A word is a verb if..."
    (d) How do you locate the subject in a sentence?

3. Demonstrate on the chalkboard or the overhead the underlining and diagramming for items 4 and 5.

4. Read aloud the instructions for the Practice.

5. Examine the example sentence and ask students these questions:

    (a) What are the helping verbs?
    (b) What was being done?
    (c) What is the complete verb?

    (d) In analyzing a sentence, what will you do to show the complete verb?
    (e) What had been barking?
    (f) What part of the sentence is *dog*?
    (g) In analyzing a sentence, what will you do to show the subject?

6. Construct diagrams for Practice items 1 and 2, for students to copy on their papers. Emphasize careful diagrams.

7. Instruct students to complete Practice items 3-10, diagramming 5, 6, and 9.

8. When all are finished, ask individual students to draw 5, 6, and 9 on the chalkboard and explain their diagrams.

9. Correct these diagrams as necessary. Then tell students to change any errors they may have made and to write the correct form. Explain that a completely correct paper earns 100% when turned in; each error not corrected lowers the grade by 5%. A paper graded 75% for 5 small errors is a high price to pay for carelessness or inattentiveness.

10. Allow a few minutes for students to write and diagram their two original subject-verb sentences; then collect papers.

11. Return the graded papers the next day.

1. The <u>girl</u> <u>sang</u>.   *girl | sang*

2. The <u>rain</u> <u>had begun</u>.   *rain | had begun*

3. The <u>sun</u> <u>sank</u>.

4. The <u>houses</u> <u>had burned</u>.

5. A <u>cat</u> <u>was meowing</u>.   *cat | was meowing*

6. The <u>men</u> <u>must have been working</u>.
    men | must have been working

7. The <u>students</u> <u>were studying</u>.

8. The <u>tree</u> <u>grew</u>.

9. The <u>eggs</u> <u>had been smashed</u>.
    eggs | had been smashed

10. The <u>band</u> <u>might play</u>.

THE BASIC SENTENCE

Simple Sentences

KNOW: 1. A simple sentence is a group of words that expresses one complete thought. It must contain a **subject** and a **verb.** It must make sense.

2. **Remember:** A word is a **verb** if it tells what is being done in the sentence or if it is one of the twenty-three helping verbs.

3. The **subject** is what or whom ~~the sentence is about.~~ *is doing something.* To find the subject, first find the verb, then ask "What?" or "Who?" before the verb. The word that answers the question is the subject.

   Example: The wind had been blowing.

   The verb is *had been blowing. What* had been blowing?
   Wind had been blowing. *Wind* is the subject.

4. In analyzing a sentence, draw two lines under the verb; draw one line under the subject:

   The <u>wind</u> <u>had been blowing.</u>

5. Diagramming is an aid to understanding the parts of a sentence:

wind	had been blowing	
(subject)	(verb)	(sentence line)

   Cross the sentence line with a short, perpendicular line to separate the subject and verb.

PRACTICE: Locating Subjects and Verbs in Simple Sentences

Part I. Instructions: Draw two lines under the verb, one under the subject in the sentences below. On the reverse side of this paper, construct diagrams for sentences 1, 2, 5, 6, and 9.

   Example: A <u>dog</u> <u>had been barking.</u>   *dog | had been barking*

1. The girl sang.

2. The rain had begun.

3. The sun sank.

4. The houses had burned.

5. A cat was meowing.

6. The men must have been working.

7. The students were studying.

8. The tree grew.

9. The eggs had been smashed.

10. The band might play.

Part II. Now write two subject-verb sentences of your own on the back of this paper, underlining subject and verb, and then construct diagrams for them.

Steps to Good Grammar

DRILL: Locating Verbs and Subjects

> This reproducible page contains two copies of one half-page drill/test. Cut each duplicated page in half; give each student one half-page.

Read aloud the Remember section and the instructions.

REMINDER: The term *predicate* is not used in this study, since it may include a variety of sentence parts in addition to the verb. This book deals separately and cumulatively with specific sentence parts.

Clarify for the students the difference between predicate and verb.

Many students, in previous years in school, have referred to the subject as "the noun." They should use the sentence part term: *subject.*

Student analysis of sentences

Students should orally identify the specific parts. They should *say:*

(a) The verb is *had been waving;* draw two lines under it.

(b) The subject is *girls;* draw one line under it.

Students' long-term retention of their learning is assured if verbal analysis is maintained to the end.

Diagramming

Diagramming forms a blueprint of a sentence. Constructing a diagram helps many students to put the parts of the sentence into clearer perspective. For many students, simply underlining and labeling the individual parts is sufficient. Diagramming is a tool and need not be tested. Underlining and labeling is the method of sentence analysis which you will test.

Students' original sentences

The sentences in the exercise are in simple subject-verb form. Instruct students to write sentences in this same pattern — especially to use an interesting "doing" verb.

Suppose a student writes a sentence with a linking verb, like this:

The children were happy.

Point out that *were* is used in a special way in that sentence — as a linking verb, which will be studied later. Suggest, instead, using a verb that tells something the subject could *do:*

The children were rehearsing.

Children can *rehearse* — they can't *happy!*

1. The boys are leaving.

2. The shipment has arrived.

3. The rooster was crowing.

4. The boy should have studied.

5. Stacy must have been helping.

6. The car swerved.

7. Snow was falling.

8. The children had eaten.

9. The package has arrived.

10. My grandparents will be visiting.

THE BASIC SENTENCE

DRILL: Locating Verbs and Subjects

REMEMBER: Every sentence must have a verb and a subject. The verb tells what is done in the sentence and/or is in the list of twenty-three helping verbs; the subject is what or whom the sentence is about. In analyzing a sentence, always locate the verb first.

Part I. Instructions: For each sentence below, draw two lines under the complete verb; draw one line under the subject; on the back of this paper, diagram the verb and subject in sentences 1, 5, and 10.

Example: The girls had been waving.　　*girls | had been waving*

1. The boys are leaving.
2. The shipment has arrived.
3. The rooster was crowing.
4. The boy should have studied.
5. Stacy must have been helping.

6. The car swerved.
7. Snow was falling.
8. The children had eaten.
9. The package has arrived.
10. My grandparents will be visiting.

Part II. On the back of this paper, write two subject-verb sentences of your own; construct diagrams for them.

NAME _____ DATE _____ 31

THE BASIC SENTENCE

DRILL: Locating Verbs and Subjects

REMEMBER: Every sentence must have a verb and a subject. The verb tells what is done in the sentence and/or is in the list of twenty-three helping verbs; the subject is what or whom the sentence is about. In analyzing a sentence, always locate the verb first.

Part I. Instructions: For each sentence below, draw two lines under the complete verb; draw one line under the subject; on the back of this paper, diagram the verb and subject in sentences 1, 5, and 10.

Example: The girls had been waving.　　*girls | had been waving*

1. The boys are leaving.
2. The shipment has arrived.
3. The rooster was crowing.
4. The boy should have studied.
5. Stacy must have been helping.

6. The car swerved.
7. Snow was falling.
8. The children had eaten.
9. The package has arrived.
10. My grandparents will be visiting.

Part II. On the back of this paper, write two subject-verb sentences of your own; construct diagrams for them.

RECOGNIZING ADJECTIVES

Review the definition of a verb and a subject with students. Then read aloud the introductory material.

Students should memorize the definition of an adjective: "An adjective is a word that modifies a noun or a pronoun. It tells *what kind, which one, how many,* or *whose* about the word it modifies."

What an adjective "tells" emphasizes its use in the sentence. Students understand it easily and learn to modify nouns very descriptively. Later in their academic years they can apply this understanding to classifying adjectives as to type.

In analyzing a sentence, students should verbalize what they are doing; for example, they should say, *"Neighbor's* is an adjective; draw a circle around it."

Encourage students to use interesting adjectives in the Practice sentences.

Diagramming examples:

3. houses | were built
   Twenty-four

4. cat | was meowing
   my cousin's

Insist that students draw the dividing line between the subject and verb perpendicular to and across the sentence line. Explain that slanted lines have special uses in diagramming.

1. (The) _____ girl sang. (which one)

2. (A) _____ rain had begun. (what kind)

3. _____ houses were built. (how many)

4. _____ cat was meowing. (whose)

5. (The) _____ tree grew. (what kind)

6. (The) _____ band might play. (which one)

7. _____ dad is coming. (whose)

8. _____ students were going. (how many)

9. _____ parents were attending. (whose)

10. (The) _____ student must have studied. (which one)

ADJECTIVES

Recognizing Adjectives

KNOW: A word that describes (modifies) a noun is an **adjective.** An adjective tells *what kind, which one, how many,* or *whose* about the noun in modifies. Some adjectives are called "determiners." The articles *a, an,* and *the* are adjectives.

1. The black dog had been barking. (*black* tells *which one*)

2. A wild dog had been barking. (*wild* tells *what kind*)

3. Six dogs had been barking. (*six* tells *how many*)

4. Our neighbor's dog had been barking. (*neighbor's* tells *whose*)

** In analyzing a sentence, draw a circle around an adjective.

** In diagramming, write the adjective on a slanted line under the word it modifies:

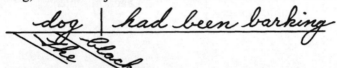

PRACTICE: In each sentence below, draw two lines under the complete verb, one under the subject. In the space before the subject, write an adjective with the meaning given in parentheses. On the back of this sheet, diagram sentences 3, 4, 5, and 6.

1. The _____ girl sang. (which one)

2. A _____ rain had begun. (what kind)

3. _____ houses were built. (how many)

4. _____ cat was meowing. (whose)

5. The _____ tree grew. (what kind)

6. The _____ band might play. (which one)

7. _____ dad is coming. (whose)

8. _____ students were going. (how many)

9. _____ parents were attending. (whose)

10. The _____ student must have studied. (which one)

Steps to Good Grammar

USING ADJECTIVES — PRACTICE

This page is suitable for a homework assignment.

Objective: To emphasize using unusual, descriptive adjectives.

Instructions for Students:

1. Sentences 1, 4, 5, 6, 8, and 10 require adjectives that tell *which one* or *what kind.*

2. Using your dictionary, scan quickly down the columns to find entries for adjectives.

Example:

rep • a • ra • ble (rep′-ə-rə-bəl) *adj.* Also

LOOK FOR

| Entry | Pronunciation | Abbreviation of *adjective* |

re • pair • a • ble (ri-pǎr′-ə-bəl).   Able to be repaired.

Meaning

3. Find a suitable adjective; on the reverse side of your paper, copy the entry, including the meaning that makes sense in the sentence.

4. Write the adjective in the blank:

The *reparable* car was being repaired.

5. Identify sentence parts: verb, subject.

6. Diagram sentences 2, 3, 4, and 5 only.

1. The _____ pie had been burned. (what kind)

2. The _____ puppy was whining. (whose)

3. _____ girls had been running. (how many)

4. Sally's _____ book has been found. (which one)

5. The _____ children had been hiking. (what kind)

6. The _____ car was being repaired. (which one)

7. _____ children had eaten. (how many)

8. The _____ plane was landing. (what kind)

9. The _____ telephone has been ringing. (whose)

10. The _____ package should have arrived. (which one)

ADJECTIVES

Using Adjectives — Practice

REMEMBER:

1. Every sentence must have a verb and a subject. Locate the **verb,** ask "Who?" or "What?" before it, and the word that answers the question is the **subject.**

2. An **adjective** modifies a noun or pronoun; it tells *which one, what kind, how many,* or *whose* about the word it modifies.

Instructions: In each sentence below, draw two lines under the complete verb; draw one line under the subject; in the space before the subject, write an adjective with the meaning given in parentheses. Diagram sentences 2, 3, 4, and 5.

Example: (The) _disappointed_ boys were leaving. (what kind)

boys | were leaving

The disappointed

1. The _____ pie had been burned. (what kind)

2. The _____ puppy was whining. (whose)

3. _____ girls had been running. (how many)

4. Sally's _____ book has been found. (which one)

5. The _____ children had been hiking. (what kind)

6. The _____ car was being repaired. (which one)

7. _____ children had eaten. (how many)

8. The _____ plane was landing. (what kind)

9. The _____ telephone has been ringing. (whose)

10. The _____ package should have arrived. (which one)

Steps to Good Grammar

FACTS ABOUT ADJECTIVE USAGE

This sheet presents important facts for students to understand, remember, and use.

1. Read aloud Remember and Fact 1 with its accompanying *Reminder.*

   (a) Elicit the fact that consonants are all the letters in the alphabet except the vowels, which are *a, e, i, o, u,* and sometimes *y.*

   (b) Call attention, in the sample sentences, to the placement of the adjectives and to the first letter of each adjective.

2. Read aloud Fact 2 and its first sample sentence, emphasizing the commas.

3. Read the second *Reminder* and the two sample sentences, which demonstrate the use of *an* and commas.

4. Read Fact 3 and the accompanying *Reminder.* In reading the sample sentences, substitute the word *and* for the commas to demonstrate the fact that commas are used between adjectives in a series if *and* would sound right in place of the commas.

5. Work with the students to complete the Practice exercise. Point out that no comma separates the final adjective in a series from the noun it modifies.

1. __An__ honest person is respected by all.

2. The dog, old and feeble, could hardly walk.

3. __a__ wide brick walkway led to __a__ fountain.

4. I love __a__ warm, clear, sunny day.

5. Dee wanted only __a__ glass of orange juice, __an__ egg, and __a__ slice of toast.

6. What is it that makes __a__ house __a__ home?

7. The President's noticing me was __an__ honor.

8. __a__ rain-soaked, discouraged team left the field.

9. __An__ excited, happy, noisy crowd of children was approaching.

10. __a__ serious-looking man was given __an__ honorary degree.

ADJECTIVES

Facts About Adjective Usage

REMEMBER: An adjective tells *which one, what kind, how many,* or *whose* about the noun it modifies.

FACT 1: Adjectives usually come before the noun they modify.

A (pretty) girl was calling.

A (uniformed) man had been watching.

A (helpful) suggestion was made.

> **Reminder:** Use *a* before words beginning with a consonant or a long *ū*.

FACT 2: Adjectives that follow a noun are separated from the noun and the rest of the sentence by commas.

Sharon, (bright-eyed) and (smiling,) arrived.

An (ugly) (little) mutt, (tail-wagging) and (lovable,) was barking.

An (elegant) woman, (well-dressed) and (poised,) was approaching.

> **Reminder:** Use *an* before words beginning with a vowel or a silent *h.*

FACT 3: Adjectives used in a series are separated by commas.

An (eager,) (immaculate,) (tall,) (lanky) sailor was waving.

The (hungry,) (tired,) (bedraggled) (little) Cub Scouts were eating.

> **Reminder:** Use a comma between adjectives where *and* sounds right.

PRACTICE: Draw a circle around each adjective; insert commas, and write *a* or *an* where appropriate.

1. _____ honest person is respected by all.

2. The dog old and feeble could hardly walk.

3. _____ wide brick walkway led to _____ fountain.

4. I love _____ warm clear sunny day.

5. Dee wanted only _____ glass of orange juice, _____ egg, and _____ slice of toast.

6. What is it that makes _____ house _____ home?

7. The President's noticing me was _____ honor.

8. _____ rain-soaked discouraged team left the field.

9. _____ excited happy noisy crowd of children was approaching.

10. _____ serious-looking man was given _____ honorary degree.

REVIEW

1. In reading the sample sentences, reestablish in your students' minds the oral routine they should follow in identifying sentence parts: ·

    (a) The verb is <u>Should be counted</u>; put two lines under it.

    (b) The subject is <u>ballots</u>; draw one line under it.

    (c) These and torn are adjectives; draw a circle around each.

2. As you duplicate the diagram on the chalkboard, stress the following:

    (a) The sentence line is cut across by a perpendicular line between the verb, *Should be counted,* and the subject, *ballots.*

    (b) *Should* is capitalized because it is the first word in the sentence.

    (c) The adjectives, *these* and *torn,* are on slanted lines under the subject, *ballots,* which they modify.

3. In *Steps to Good Grammar,* a conjunction (*and* in sentence 12) is given no marking. Point out to students the placement of *and* in the diagram — on a dotted line between the words it connects.

4. Checking students' work:

    (a) A representative section to check on this paper includes sentences 8 through 13.

    (b) Check the diagrams for accuracy and neatness. Make suggestions for improvement where necessary, *or* write a compliment!

2.

everyone | Has eaten

3.

neighbors | Have arrived
new
your

6.

hotdogs | have been eaten
All the Oscar Mayer

9.

girl | has won
The clever little

10.

vase | Was broken
Edna's favorite cut-glass

1. <u>Can</u> Hal <u>come</u>?

2. <u>Has</u> everyone <u>eaten</u>?

3. <u>Have</u> your new neighbors <u>arrived</u>?

4. A few girls <u>had been skating</u>.

5. <u>Were</u> the two prisoners <u>freed</u>?

6. All the foot-long hot dogs <u>have been eaten</u>.

7. Several delicious cakes <u>will be sold</u>.

8. <u>Could</u> all the chocolate ice cream <u>have been eaten</u>?

9. The clever little girl <u>has won</u>.

10. <u>Was</u> Edna's favorite cut-glass vase <u>broken</u>?

11. <u>Did</u> that beautiful Dalmatian dog <u>win</u>?

12. Alicia, excited and happy, <u>had arrived</u>.

13. My Uncle Pete <u>has moved</u>.

REVIEW: VERBS, SUBJECTS, AND ADJECTIVES

Instructions: Draw two lines under each complete verb and one line under each subject. Draw a circle around each adjective. Diagram all words in sentences 2, 3, 6, 9, and 10.

Example: Should (these) (torn) ballots be counted?

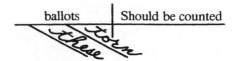

1. Can Hal come?

2. Has everyone eaten?

Reminder: Many questions begin with a "helping" verb; be sure to underline twice!

3. Have your new neighbors arrived?

4. A few girls had been skating.

5. Were the two prisoners freed?

6. All the foot-long hot dogs have been eaten.

7. Several delicious cakes will be sold.

8. Could all the chocolate ice cream have been eaten?

9. The clever little girl has won.

10. Was Edna's favorite cut-glass vase broken?

11. Did that beautiful Dalmatian dog win?

12. Alicia, excited and happy, had arrived.

13. My Uncle Pete has moved.

Steps to Good Grammar

MEMORY CHECK AND RECOGNITION DRILL

In completing this page, point out:

Sentence 6: *Borrowed* is usually used as a verb.

Dan borrowed some books.

Remind students that the "part of speech" of any word depends upon its use in the sentence. In this sentence, *borrowed* is an adjective that tells *what kind* of books.

Sentence 8: Even though four adjectives precede *truck,* "and" spoken between them sounds awkward; hence, no commas.

Sentence 10: The comma following *tired* demonstrates the rule that a comma is used where *and* could sensibly be used instead.

When students have completed work on the page:

1. If they want more practice before taking a test, use the Trial Test (page 43) next. Follow it the next day with the actual Test (page 45).

2. If they feel fully prepared to take a test now, announce one for the next day; omit the Trial Test and use the actual Test.

Memory Check

1. verb, subject
2. verb
3. subject
4. which one, what kind, how many, whose

5. is, am, are, was, were, be, being, been, has, have, had, do, does, did, shall, will, should, would, may, might, must, can, could

1. (Those)(four) students <u>must have studied</u>.

2. <u>Should</u> (the)(girls') (softball) team <u>practice</u>?

3. <u>Will</u> (your) parents <u>come</u>?

4. (Your)(family) doctor <u>should have been called</u>.

5. <u>Have</u> (all)(the)(borrowed) books <u>been returned</u>? (*What kind* of books?)

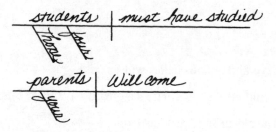

6. (New)(student body) officers <u>have been elected</u>.

7. <u>Did</u> (your)(little) sister <u>leave</u>?

8. <u>Was</u> [your] [dad's] [new] [panel] truck <u>wrecked</u>?

9. (The)(rain-soaked) spectators <u>were leaving</u>.

10. (Many) (tired,)(hungry,) and (hopeless) refugees <u>had arrived</u>.

REVIEW: VERBS, SUBJECTS, AND ADJECTIVES

Memory Check and Recognition Drill

Memory Check

Instructions: Write the words that correctly complete these sentences.

1. Every sentence must have a _____ and a _____.

2. The word that tells what is being done in a sentence is the _____.

3. The word that answers "Who?" or "What?" before the verb is the _____.

4. An adjective may tell _____ _____, _____

    _____, _____ _____, or _____

    about the word it modifies.

5. Write, in order, the twenty-three helping verbs:

Recognition Drill

Instructions: In each sentence below, draw two lines under the verb, one under the subject. Draw a circle around each adjective. On the reverse side of this paper, construct diagrams for the odd-numbered sentences.

1. Those four students must have studied.

2. Should the girls' softball team practice?

3. Will your parents come?

4. Your family doctor should have been called.

5. Have all the borrowed books been returned? (*What kind* of books?)

6. New student body officers have been elected.

7. Did your little sister leave?

8. Was your dad's new panel truck wrecked?

9. The rain-soaked spectators were leaving.

10. Many tired, hungry, and hopeless refugees had arrived.

Steps to Good Grammar

TRIAL TEST

This page may be used either as a trial test or as a unit test.

Announce, before students take the test, that one point of extra credit will be awarded for each *completely* correct diagram.

Suggestions for grading:

1. The complete verb is counted as 1 point.

    (a) If the doing verb is not underlined, subtract ½ point.

(b) If the helping verbs are not underlined correctly, subtract ½ point.

2. Grading scale: 30 identification symbols
    5 list of helping verbs
    5 written answers
    40

-1, 97	-4, 89	-7, 81	-10, 73	-13, 65
-2, 94	-5, 86	-8, 78	-11, 70	-14, 62
-3, 92	-6, 84	-9, 76	-12, 68	-15, 60

1. The two suspects were released.

2. Alicia, excited and happy, had arrived.

3. All the peaches have been picked.

4. Is your new house being built?

5. Their neighbor's new van was wrecked.

6. Did the Alhambra jazz band play?

7. Have the spelling tests been graded?

REVIEW: VERBS, SUBJECTS, AND ADJECTIVES

TRIAL TEST

Definitions

Instructions: Write the words you have memorized to complete these sentences.

1. Every sentence must have a _____ and a _____.

2. The _____ is the word that tells what is being done.

3. The _____ is the word that the sentence is about.

4. An _____ describes or modifies a noun.

5. On the reverse side of this paper, write the twenty-three helping verbs in order.

Recognizing Verbs, Subjects, and Adjectives

Instructions: In the following sentences, draw two lines under the verb, one under the subject; draw a circle around each adjective; beside each sentence, construct a diagram showing all the words.

1. The two suspects were released.

2. Alicia, excited and happy, had arrived.

3. All the peaches have been picked.

4. Is your new house being built?

5. Their neighbor's new van was wrecked.

6. Did the Alhambra jazz band play?

7. Have the spelling tests been graded?

Steps to Good Grammar

TEST

This reproducible page contains two copies of one half-page drill/test. Cut each duplicated page in half; give each student one half-page.

Announce, before students take the test, that one point of extra credit will be awarded for each *completely* correct diagram.

Suggestions for grading:

1. The complete verb is counted as 1 point.

   (a) If the doing verb is not underlined, take off ½ point (for example, *built* in *will be built*).

   (b) If any helping verbs are not underlined, take off ½ point (for example, *will* or *be* in *will be built*).

2. Grading scale:

   (a) Number of items: 38 identification symbols

   <u> 5</u> written answers

   43 total points

-1, 98	-4, 91	-7, 84	-10, 77	-13, 70
-2, 95	-5, 88	-8, 81	-11, 74	-14, 67
-3, 93	-6, 86	-9, 79	-12, 72	-15, 65

   (b) If a student has missed 7 of the 43 points but has constructed two completely correct diagrams, the grade would be -5 = 88.

Diagrams:

2.

6.

8.

Part II.

1. verb, subject
2. verb
3. subject
4. adjective

1. The studious girl had been reading.

2. Sixteen new houses will be built.

3. Our team won!

4. Did the Alhambra jazz band play?

5. The frightened little boy has left.

6. That small, smiling, confident blond girl will audition.

7. The four barefoot children were wading.

8. Has your sister's sports car been repaired?

REVIEW: VERBS, SUBJECTS, AND ADJECTIVES

TEST

Part I. Instructions: Draw two lines under each verb, one under each subject; draw a circle around each adjective; on the reverse side of this page, diagram sentences 2, 6, and 8.

1. The studious girl had been reading.

2. Sixteen new houses will be built.

3. Our team won!

4. Did the Alhambra jazz band play?

5. The frightened little boy has left.

6. That small, smiling, confident blond girl will audition.

7. The four barefoot children were wading.

8. Has your sister's sports car been repaired?

Part II. Fill in the blanks.

1. Every sentence must have a _____ and a _____ .

2. The word that tells what is being done is the _____ .

3. The word that answers "Who?" or "What?" before a verb is the _____ .

4. A word that describes or modifies a noun is an _____ .

REVIEW: VERBS, SUBJECTS, AND ADJECTIVES
TEST

Part I. Instructions: Draw two lines under each verb, one under each subject; draw a circle around each adjective; on the reverse side of this page, diagram sentences 2, 6, and 8.

1. The studious girl had been reading.

2. Sixteen new houses will be built.

3. Our team won!

4. Did the Alhambra jazz band play?

5. The frightened little boy has left.

6. That small, smiling, confident blond girl will audition.

7. The four barefoot children were wading.

8. Has your sister's sports car been repaired?

Part II. Fill in the blanks.

1. Every sentence must have a _____ and a _____ .

2. The word that tells what is being done is the _____ .

3. The word that answers "Who?" or "What?" before a verb is the _____ .

4. A word that describes or modifies a noun is an _____ .

Steps to Good Grammar

RECOGNIZING ADVERBS

Review the definitions of a verb, a subject, and an adjective. Then instruct students to memorize this definition: An adverb is a word that modifies a verb, an adjective, or another adverb. It tells *how, when,* and *where* about verbs; it tells *how much* about adjectives and adverbs.

1. In reading and analyzing the sample sentences, point out:

   (a) In all sentences, *was ringing* is underlined twice as the verb, *bell* is underlined once as the subject, and *A* is circled as an adjective.

   (b) *Loudly* is bracketed as an adverb and tells *how* about *was ringing; already* is bracketed . . . , and so on.

2. In duplicating the sample diagram on the chalk-board, point out:

   (a) *Slightly* is on a slanted adverb line.

   (b) The adverb line angles to touch the slanted line of the adjective *cracked* because *slightly* tells

how much about *cracked.*

3. Student analysis of practice sentences:

   (a) Instruct students to identify:
   - The word that is modified by each adverb.

   - What the adverb "tells" about that word.

   Example — Sentence 3:
   Sleepily is an adverb. Bracket it.
   It tells *how* about the verb *had eaten.*

   (b) In completing the all-inclusive diagram at the bottom of the page, instruct students to write *sleepily* on the last slanted line under *had eaten.*

   Doing this will avoid confusion as the other adverbs are written in their correct order on slanted lines.

   And, of course, is on the dotted line connecting *sleepily* and *slowly,* as explained in the **Reminder** box.

1. The children had eaten .

2. The three exhausted children had eaten .

3. The three exhausted children had eaten [sleepily].

4. The three [completely] exhausted children had eaten [very] [sleepily].

5. The three [completely] exhausted children had eaten [slowly] and [very] [sleepily].

Fill in this diagram with the words from sentences 1-5, starting with sentence 1. Use the sample diagram as a model.

ADVERBS

Recognizing Adverbs

LEARN: An **adverb** is a word that modifies a verb, an adjective, or another adverb. It tells *how, when, where,* or *how much* about the word it modifies. In analyzing sentences, bracket adverbs. *Examples:*

1. (A) bell was ringing [loudly]. (*loudly* tells *how* about the verb)
2. (A) bell was ringing [already]. (*already* tells *when* about the verb)
3. (A) bell was ringing [somewhere]. (*somewhere* tells *where* about the verb)
4. (A) bell was ringing [very][loudly]. (*very* tells *how much* about the adverb *loudly*)
5. (A)[slightly](cracked) bell was ringing . (*slightly* tells *how much* about the adjective *cracked*)

Adjectives and adverbs are diagrammed on slanted lines under the words they modify; the line for an adverb that tells *how much* touches the line of the adjective or adverb it modifies:

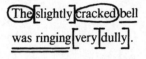 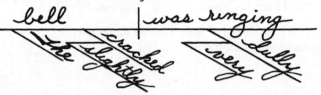

(The)[slightly](cracked) bell
was ringing [very][dully].

PRACTICE: In each sentence below, draw two lines under the verb, one under the subject; draw a circle around adjectives, brackets around adverbs.

1. The children had eaten .

2. The three exhausted children had eaten .

> **Reminder:** In sentence analysis, no mark is given to conjunctions: *and, but,* etc. Diagram them on dotted lines.

3. The three exhausted children had eaten sleepily .

4. The three completely exhausted children had eaten very sleepily .

5. The three completely exhausted children had eaten slowly and very sleepily .

Fill in this diagram with the words from sentences 1-5, starting with sentence 1. Use the sample diagram as a model.

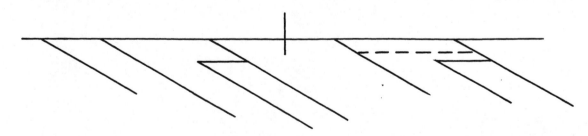

Steps to Good Grammar

RECOGNIZING ADVERBS — PRACTICE

This reproducible page contains two copies of one half-page drill/test. Cut each duplicated page in half; give each student one half-page.

1. Write the sample sentence on the chalkboard to demonstrate the marks for identification:

   (a) Point out the two verbs, two things Randy did: *worked* and *did finish.*

   (b) Make clear the fact that *n't,* a contraction of *not,* is bracketed as an adverb even though it is part of the word *didn't.*

2. Duplicate the sample diagram on the chalkboard:

   (a) Carefully construct a *wide* fork in the verb position for the two verbs.

   (b) In the wide space under *worked,* show clearly the placement of the slanted adverb lines.

   (c) Point out the conjunctions, *and* and *but,* on the dotted lines between the words they join.

3.

9.

10.

---

1. Larry was [severely] injured.

2. (The) campfire blazed [brightly].

3. Will (our) car be repaired [today]?

4. (The) team played [unusually] [well].

5. (Several) teachers were talking [quietly].

6. [Not] (many) houses have been built [around] [here].

7. [Hardly] (any) people live [nearby].

8. Did (many) students arrive [promptly]?

9. (The) flame flickered [feebly] and [then] went [out].

10. Ellen was driving [extremely] [slowly] and [cautiously].

ADVERBS

Recognizing Adverbs — Practice

REMEMBER: An adverb tells *how, when, where* about a verb; *how much* about an adjective or another adverb.

Instructions: In each sentence below, draw two lines under the verb, one under the subject; circle adjectives, bracket adverbs. Diagram sentences 3, 9, and 10.

Example:
Randy worked[very][slowly]and
[carefully]but did n't finish.

1. Larry was severely injured.
2. The campfire blazed brightly.
3. Will our car be repaired today?
4. The team played unusually well.
5. Several teachers were talking quietly.
6. Not many houses have been built around here.

7. Hardly any people live nearby.
8. Did many students arrive promptly?
9. The flame flickered feebly and then went out.
10. Ellen was driving extremely slowly and cautiously.

NAME _____ DATE _____ 49

ADVERBS

Recognizing Adverbs — Practice

REMEMBER: An adverb tells *how, when, where* about a verb; *how much* about an adjective or another adverb.

Instructions: In each sentence below, draw two lines under the verb, one under the subject; circle adjectives, bracket adverbs. Diagram sentences 3, 9, and 10.

Example:
Randy worked[very][slowly]and
[carefully]but did n't finish.

1. Larry was severely injured
2. The campfire blazed brightly.
3. Will our car be repaired today?
4. The team played unusually well.
5. Several teachers were talking quietly.
6. Not many houses have been built around here.

7. Hardly any people live nearby.
8. Did many students arrive promptly?
9. The flame flickered feebly and then went out.
10. Ellen was driving extremely slowly and cautiously.

Steps to Good Grammar

DRILL: RECOGNIZING AND DIAGRAMMING ADVERBS AND OTHER SENTENCE PARTS

It is important that students say the words *adjective* and *adverb*, not just *circle* and *bracket*. In later years in school, teachers will expect them to say the grammatical terms.

Somewhat simplified oral identification is appropriate. For example, for sentence 1:

1. Draw two lines under the verb, *trudged,* one line under the subject, *hikers.*

2. Circle the adjectives, *The, sunburned,* and *thirsty.*

3. Bracket the adverbs, *along* and *slowly.*

One reason for continuing to diagram is that it provides visual analysis of the relationship between all sentence parts:

- It establishes the position of verb and subject.

- It places adjectives and adverbs on slanted lines that touch the lines of the words they modify.

1. The hikers, sunburned and thirsty, trudged along slowly.

2. The old Victorian house has been completely rebuilt.

3. All the little campers will be going home tomorrow.

4. Have your parents arrived already?

5. The boys were working fast but very carefully.

6. Our school band will play tomorrow.

7. The spectators were cheering wildly.

8. Tina spoke softly but quite distinctly.

9. The men must have worked quickly and have already left.

10. A rather embarrassed girl came in quietly and sat down.

11. The two really excited little boys were leaving.

12. A gentle, warm breeze had come up suddenly.

13. Shouldn't Dad be arriving soon?

14. Several students should have studied more regularly and carefully.

15. Why aren't those three little girls playing now?

2.

5.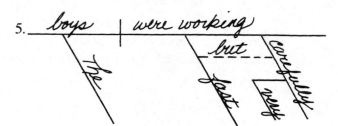

10.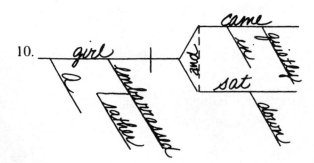

14.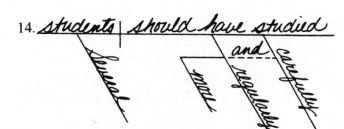

ADVERBS

DRILL: Recognizing and Diagramming Adverbs and Other Sentence Parts

Instructions: Underline each verb twice, each subject once; circle adjectives, bracket adverbs. Diagram sentences 2, 5, 10, and 14 on the other side of this page.

1. The hikers, sunburned and thirsty, trudged along slowly.

2. The old Victorian house has been completely rebuilt.

3. All the little campers will be going home tomorrow.

4. Have your parents arrived already?

5. The boys were working fast but very carefully.

6. Our school band will play tomorrow.

7. The spectators were cheering wildly.

8. Tina spoke softly but quite distinctly.

9. The men must have worked quickly and have already left.

10. A rather embarrassed girl came in quietly and sat down.

11. The two really excited little boys were leaving.

12. A gentle, warm breeze had come up suddenly.

13. Shouldn't Dad be arriving soon?

14. Several students should have studied more regularly and carefully.

15. Why aren't those three little girls playing now?

© 1988, 1997 J. Weston Walch, Publisher

Steps to Good Grammar

TEST

Part I

1. verb, subject
2. verb
3. subject
4. adjective
5. adverb

1. The three little boys were sleeping peacefully.

2. The Alhambra jazz band will play tomorrow.

3. The handsome man walked very quickly away.

4. Have the five cheerleaders arrived yet?

5. The smiling and very happy winners walked forward.

6. Sue's homework is always done promptly and neatly.

ADVERBS

TEST: Recognizing and Diagramming Adverbs and Other Sentence Parts

Part I. Instructions: Write the correct word in the spaces below.

1. Every sentence must have a _____ and a _____ .

2. The _____ is the word that tells what is being done.

3. The word that answers the question "Who?" or "What?" before the verb is the

   _____ .

4. A word that modifies a noun is an _____ .

5. An _____ modifies a verb, an adjective, or another adverb.

Part II. Instructions: In each sentence below, draw two lines under the verb, one under the subject; circle adjectives, bracket adverbs. Diagram each sentence.

1. The three little boys were sleeping peacefully.

2. The Alhambra jazz band will play tomorrow.

3. The handsome man walked very quickly away.

4. Have the five cheerleaders arrived yet?

5. The smiling and very happy winners walked forward.

6. Sue's homework is always done promptly and neatly.

© 1988, 1997 J. Weston Walch, Publisher

Steps to Good Grammar

REVIEW

This page may serve two purposes:

1. It may be a real review for students who need to have all the concepts condensed into a brief, compact unit.

2. As so often happens, students may transfer into the class some time after work on this course of study has been started. Careful study of the material presented here could help them to gain a secure base of understanding.

1. The <u>students</u> <u>are reading</u>.

| students | are reading |

2. <u>Will</u> the <u>test</u> <u>be given</u>?

| test | Will be given |

3. The <u>game</u> <u>has been played</u>.

| game | has been played |

1. (Our)(big)(black) <u>dog</u> <u>was growling</u>.

| dog | was growling |
Our / big / black

2. <u>Will</u> (your)(school's)(girls') <u>chorus</u> <u>sing</u>?

| chorus | Will sing |
your / school's / girls'

1. (A)(mistlike) <u>rain</u> <u>has been falling</u> [very][gently][today].

| rain | has been falling |
a / mistlike / very / gently / today

2. (Five)[really](tired) and (hungry)(little) <u>girls</u> <u>walked</u> [slowly][in].

| girls | walked |
Five / really / tired / and / hungry / little / slowly / in

REVIEW: VERBS, SUBJECTS, ADJECTIVES, AND ADVERBS

Verbs and Subjects

KNOW: The word or words that tell *what is done* is the **verb**. The word that tells *who or what does the verb* is the **subject**.

PRACTICE: Underline the verb twice, the subject once; diagram.

Example: The <u>boy</u> <u>is running</u>.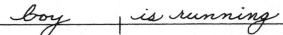

1. The students are reading.

2. Will the test be given?

3. The game has been played.

Adjectives

KNOW: An **adjective** modifies a noun; it tells *which one, what kind, how many,* or *whose* about the noun or pronoun it modifies.

PRACTICE: Underline verb twice, subject once; circle adjectives; diagram.

Example: The frightened little <u>boy</u> <u>is running</u>.

> **Reminder:** The line of a modifier touches the line of the word it modifies.

1. Our big black dog was growling.

2. Will your school's girls' chorus sing?

Adverbs

KNOW: An **adverb** tells *how, when,* and *where* about verbs and *how much* about adjectives and other adverbs.

PRACTICE: Underline verb twice, subject once; circle adjectives, bracket adverbs; diagram.

Example: The [very] frightened little boy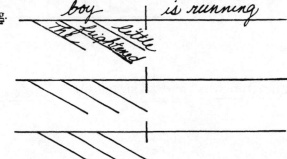
is running [extremely] [fast].

1. A mistlike rain has been falling very gently today.

2. Five really tired and hungry little girls walked slowly in.

Steps to Good Grammar

TEST

Suggested grading if this page is used as a test: Use grading scale on page 24.

    29 identification symbols
    <u> 6 written answers</u>
    35 total points

Part I

1. verb, subject
2. first
3. end
4. verb
5. subject

1. The tired and hungry little boys were eating.

2. Has the bell rung yet?

3. The three teachers were talking quietly.

4. Four girls are working slowly and very carefully.

5. A rather surprised student came in quite quickly.

REVIEW: VERBS, SUBJECTS, ADJECTIVES, AND ADVERBS

TEST

Part I. Instructions: Write the correct word in each space below.

1. Every sentence must have a _____ and a _____ .

2. The _____ word in every sentence must be capitalized.

3. There must be a mark of punctuation at the _____ of every sentence.

4. The _____ is the word that tells what is being done in the sentence.

5. The _____ is the word that *does* the verb.

Part II. Instructions: In each sentence below, draw two lines under the verb, one under the subject; draw a circle around each adjective, brackets around each adverb. In the space under the sentence, construct a diagram.

1. The tired and hungry little boys were eating.

2. Has the bell rung yet?

3. The three teachers were talking quietly.

4. Four girls are working slowly and very carefully.

5. A rather surprised student came in quite quickly.

PRETEST

> This reproducible page contains two copies of one half-page drill/test. Cut each duplicated page in half; give each student one half-page.

Remind students that the scores they receive on this pretest in no way affect their report card grades. The results will simply indicate what they understand and what they need to learn about the use of pronouns as subjects in sentences.

Before they start the pretest, call attention to sentences 8 and 9.

In sentence 8, explain that four choices, each containing three words, are separated by semicolons; students are to underline one set of three words.

In sentence 9, students are to underline *one* of the two words given in *each* set.

Grading suggestion:

The pretest requires recognition of correct subject words. Because 2 separate choices are given in sentence 9, there are 11 subjects to consider.

Since so few items are being considered, *word* grades are suggested:

10 or 11 correct	Excellent
8 or 9 correct	Good
6 or 7 correct	Fair
5 or fewer correct	Better study!

You can use the same word grades to evaluate students' recognition of complete verbs in the sentences.

1.   (Him and Bill, Bill and he, Bill and him) are going out for football.

2.   (Us, We) girls won the tug-of-war!

3.   Were Jim and (he, him) elected?

4.   (You and her, Her and you, She and you, You and she) were chosen.

5.   Certainly (we and them, them and us, they and we) should practice now.

6.   Pat or (she, her) could be our class president.

7.   Could (I, you, and she; her, me, and you; me, you, and she; you, she, and I) come early?

8.   Weren't (he and I, me and him, him and I, he and me) invited?

9.   (Her, She) and (him, he) have already volunteered.

10.   Will (you and Mom, Mom and you) wait?

PRONOUNS USED AS SUBJECTS

PRETEST: Using Pronouns as Subjects

Instructions: Draw two lines under each verb; draw one line under the correct form of the choices given in parentheses.

1. (Him and Bill, Bill and he, Bill and him) are going out for football.

2. (Us, We) girls won the tug-of-war!

3. Were Jim and (he, him) elected?

4. (You and her, Her and you, She and you, You and she) were chosen.

5. Certainly (we and them, them and us, they and we) should practice now.

6. Pat or (she, her) could be our class president.

7. Could (I, you, and she; her, me, and you; me, you, and she; you, she, and I) come early?

8. Weren't (he and I, me and him, him and I, he and me) invited?

9. (Her, She) and (him, he) have already volunteered.

10. Will (you and Mom, Mom and you) wait?

NAME _____ DATE _____ 59

PRONOUNS USED AS SUBJECTS

PRETEST: Using Pronouns as Subjects

Instructions: Draw two lines under each verb; draw one line under the correct form of the choices given in parentheses.

1. (Him and Bill, Bill and he, Bill and him) are going out for football.

2. (Us, We) girls won the tug-of-war!

3. Were Jim and (he, him) elected?

4. (You and her, Her and you, She and you, You and she) were chosen.

5. Certainly (we and them, them and us, they and we) should practice now.

6. Pat or (she, her) could be our class president.

7. Could (I, you, and she; her, me, and you; me, you, and she; you, she and I) come early?

8. Weren't (he and I, me and him, him and I, he and me) invited?

9. (Her, She) and (him, he) have already volunteered.

10. Will (you and Mom, Mom and you) wait?

Steps to Good Grammar

RECOGNIZING NOMINATIVE PRONOUNS

Introducing Pronouns

Students now have a firm understanding of the subject of a sentence. They should add to that a firm understanding of the correct pronouns to use in that position.

Plan to counter every bit of resistance to learning to use pronouns correctly. Suggested approaches:

1. "That was then, this is now!"

   Very early in their lives students learned to speak "playground" language:

   "Me and him is next!" "Give it to John and I!"

   The children's attitude toward grammatical corrections may have been: "*Me*'s right sometimes. *I*'s right sometimes. Who cares!" Now they have the reasoning ability to understand parts of sentences. Now is the time to give up playground language!

2. There is value in "being different!"

   Junior high age students are especially eager to be accepted and try earnestly not to be "different." A student might say, "'They and we are going' sounds weird. If I say that, my friends will think I'm weird."

Assure the student that in a few years his friends will have learned correct usage and might, indeed, think he was a little weird if he were to say, "Them and us are going."

More convincingly, assure students that using language correctly is a valuable difference to establish. Future employers will seek them out because of it.

3. Then there's the appeal to pride!

   It seems a shame that average citizens in the United States use their language less well than educated people in other countries who learn English merely as a second language.

Student Page Guide:

1. Read aloud carefully every item in **Know** as students read silently.

2. Quiz students as you read to establish their understanding: What is the meaning of *pro*? What is a pronoun? What is the meaning of *nominative*? What are the nominative or *subjective* pronouns? And so on!

3. Note to students that objective pronouns — *me, him, her, us, them* — are never used as subjects. Students will study pronouns in the object position later.

1. We had already gone. Dale had already gone. *Dale* and *we* had already gone.

2. I left quickly. Derek left quickly. *Derek* and *I* left quickly.

3. Has Karen decided? Have you decided? Have *you* and *Karen* decided?

4. My little sister and (me, I) talked quietly.

5. (They, Them) and (us, we) may go in.

6. You, (she, her), and (me, I) could work together.

7. Have (he, him) and (her, she) finished?

8. The other girls and (we, us) ate hurriedly and left.

9. You, Alison, and (I, me) should arrive early.

10. Have (them, they) and (her, she) gone?

PRONOUNS USED AS SUBJECTS

Recognizing Nominative Pronouns

KNOW: 1. A **pronoun** is a word used to take the place of a noun. *Pro* means "for"; a pronoun stands for a noun. When you use a pronoun, it should refer clearly to a noun you used earlier.

2. **Nominative** means **subjec**tive. The nominative pronouns are:

MEMORIZE: **I, YOU, HE, SHE, WE, THEY**

They are correct in the subject position — used as subjects.

Simple subject: **She** arrived. **I** just arrived.
Compound subject: **She** and **I** just arrived.

3. To use the correct pronouns in compound subjects (subjects with two or more parts), say each pronoun by itself with the verb:

(Him, He), (she, her), and (me, I) will leave soon.

Obviously incorrect: *Him* will leave, *her* will leave, *me* will leave.
Obviously correct: **He** will leave, **she** will leave, **I** will leave.

4. Remember, **polite order** in using pronouns in compound subjects:
First: *you,* as the person *to whom* you are talking.
Second: *she, he, they,* or **nouns**, persons *about whom* you are talking.
Last: *I* and *we.*

PRACTICE: As in the examples below, draw two lines under each verb, one under each subject. Using polite order, write the pronouns/nouns in the compound subject for sentences 1–3; choose the correct pronouns for sentences 5–10.

Example: I went in. My mom went in. My mom and I went in.

1. We had already gone. Dale had already gone. _____ and _____ had already gone.

2. I left quickly. Derek left quickly. _____ and _____ left quickly.

3. Has Karen decided? Have you decided? Have _____ and _____ decided?

4. My little sister and (me, I) talked quietly.

5. (They, Them) and (us, we) may go in.

6. You, (she, her), and (me, I) could work together.

7. Have (he, him) and (her, she) finished?

8. The other girls and (we, us) ate hurriedly and left.

9. You, Alison, and (I, me) should arrive early.

10. Have (them, they) and (her, she) gone?

  Steps to Good Grammar

USING NOMINATIVE PRONOUNS — PRACTICE

Call on students to recite the list of subject pronouns and the order of polite usage.

Part I, sentence 7: If a student questions the use of the verb *like* after the second part of the subject, point out that the compound subject, *he and she*, means that *more* than one *like* apple pie; therefore, the thought is *"they like"*.

Part I, sentence 9: This sentence uses a linking verb, which will be studied later. Simply point out that a person can't do

tardy; the word is an adjective that describes the subject and should not be underlined as a verb.

In Part II, sentences 1–5, instruct students to write *appos.* (appositive) above the words *students, cheerleaders, four,* and *Californians*.

To reinforce learning, continue rewarding students who turn in perfect drill/practice papers with 100%; continue to deduct 5% for each error a student has not corrected.

1. (Her, She) is going. (We, Us) are going. _____She_____ and _____we_____ are going.
2. Mom is leaving. (Me, I) am leaving. Dad is leaving. _____Mom_____, _____Dad_____, and _____I_____ are leaving.
3. Gene should practice. You should practice. _____You_____ and _____Gene_____ should practice.
4. (Me, I) have been elected. You have been elected. _____You_____ and _____I_____ have been elected.
5. (They, Them) are working hard. (We, Us) are working hard. _____They_____ and _____we_____ are working hard.
6. (I, Me) play tennis. Alice plays tennis. _____Alice_____ and _____I_____ play tennis.
7. (He, Him) likes apple pie. (Her, She) likes apple pie. _____He_____ and _____she_____ like apple pie.
8. (We, Us) have bought a new car. Our neighbors have bought a new car. _____Our neighbors_____ and _____we_____ have bought new cars.
9. (Me, I) am often tardy. You are often tardy. Danny is often tardy. _____You_____, _____Danny_____, and _____I_____ are often tardy.
10. (Them, They) could volunteer. You could volunteer. (I, Me) could volunteer. _____You_____, _____they_____, and _____I_____ could volunteer.

1. (Us, We) junior high students have our opinions. *appos.*
2. (We, Us) students like vacations. *appos.*
3. (We, Us) cheerleaders rode on the bus. *appos.*
4. (We, Us) four asked for library passes. *appos.*
5. (Us, We) Californians like our state. *appos.*

PRONOUNS USED AS SUBJECTS

Using Nominative Pronouns — Practice

I, YOU, HE, SHE, WE, THEY

REMEMBER: Polite order: *First:* you
Second: he, she, they, nouns
Last: I, we

Part I. Instructions: In each sentence below, draw two lines under the verb, one under the subject; underline the correct word in parentheses. In the spaces, write the subjects in polite order.

Example: Sue was chosen. (Me, I) was chosen. You were chosen. *You, Sue,* and *I* were chosen.

1. (Her, She) is going. (We, Us) are going. _____ and _____ are going.

2. Mom is leaving. (Me, I) am leaving. Dad is leaving. _____ , _____ , and _____ are leaving.

3. Gene should practice. You should practice. _____ and _____ should practice.

4. (Me, I) have been elected. You have been elected. _____ and _____ have been elected.

5. (They, Them) are working hard. (We, Us) are working hard. _____ and _____ are working hard.

6. (I, Me) play tennis. Alice plays tennis. _____ and _____ play tennis.

7. (He, Him) likes apple pie. (Her, She) likes apple pie. _____ and _____ like apple pie.

8. (We, Us) have bought a new car. Our neighbors have bought a new car. _____ and _____ have bought new cars.

9. (Me, I) am often tardy. You are often tardy. Danny is often tardy. _____ , _____ , and _____ are often tardy.

10. (Them, They) could volunteer. You could volunteer. (I, Me) could volunteer. _____ , _____ , and _____ could volunteer.

Part II. Instructions: In the following sentences, the pronoun is the subject. The noun that follows the pronoun is an appositive, which we will study later; it identifies the pronoun, tells *who* the pronoun is. Underline verb and subject as above.

1. (Us, We) junior high students have our opinions.

2. (We, Us) students like vacations.

3. (We, Us) cheerleaders rode on the bus.

4. (We, Us) four asked for library passes.

5. (Us, We) Californians like our state.

Steps to Good Grammar

DRILL 1

Students often say, "That doesn't sound right!"

Establishing the sound of correct usage is important. After the correct pronouns have been selected, instruct students to reread each sentence aloud.

In Part II, sentences 9 and 15, instruct students to write *appos.* (appositive) above the words *citizens* and *students*.

1. You may leave. (Her, She) may leave. ___*You*___ and ___*she*___ may leave.

2. (Me, I) am buying new shoes. (She, Her) is buying new shoes. ___*She*___ and ___*I*___ are buying new shoes.

3. Tony had arrived on time. (Us, We) had arrived on time. ___*Tony*___ and ___*we*___ had arrived on time.

4. (He, Him) often rides his motorcycle. (They, Them) often ride their motorcycles. ___*He*___ and ___*they*___ often ride their motorcycles.

5. Jill bought a blouse. (Me, I) bought a blouse. ___*Jill*___ and ___*I*___ bought blouses.

1. (Them, They) and (us, we) both won our playoff game.

2. (Sally and me) (Sally and I) (Me and Sally) hurried home.

3. (You, him, and me) (He, you, and I) (You, he, and I) won the election.

4. (Me and my brothers) (My brothers and I) (I and my brothers) enjoy hockey.

5. (He, she, and you) (You, she, and he) will be squad leaders.

6. (Us and them) (Them and us) (We and they) (They and we) walk to school.

7. (Him and her) (She and him) (She and he) are the best dancers.

8. Usually (me and Jody) (Jody and I) (I and Jody) mow the lawn.

9. (Us, We) citizens *appos.* are very fortunate people.

10. Are (you, them, and me) (they, you, and I) (you, they, and I) going now?

11. (Him and me) (Me and he) (He and I) are going to the library.

12. Have (you and they) (them and you) (you and them) finished your homework?

13. Shouldn't (you, her, and me) (you, she, and I) (her, you, and me) leave?

14. (My parents and I) (Me and my parents) (I and my parents) seldom argue.

15. Are (us, we) students *appos.* learning to use pronouns correctly?

PRONOUNS USED AS SUBJECTS

DRILL 1: Using Pronouns as Subjects

Part I. Instructions: Draw two lines under each verb, one under each subject; in the spaces, write the subject words in polite order.

1. You may leave. (Her, She) may leave. _____ and _____ may leave.

2. (Me, I) am buying new shoes. (She, Her) is buying new shoes. _____ and _____ are buying new shoes.

3. Tony had arrived on time. (Us, We) had arrived on time. _____ and _____ had arrived on time.

4. (He, Him) often rides his motorcycle. (They, Them) often ride their motorcycles. _____ and _____ often ride their motorcycles.

5. Jill bought a blouse. (Me, I) bought a blouse. _____ and _____ bought blouses.

Part II. Instructions: Draw two lines under each verb, one under the correct subject words.

1. (Them, They) and (us, we) both won our playoff game.

2. (Sally and me) (Sally and I) (Me and Sally) hurried home.

3. (You, him, and me) (He, you, and I) (You, he, and I) won the election.

4. (Me and my brothers) (My brothers and I) (I and my brothers) enjoy hockey.

5. (He, she, and you) (You, she, and he) will be squad leaders.

6. (Us and them) (Them and us) (We and they) (They and we) walk to school.

7. (Him and her) (She and him) (She and he) are the best dancers.

8. Usually (me and Jody) (Jody and I) (I and Jody) mow the lawn.

9. (Us, We) citizens are very fortunate people.

10. Are (you, them, and me) (they, you, and I) (you, they, and I) going now?

11. (Him and me) (Me and he) (He and I) are going to the library.

12. Have (you and they) (them and you) (you and them) finished your homework?

13. Shouldn't (you, her, and me) (you, she, and I) (her, you, and me) leave?

14. (My parents and I) (Me and my parents) (I and my parents) seldom argue.

15. Are (us, we) students learning to use pronouns correctly?

© 1988, 1997 J. Weston Walch, Publisher

Steps to Good Grammar

DRILL 2

After students have named the correct subject words in polite order, have them reread the sentences aloud to establish the correct "sound."

Sentences 3 and 13 have appositives, which students should label *appos.*

Sentences 5, 7, and 17 have adjectives: *my* tells *whose*; *only* tells *how many*; *Our* tells *whose.*

Sentence 15: Students may be surprised that *home* is an adverb telling *where.*

1. *Lisa* and *I* were [there] early. (me, I) (Lisa)

2. Shall *they* and *we* wait [here]? (us, we) (they, them)

3. *We* girls will practice [tomorrow] (We, Us)

4. *You*, *he*, and *I* should listen [more] carefully. (me, I) (he, him) (you)

5. [Frequently] *my brother* and *I* arrive [early] (me, I) (my brother)

6. *They* and *we* were appointed. (them, they) (we, us)

7. Only *she* and *I* have been excused. (I, me) (her, she)

8. Can *you* and *she* leave [right] now? (you) (she, her)

9. *Sara*, *he*, and *I* have agreed [completely] (Sara) (he, him) (me, I)

10. Have *you* and *they* volunteered? (them, they) (you)

11. [Suddenly] *he* and *she* ran [in] and sat [down] (he, him) (her, she)

12. [Unfortunately] *you* and *Rick* weren't chosen. (Rick) (you)

13. *We* boys will sign [up] (We, Us)

14. Diane and *she* were playing [very] well. (her, she)

15. *You*, *Nancy*, and *I* should hurry [home] (Nancy) (me, I) (you)

16. *You* and *we* could study [now] (we, us) (you)

17. Our parents and *we* [usually] agree. (us, we) (our parents)

18. *She* and *we* will walk [out] quietly and leave [quickly] (we, us) (her, she)

19. [Why] were *he* and *I* arguing? (he, him) (me, I)

20. Have *she* and *he* been appointed? (her, she) (he, him)

PRONOUNS USED AS SUBJECTS

DRILL 2: Using Pronouns as Subjects

Instructions: Draw two lines under each verb. Choose the correct words to use as subjects from the parentheses at the end of each sentence. Write them in the blanks in polite order. Bracket adverbs; circle adjectives. Write **appos.** above each appositive.

1. _____ and _____ were there early. (me, I) (Lisa)

2. Shall _____ and _____ wait here? (us, we) (they, them)

3. _____ girls will practice tomorrow. (We, Us)

4. _____, _____, and _____ should listen more carefully. (me, I) (he, him) (you)

5. Frequently _____ and _____ arrive early. (me, I) (my brother)

6. _____ and _____ were appointed. (them, they) (we, us)

7. Only _____ and _____ have been excused. (I, me) (her, she)

8. Can _____ and _____ leave right now? (you) (she, her)

9. _____, _____, and _____ have agreed completely. (Sara) (he, him) (me, I)

10. Have _____ and _____ volunteered? (them, they) (you)

11. Suddenly _____ and _____ ran in and sat down. (he, him) (her, she)

12. Unfortunately, _____ and _____ weren't chosen. (Rick) (you)

13. _____ boys will sign up. (We, Us)

14. Diane and _____ were playing very well. (her, she)

15. _____, _____, and _____ should hurry home. (Nancy) (me, I) (you)

16. _____ and _____ could study now. (we, us) (you)

17. _____ and _____ usually agree. (us, we) (our parents)

18. _____ and _____ will walk out quietly and leave quickly. (we, us) (her, she)

19. Why were _____ and _____ arguing? (he, him) (me, I)

20. Have _____ and _____ been appointed? (her, she) (he, him)

Steps to Good Grammar

FINAL DRILL AND TEST

You will need one copy of this page for each student in your class(es). The top half is the final drill, and the bottom half is the test to determine your students' understanding of pronouns correctly used as subjects.

Final Drill:

1. Emphasize the Reminder item, since a sentence using *neither-nor* is included in the test.

2. Sentence 7: Call attention to *n't* being marked as an adverb. The test has a similar sentence.

3. Have students take the drill home and read it aloud several times to firm up their "hearing" of correct pronoun subjects.

Suggestions for grading:

You may give two grades, one for pronoun usage and the other for recognition of other sentence parts; using two colors for the two grades is helpful.

Pronoun usage: -3 for each error in choice of pronouns and/or incorrect order.

Identification of other sentence parts: -4 for each error.

1.   _____*We*_____ students should win! (Us, We)

2.   _____*Dad*_____ and _____*I*_____ should eat [later] (Me, I) (Dad)

3.   Neither _____*they*_____ nor _____*we*_____ can go. (them, they) (we, us)

4.   [Suddenly] _____*Patty*_____ and _____*she*_____ hurried [out] (she, her) (Patty)

5.   _____*You*_____, _____*Lex*_____, and _____*I*_____ should start [now] (Lex) (me, I) (you)

6.   _____*You*_____, _____*she*_____, and _____*he*_____ will be helping. (her, she) (you) (he, him)

7.   Have [n't] _____*you*_____ and _____*he*_____ finished [yet] (he, him) (you)

8.   [Surprisingly] _____*Tony*_____ and _____*we*_____ had arrived [early] (us, we) (Tony)

9.   Could _____*you*_____, _____*she*_____, and _____*I*_____ leave [now]? (me, I) (you) (she, her)

10.   [Luckily] _____*Laura*_____ and _____*I*_____ have been chosen. (I, me) (Laura)

1.   Are _____*you*_____ and _____*they*_____ coming [now]? (them, they) (you)

2.   _____*They*_____ and _____*we*_____ [often] vacation [together] (us, we) (them, they)

3.   _____*You*_____, _____*he*_____, and _____*I*_____ should work [together] (you) (me, I) (he, him)

4.   Are [n't] _____*he*_____ and _____*she*_____ swimming [now]? (him, he) (she, her)

5.   Neither _____*Dale*_____ nor _____*we*_____ have left [yet] (us, we) (Dale)

6.   _____*He*_____, _____*she*_____, and _____*I*_____ should have practiced. (him, he) (me, I) (she, her)

7.   _____*They*_____ and _____*we*_____ were working [very] [hard] (us, we) (they, them)

8.   [Certainly] _____*you*_____, _____*she*_____, and _____*I*_____ might win. (she, her) (you) (me, I)

9.   Will _____*they*_____ or _____*we*_____ play [first]? (them, they) (us, we)

10.   _____*We*_____ Californians like our state. (Us, We)

PRONOUNS USED AS SUBJECTS

FINAL DRILL

Instructions: Draw two lines under each verb. Subject words to use in the blanks are in parentheses at the end of each sentence. Choose and write the correct words in polite order. Bracket adverbs; label appositives **appos.**

> **Reminder:** Use no label for the two-word conjunction *Neither-nor* in sentence 3.

1. _____ students should win! (Us, We)

2. _____ and _____ should eat later. (Me, I) (Dad)

3. Neither _____ nor _____ can go. (them, they) (we, us)

4. Suddenly, _____ and _____ hurried out. (she, her) (Patty)

5. _____, _____, and _____ should start now. (Lex) (me, I) (you)

6. _____, _____, and _____ will be helping. (her, she) (you) (he, him)

7. Haven't _____ and _____ finished yet? (he, him) (you)

8. Surprisingly, _____ and _____ had arrived early. (us, we) (Tony)

9. Could _____, _____, and _____ leave now? (me, I) (you) (she, her)

10. Luckily, _____ and _____ have been chosen. (I, me) (Laura)

NAME _____ DATE _____ 69

PRONOUNS USED AS SUBJECTS

TEST

Instructions: Draw two lines under each verb. Subject words to use in the blanks are in parentheses at the end of each sentence. Choose and write the correct words in polite order. Bracket adverbs; label appositives **appos.**

1. Are _____ and _____ coming now? (them, they) (you)

2. _____ and _____ often vacation together. (us, we) (them, they)

3. _____, _____, and _____ should work together. (you) (me, I) (hc, him)

4. Aren't _____ and _____ swimming now? (him, he) (she, her)

5. Neither _____ nor _____ have left yet. (us, we) (Dale)

6. _____, _____, and _____ should have practiced. (him, he) (me, I) (she, her)

7. _____ and _____ were working very hard. (us, we) (they, them)

8. Certainly, _____, _____, and _____ might win. (she, her) (you) (me, I)

9. Will _____ or _____ play first? (them, they) (us, we)

10. _____ Californians like our state. (Us, We)

Steps to Good Grammar

RECOGNIZING NOUNS USED AS DIRECT OBJECTS

Students should memorize this statement: A direct object receives the action of a "doing" verb.

1. The term "doing" is used here instead of the generally accepted term "action" so students understand that they can *do* a "doing" verb.

    Also, consider this sentence: "The pyramids have stood there for centuries." The pyramids haven't been performing much *action*. But the pyramids have *done* something. They have stood there.

2. As the students analyze the sentences, point out these related reminders:

(a) Many questions begin with a helping verb (sentences 4 and 5).

(b) *Ben's* is a possessive noun used as an adjective (sentence 2).

(c) Use quotation marks to call attention to song titles (sentence 5).

(d) *Ford* is a trade name and proper noun used as an adjective (sentence 7).

(e) A direct object may be compound; if so, it is diagrammed as shown for sentence 9.

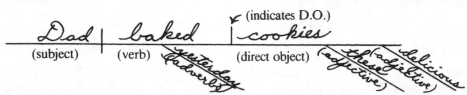

1. Aunt Gail is wearing her new leather coat.
2. Ben's older brother is playing tennis.
3. I am saving all my allowance.
4. Have you finished your homework yet?
5. Will the chorus sing "Silent Night"?

6. When is your mom taking her vacation?
7. My grandfather recently bought a new Ford pickup.
8. The hungry little puppies were eating their supper.
9. Carol will invite Lori and Angela.
10. The team, tired but victorious, left the field slowly.

DIRECT OBJECTS—NOUNS

Recognizing Nouns Used as Direct Objects

KNOW: 1. A **direct object** (abbreviated **D.O.**) receives the action of a "doing" verb.

Example: The little boy had thrown the ball.

The *ball* was the *object* the little boy had thrown.

2. To locate a direct object, say the subject and verb and ask, "What object?" The word that answers the question is the direct object, the **D.O.**

Example: Dad baked these delicious cookies yesterday.

Write the subject and the verb: _____

What object? _____ is the direct object.

3. In a diagram, the direct object follows the verb and is separated from it by a short perpendicular line that stops at the sentence line.

Underline and label the sentence parts in example 2 above; then complete this diagram:

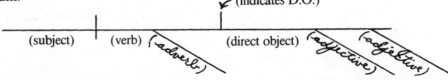

(indicates D.O.)

(subject)   (verb) *(adverb)*   (direct object) *(adjective) (adjective)*

PRACTICE: In the sentences below, mark as usual: verbs, subject, adjectives, adverbs. Write **D.O.** above the word that answers "What object?" On the reverse side of this page, diagram sentences 2, 4, 6, 8, and 10.

1. Aunt Gail is wearing her new leather coat.

2. Ben's older brother is playing tennis.

3. I am saving all my allowance.

4. Have you finished your homework yet?

5. Will the chorus sing "Silent Night"?

6. When is your mom taking her vacation?

7. My grandfather recently bought a new Ford pickup.

8. The hungry little puppies were eating their supper.

9. Carol will invite Lori and Angela.   *Carol | will invite Lori Angela*

10. The team, tired but victorious, left the field slowly.

Steps to Good Grammar

DRILL

After students complete the analysis of the first eight sentences in class, you could assign the rest of the page for homework and go over it at the beginning of class the next day.

The statements at the bottom of the page appeared on the previous worksheet. Students should have no trouble completing them without assistance.

As the students analyse the sentences, point out these related reminders:

1. The plural of *Jones* is *Joneses;* the plural ends in *s,* so the possessive is formed by adding only an apostrophe — *Joneses'* (sentence 1). You might go through a few other examples of this if students have difficulty with it.

2. Call attention to the title of a book by underlining it; in print, underlining becomes italics, as shown in sentence 13.

3. Construct a "fork" to diagram a compound subject (sentences 6, 12, 15, and 17).

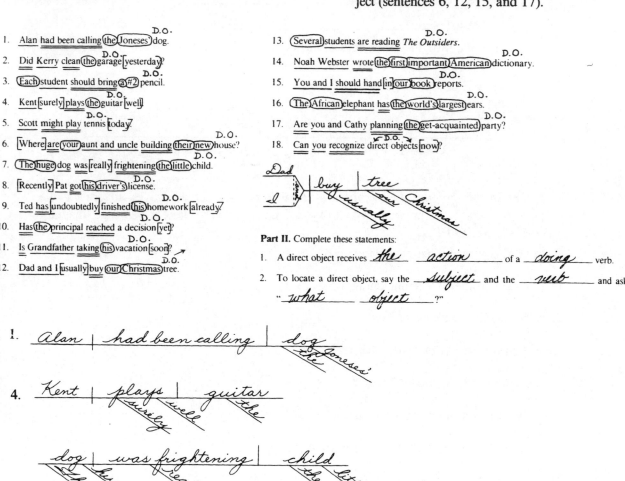

1. Alan had been calling the Joneses dog.   D.O.
2. Did Kerry clean the garage yesterday?   D.O.
3. Each student should bring a #2 pencil.   D.O.
4. Kent surely plays the guitar well.   D.O.
5. Scott might play tennis today?
6. Where are your aunt and uncle building their new house?   D.O.
7. The huge dog was really frightening the little child.   D.O.
8. Recently Pat got his driver's license.   D.O.
9. Ted has undoubtedly finished his homework already.   D.O.
10. Has the principal reached a decision yet?   D.O.
11. Is Grandfather taking his vacation soon?   D.O.
12. Dad and I usually buy our Christmas tree.   D.O.

13. Several students are reading *The Outsiders*.   D.O.
14. Noah Webster wrote the first important American dictionary.   D.O.
15. You and I should hand in our book reports.   D.O.
16. The African elephant has the world's largest ears.   D.O.
17. Are you and Cathy planning the get-acquainted party?   D.O.
18. Can you recognize direct objects now?   D.O.

Part II. Complete these statements:

1. A direct object receives *the* _____ *action* _____ of a _____ *doing* _____ verb.
2. To locate a direct object, say the _____ *subject* _____ and the _____ *verb* _____ and ask, " _____ *what* _____ *object* _____ ?"

DIRECT OBJECTS — NOUNS

DRILL: Recognizing Direct Objects and Other Sentence Parts

Part I. Instructions: Mark as usual: verbs, subjects, adjectives, adverbs. Write **D.O.** above direct objects. Diagram sentences 1, 4, 7, 10, 12, and 15.

1. Alan had been calling the Joneses' dog.

2. Did Kerry clean the garage yesterday?

3. Each student should bring a #2 pencil.

4. Kent surely plays the guitar well.

5. Scott might play tennis today.

6. Where are your aunt and uncle building their new house?

7. The huge dog was really frightening the little child.

8. Recently Pat got his driver's license.

9. Ted has undoubtedly finished his homework already.

10. Has the principal reached a decision yet?

11. Is Grandfather taking his vacation soon?

12. Dad and I usually buy our Christmas tree.

13. Several students are reading *The Outsiders*.

14. Noah Webster wrote the first important American dictionary.

15. You and I should hand in our book reports.

16. The African elephant has the world's largest ears.

17. Are you and Cathy planning the get-acquainted party?

18. Can you recognize direct objects now?

Part II. Complete these statements:

1. A direct object receives _____ _____ of a _____ verb.

2. To locate a direct object, say the _____ and the _____ and ask,

   "_____ _____?"

© 1988, 1997 J. Weston Walch, Publisher

Steps to Good Grammar

FINAL DRILL

Some of the sentences on this final drill are purposely more complicated than earlier ones. For two of them, sentences 8 and 16, the diagrams have been constructed.

Sentence 8: *Homework* is a direct object only to the verb *do,* and the adverb *carefully* modifies only the verb *listen. Most* is an adverb that modifies the adjective *successful.*

Sentence 14: Of the two parts of the compound

verb, *school* is the direct object to the verb *has left,* and *home* is the adverb that tells *where* about the verb *gone.* Also note that *has* is a helping verb to both *left* and *gone; has* immediately follows the dividing line in the diagram; the doing verbs are placed on the forked lines.

Sentence 16: *Car* is the direct object to both verbs and is shown that way in the diagram.

Announce a test for the next day.

1. Yesterday my little sister lost her new soccer ball.
2. Rosie plays the piano [very] [well.]
3. Is Ted doing his homework [now]?
4. Alan [really] should have read the book.
5. Leo is [still] eating his lunch.
6. Dad has [just] bought a new pickup.
7. Have the freshmen [ever] won the tournament?
8. The most successful students listen [carefully] and do their homework.
9. Our new neighbors have a sailboat.

10. The dog's barking must have awakened my little brother.
11. Do the students elect new officers [tomorrow]?
12. Did Terry buy a Harley-Davidson motorcycle?
13. The librarian was describing some new books.
14. Bill has [already] left the school and gone [home.]
15. My little nephew [just] got his first haircut.
16. Dad [just] washed and waxed the car.
17. Pocahontas's pleas may have saved Captain John Smith.
18. Has everyone finished this worksheet?

Part II. Complete these statements:

1. A direct object receives _the action of a doing verb._

2. To locate a direct object, say _the subject and the verb and ask,_ _"What object?"_ ?

DIRECT OBJECTS — NOUNS

FINAL DRILL: Recognizing Direct Objects and Other Sentence Parts

Part I. Instructions: Mark as usual: <u>verbs</u>, <u>subjects</u>, (adjectives) [adverbs] Write **D.O.** above direct objects. Diagram sentences 1, 8, 9, 10, 14, and 16.

1. Yesterday my little sister lost her new soccer ball.

2. Rosie plays the piano very well.

3. Is Ted doing his homework now?

4. Alan really should have read the book.

5. Leo is still eating his lunch.

6. Dad has just bought a new pickup.

7. Have the freshmen ever won the tournament?

8. The most successful students listen carefully and do their homework?

9. Our new neighbors have a sailboat.

10. The dog's barking must have awakened my little brother.

11. Do the students elect new officers tomorrow?

12. Did Terry buy a Harley-Davidson motorcycle?

13. The librarian was describing some new books.

14. Bill has already left the school and gone home.

15. My little nephew just got his first haircut.

16. Dad just washed and waxed the car. →

17. Pocahontas's pleas may have saved Captain John Smith.

18. Has everyone finished this worksheet?

> **Reminders:**
> 1. All singular nouns add *'s* to show possession (sentences 10 and 17).
> 2. Some adverbs tell *where* (sentence 14). Don't confuse this with "What object?"

Part II. Complete these statements:

1. A direct object receives _____ .

2. To locate a direct object, say _____ ?

Steps to Good Grammar

TEST 1

Test 2 on page 79 is an alternate test of nearly equal difficulty. You can use Test 2 as a makeup test for students who are absent the day of Test 1.

Suggested grading:

As on previous tests, count complete verbs as one item. If a student fails to underline either the doing verb *or* the helping verb(s), the complete verb is half wrong.

34 identification symbols
 9 written answers
43 total items

The grading scale for 43 items is given on page 44.

You can give extra credit for perfect diagrams.

Part I

1. verb, subject

2. verb

3. subject

4. adjective

5. adverb

6. subject, verb, "What object?"

Part II.

1. (All)(the) clouds have [finally] drifted [away].

2. Someone must have put (Joe's) report [there].   **D.O.**

3. [Probably] Kristy has [already] finished (all)(her) homework.   **D.O.**

4. Is (your) brother [really] buying (that)[very](expensive) watch?   **D.O.**

5. (Many) students had listened [carefully] and completed (the) assignment [correctly].   **D.O.**

DIRECT OBJECTS — NOUNS

TEST 1: Recognizing Direct Objects and Other Sentence Parts

Part I. Instructions: Write the correct words in the spaces in the following sentences.

1. Every sentence must have a _____ and a _____ .

2. The _____ is the word that tells what is being done.

3. The _____ is what or whom the sentence is about.

4. An _____ modifies a noun or pronoun.

5. An _____ modifies a verb, an adjective, or an adverb.

6. To find the direct object, say the _____ and _____ and ask,

    _____ ?

Part II. Instructions: In each sentence below, mark: <u>verbs</u>, <u>subjects</u>, (adjectives), [adverbs], label **D.O.** if there is one; construct diagrams.

1. All the clouds have finally drifted away.

2. Someone must have put Joe's report there.

3. Probably Kristy has already finished all her homework.

4. Is your brother really buying that very expensive watch?

5. Many students had listened carefully and completed the assignment correctly.

Steps to Good Grammar

TEST 2

This reproducible page contains two copies of one half-page drill/test. Cut each duplicated page in half; give each student one half-page.

2.   35 identification symbols
          7 written answers
        42 total items

See page 44 for grading scale.

Suggested grading:

1. See previous teacher page for information about scoring complete verbs.

Part I

1. verb, subject

2. verb

3. subject

4. adjective

5. adverb

6. direct object

2.

3.

4.

Part II

1. All the students had finally settled down.
2. My older brother probably finished that job today.
3. Lon had already picked all the peaches.
4. Did your uncle really buy that black van?
5. Some teachers explain clearly and really help the students.

DIRECT OBJECTS — NOUNS

TEST 2: Recognizing Direct Objects and Other Sentence Parts

Part I. Instructions: Complete these statements.

1. Every sentence must have a _____ and _____ .
2. The word that tells what is being done is the _____.
3. The word that tells what the sentence is about is the _____.
4. An _____ modifies a noun.
5. An _____ modifies a verb, an adjective, or an adverb.
6. When you say the subject and verb and ask, "What object?" you find the _____ _____.

Part II. Instructions: Mark: <u>verbs</u>, <u>subjects</u>, adjectives, adverbs, label **D.O.** On the reverse side of this page, diagram sentences 2, 3, and 4.

1. All the students had finally settled down.
2. My older brother probably finished that job today.
3. Lon had already picked all the peaches.
4. Did your uncle really buy that black van?
5. Some teachers explain clearly and really help the students.

DIRECT OBJECTS — NOUNS

TEST 2: Recognizing Direct Objects and Other Sentence Parts

Part I. Instructions: Complete these statements.

1. Every sentence must have a _____ and _____ .
2. The word that tells what is being done is the _____.
3. The word that tells what the sentence is about is the _____.
4. An _____ modifies a noun.
5. An _____ modifies a verb, an adjective, or an adverb.
6. When you say the subject and verb and ask, "What object?" you find the _____ _____.

Part II. Instructions: Mark: <u>verbs</u>, <u>subjects</u>, adjectives, adverbs, label **D.O.** On the reverse side of this page, diagram sentences 2, 3, and 4.

1. All the students had finally settled down.
2. My older brother probably finished that job today.
3. Lon had already picked all the peaches.
4. Did your uncle really buy that black van?
5. Some teachers explain clearly and really help the students.

© 1988, 1997 J. Weston Walch, Publisher

Steps to Good Grammar

SHORT SENTENCES

1. Emphasize the fact that students' sentences are to include only verb, subject, direct object, adjectives, and adverbs.

2. Undoubtedly, as students have been working their way through this course of study, they have been given original writing assignments. Probably they have expressed their ideas in more sophisticated sentences than they have been studying in *Steps to Good Grammar.*

3. This assignment may be a real challenge to your students to structure sentences that include only the sentence parts they have studied. Other students have enjoyed finding they can write interesting short sentences within these limits.

4. Ask volunteers to identify the sentence parts of the "Short, choppy sentences" examples. Realizing that those sentences were written within the requirements of the assignment should make it easier for your students to write similar sentences.

WRITTEN EXPRESSION

Short Sentences

Now you can easily recognize verbs, subjects, direct objects, adjectives, and adverbs. You will now study a few methods you can use to express your ideas in interesting sentences.

Short, choppy sentences are not "bad." Use them *on purpose* to express:

1. Excitement:

    "Emergency lights flashed. Doors banged. Buzzers grated harshly. People rushed frantically past. My feet joined them. Why, I certainly didn't know!"

2. Simple facts:

    "Firmly, Mom said, 'No.' I couldn't argue. I wouldn't win. Actually, I understood."

3. Fear or terror:

    "There stood a weather-beaten old mansion. Its windows were boarded up. The front door hung loosely. Bill and I crept forward. Hesitantly, we mounted the sagging steps. . . ."

Use your imagination to complete this three-part assignment.

Instructions: Write three or four short sentences about:

1. An *exciting* game; write either as a member of the team *or* as a spectator.

2. A *simple fact:* The need to complete a writing assignment *or* a chore at home; *or* the need to practice an instrument *or* a sport in order to play either one well.

3. A *frightening* situation: choose your own subject *or* use one of these suggestions: your real *or* an imagined experience during a fire, a lightning storm, an earthquake, *or* a cyclone.

Instructions for writing:

1. Develop sentences that include only the sentence parts you have studied so far. Be able to identify the verb and subject, a direct object if you use one, adjectives, and adverbs.

2. Use a separate sheet of paper.

3. Work individually.

4. Read again the examples above to help you get started.

5. Volunteer to read your sentences to the class. It will be very interesting to hear the great variety of topics and ideas that have been expressed.

© 1988, 1997 J. Weston Walch, Publisher

Steps to Good Grammar

SENTENCES WITH COMPOUND PARTS

1. Students need to remember the meaning of *compound,* as well as the abbreviation of *Cd.* Both the word and the abbreviation will be used often in this unit.

2. You can offer these examples to demonstrate the meaning of the conjunctions:

   (a) Lee **and** Ted can go: Ted is definitely in *addition* to Lee.

   (b) Not Fran, **but** Carrie was elected: Carrie is *different* from Fran!

   (c) Shall we walk there **or** ride our bikes: We have a *choice*!

   (d) Neither today **nor** tomorrow can I go: There is no *alternative.*

3. Students should understand that all parts of sentences can be compound, can be made up of more than one word.

WRITTEN EXPRESSION

Sentences with Compound Parts

Reading a story written completely with short, choppy sentences becomes tiresome. One way to avoid this problem in your writing is to practice using compound parts in sentences.

Understanding Compound Parts

1. **Compound** means "more than one." It is abbreviated **Cd.**

2. Conjunctions are used to join compound parts of sentences:

> Use **and** to show an *addition.*
> Use **but** to show a *contrast* or difference.
> Use **or** and **nor** to show an *alternative* or choice.

Using Compound Parts

You can rewrite several short sentences into one longer sentence using compound parts.

1. Mark <u>likes</u> science. He <u>likes</u> U.S. history.

    In the second sentence, the words that are the same, or mean the same, as words in the first sentence have been crossed out. The words that are left can be joined to form one longer sentence with a **compound direct object:**

    Mark <u>likes</u> science and U.S. history.

2. Alison <u>has finished</u> her report. Teresa has finished her report.

    <u>Alison and Teresa</u> <u>have finished</u> their reports. (Here, the verb and possessive pronoun have been changed to agree with the **compound subject.**)

3. <u>Dad</u> <u>awakened</u> [early]. He didn't eat breakfast.
    <u>Dad</u> <u>awakened</u> [early] but didn't eat breakfast.

    Compound Verb

4. <u>Tami</u> had [not] read the book. Katie had not read the book.
    Neither <u>Tami</u> nor <u>Katie</u> had read the book.

    Compound Subject

(Here, the two-word negative conjunction, *Neither-nor,* joins the parts of the compound subject and replaces the negative word *not.*)

Steps to Good Grammar

USING COMPOUND PARTS
TO COMBINE SHORT SENTENCES

This page should present no real problem to students.

If there is confusion in anyone's mind, the diagrams, which should be constructed on the chalkboard, give very clear pictures of the compound parts.

1. Elaine will give a speech. Donna will give a speech.

  Elaine and Donna will give speeches.

2. I didn't study the spelling words. I didn't study the vocabulary words. (Use the conjunction *or*.)

  I didn't study the spelling or vocabulary words.

3. My brother raked the leaves. He mowed the lawn.

  My brother raked the leaves and mowed the lawn.

4. Luis baked a delicious chocolate cake. He frosted it. (Use only *frosted* from this sentence.)

  Luis baked and frosted a delicious chocolate cake.

5. The TAB books finally arrived. They were distributed immediately.

  The TAB books finally arrived and were distributed immediately.

6. We planned a party. We couldn't have it. (Leave out only *We* in the second sentence; use *but* as the conjunction.)

  We planned a party but couldn't have it.

7. Sue awakened early. She delivered her papers. Then she ate breakfast.

  Sue awakened early, delivered her papers, and then ate breakfast.

8. Beth played tennis. She walked home. Kurt played tennis. He walked home. (Write a sentence with a compound subject and a compound verb.)

  Beth and Kurt played tennis and walked home.

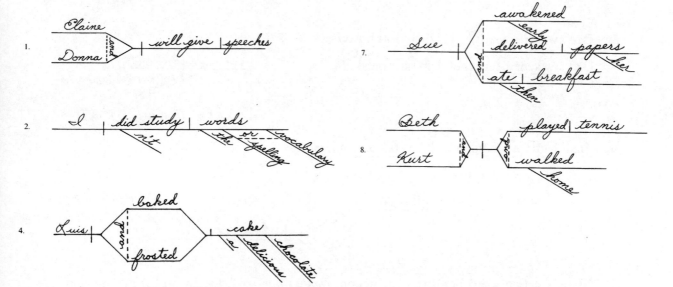

WRITTEN EXPRESSION

Using Compound Parts to Combine Short Sentences

Instructions: For each given sentence, mark: verbs, subjects, adjectives, adverbs, label **D.O.** Then, for each group of sentences, write a single sentence using a compound part; mark/label its parts. On the reverse side of this page, diagram sentences 1, 2, 4, 7, and 8.

1. Elaine will give a speech. Donna will give a speech.

2. I didn't study the spelling words. I didn't study the vocabulary words. (Use the conjunction *or*.)

3. My brother raked the leaves. He mowed the lawn.

4. Luis baked a delicious chocolate cake. He frosted it. (Use only *frosted* from this sentence.)

5. The **TAB** books finally arrived. They were distributed immediately.

6. We planned a party. We couldn't have it. (Leave out only *We* in the second sentence; use *but* as the conjunction.)

7. Sue awakened early. She delivered her papers. Then she ate breakfast.

8. Beth played tennis. She walked home. Kurt played tennis. He walked home. (Write a sentence with a compound subject and a compound verb.)

Steps to Good Grammar

RECOGNIZING COMPOUND PARTS

If any sentences present a problem for students,
construct diagrams on the chalkboard.

1.   Todd and Pete are riding their new bikes. _____ Cd. subj._____

2.   Some teachers and the principal will supervise the students. _____ Cd. subj._____

3.   Dad had thoroughly cleaned and waxed our skis. _____ Cd. verb_____

4.   Rosalie looked around casually and walked on. _____ Cd. verb_____

5.   The children had eaten all the ice cream and cake. _____ Cd. D. O._____

6.   The teacher handed out the test booklets and pencils. _____ Cd. D. O._____

7.   Laura and Kim are practicing their ice-skating routine. _____ Cd. subj._____

8.   We went in quietly and sat down. _____ Cd. verb_____

9.   Tom pruned the bushes and raked the leaves. _____ Cd. verb / D. O._____

10. Emily was thoughtfully wording and carefully printing the invitations. _____ Cd. verb_____

11. The librarian and his assistant sorted and shelved the books. _____ Cd. subj. & Cd. verb_____

12. I ran out and helped my brother. _____ Cd. verb_____

13. The contestants may either stand or sit. _____ Cd. verb_____

14. Lisa pushed open the door but remained outside. _____ Cd. verb_____

15. My parents and my grandparents are planning a Hawaiian vacation. _____ Cd. subj._____

WRITTEN EXPRESSION

Recognizing Compound Parts

Instructions: Mark: verbs, subjects, adjectives, adverbs, label **D.O.** At the end of each sentence, write the compound part: **Cd. Verb, Cd. Subject, Cd. D.O., Cd. Verb/D.O.**

1. Todd and Pete are riding their new bikes. _____

2. Some teachers and the principal will supervise the students. _____

3. Dad had thoroughly cleaned and waxed our skiis. _____

4. Rosalie looked around casually and walked on. _____

5. The children had eaten all the ice cream and cake. _____

6. The teacher handed out the test booklets and pencils. _____

7. Laura and Kim are practicing their ice-skating routine. _____

8. We went in quietly and sat down. _____

9. Tom pruned the bushes and raked the leaves. _____

10. Emily was thoughtfully wording and carefully printing the invitations. _____

11. The librarian and his assistant sorted and shelved the books. _____

12. I ran out and helped my brother. _____

13. The contestants may either stand or sit. _____

14. Lisa pushed open the door but remained outside. _____

15. My parents and my grandparents are planning a Hawaiian vacation. _____

Steps to Good Grammar

FINAL DRILL AND TEST

Recognizing and Writing Sentences with Compound Parts

You will need one copy of this page for each student; the top half is the final drill, and the bottom half is the test.

Instruct students to complete the final drill as though it were a test. Have students correct their own papers; tell them what grade they would have gotten if it had been a test.

Grading suggestions for the test:

1. Each part in a compound part of a sentence is given 1 point.

2. *Will bring* is a complete verb and receives 1 point.
3. No mark is given to conjunctions, which have no point value.
4. In Part II, sentence 2, an alternate correct form of the written sentence is:

Alex and Jerry were [not] elected.

Grading scale:

The drill has 38 points, and the test has 37 points:

-1, 97	-4, 89	-7, 81	-10, 73	-13, 65
-2, 95	-5, 86	-8, 78	-11, 70	-14, 62
-3, 92	-6, 84	-9, 76	-12, 68	-15, 59

Part I.
1. Julie brought the ice cream and the cookies. *(D.O. / D.O.)*

2. Two boys and I have finished the assignment. *(D.O.)*

3. Brent has read the book and has written his report. *(D.O. / D.O.)*

Part II.
1. The man stopped his car. He shook his fist. *(D.O. / D.O.)*
    The man stopped his car and shook his fist. *(D.O. / D.O.)*
2. My brothers are going home now. Their friends are going home now.
    My brothers and their friends are going [home] [now].
3. Lin has invited Kathy. She has invited Sarah.
    Lin has invited Kathy and Sarah. *(D.O. / D.O.)*

Part I.
1. Will Teresa bring the bat and the ball? *(D.O. / D.O.)*

2. My dad and my uncle have bought a boat. *(D.O.)*

3. Greg has bought a new jacket and is buying some new shoes. *(D.O. / D.O.)*

Part II.
1. Mom washed the car. She polished it.
    Mom washed and polished the car. *(D.O.)*
2. Alex was not elected. Jerry was not elected.
    Neither Alex nor Jerry was elected.
3. Allen has finished his algebra homework. He has finished his report.
    Allen has finished his algebra homework and his reports. *(D.O. / D.O.)*

WRITTEN EXPRESSION

FINAL DRILL: Recognizing and Writing Sentences with Compound Parts

Part I. Instructions: Mark: <u>verbs</u>, <u>subjects,</u> (adjectives) [adverbs] label **D.O.**

1.   Julie brought the ice cream and the cookies.

2.   Two boys and I have finished the assignment.

3.   Brent has read the book and has written his report.

Part II. Instructions: Write each following pair of sentences as one, using a compound subject, verb, or direct object joined by *and, but,* or *or.* In each sentence you write, mark/label sentence parts as in Part I.

1.   The man stopped his car. He shook his fist.

2.   My brothers are going home now. Their friends are going home now.

3.   Lin has invited Kathy. She has invited Sarah.

WRITTEN EXPRESSION

TEST: Recognizing and Writing Sentences with Compound Parts

Part I. Instructions: Mark: <u>verbs</u>, <u>subjects,</u> (adjectives) [adverbs] label **D.O.**

1.   Will Teresa bring the bat and the ball?

2.   My dad and my uncle have bought a boat.

3.   Greg has bought a new jacket and is buying some new shoes.

Part II. Instructions: Write each following pair of sentences as one, using a compound subject, verb, or direct object joined by *and, but,* or *or.* In each sentence you write, mark/label sentence parts as in Part I.

1.   Mom washed the car. She polished it.

2.   Alex was not elected. Jerry was not elected.

3.   Allen has finished his algebra homework. He has finished his report.

Steps to Good Grammar

RECOGNIZING COMPOUND SENTENCES

Students should understand the term **compound sentence** and the abbreviation **Cd. Sen.**

Emphasize placing the comma *before* the conjunction. Students frequently put one after it because, they say, "That's where I hear a pause!"

1. Tom played tennis, but Mike cleaned the garage.

2. Grandma was canning peaches, and my brother and I were helping her.

3. The boys should leave now, or they will miss their ride.

4. The class chose the play, Duncan built the sets, and Ken and Lenore played the lead roles.

5. The ice has frozen solidly, so we can skate today.

3.

4.

5.

WRITTEN EXPRESSION

Recognizing Compound Sentences

REMEMBER:

1. A **simple sentence** is a group of words that expresses one complete thought. It must contain at least one subject and one verb. It must make sense.

2. **Compound** means more than one.

KNOW:

1. A **compound sentence** is made up of two or more simple sentences—two or more grammatically complete thoughts, each having its own subject and verb.

2. Two simple sentences are joined with a conjunction: *and, but, or,* or *so;* a comma is usually placed before the conjunction.

   Example:

   The whistle blew shrilly,
   and the game began.

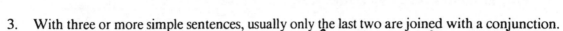

3. With three or more simple sentences, usually only the last two are joined with a conjunction.

   Example:

   I waved my arms, Ed shouted but no one saw or heard us. **D.O.**

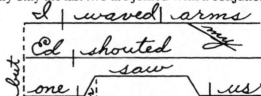

PRACTICE: Mark: verbs, subjects, adjectives, adverbs; label **D.O.** To help you remember to use the comma, draw a box around the comma and conjunction. On the reverse side of this page, diagram sentences 3, 4, and 5.

1. Tom played tennis, but Mike cleaned the garage.

2. Grandma was canning peaches, and my brother and I were helping her.

3. The boys should leave now, or they will miss their ride.

4. The class chose the play, Duncan built the sets, and Ken and Lenore played the lead roles.

5. The ice has frozen solidly, so we can skate today.

Steps to Good Grammar

WRITING COMPOUND SENTENCES

Emphasize:

1. Sentences joined to form a compound sentence must be closely related in thought.

2. The subject in a command or request is often the "understood" *you*.

3. Very short, closely related sentences joined by *and* do not require a comma before the conjunction.

   In completing the practice sentences, students may select conjunctions different from the ones used in the answer key sentences.

1. The sun is shining [brightly], and the rain puddles are drying [up.]
2. I watched the door [carefully], but no one came [out].
3. This house has its drawbacks, but we like it [anyway].
4. (You) follow these directions, or you will lose your way.
5. You must leave [immediately], or you will miss your bus.
6. I mowed the lawn and Joe helped me.

WRITTEN EXPRESSION

Writing Compound Sentences

In writing compound sentences, be sure that the sentences you join are closely related in thought:

Related: The wind was blowing wildly, and the rain was swirling around.

Not related: The wind was blowing wildly, and the flowers were blooming.

You speak and write many sentences that are requests or commands. Often the subject *you* is left out. In practice sentences, write *(You)* before the verb:

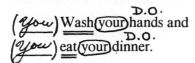

> **Reminder:** No comma is used before *and* when the two sentences (independent clauses) are *very* short and closely related.

PRACTICE: Find the sentence in the right-hand column below that makes sense when added to a sentence in the left-hand column. On the lines provided, write each compound sentence, using an appropriate conjunction — like *and, but, or, so* — and punctuating correctly. Mark/label sentence parts in the sentences you write.

Example:

The mists rolled away.   The sun shone brightly.

The mists rolled [away] and the sun shone [brightly].

1. The sun is shining brightly.   The rain puddles are drying up.
2. I watched the door carefully.   You will lose your way.
3. This house has its drawbacks.   No one came out.
4. Follow these directions.   We like it anyway.
5. You must leave immediately.   Joe helped me.
6. I mowed the lawn.   You will miss your bus.

1. _____

2. _____

3. _____

4. _____

5. _____

6. _____

Steps to Good Grammar

FINAL DRILL

Both sections of this final drill should be reviewed carefully in preparation for the test the next day. Go over the abbreviations with students: *Cd. Verb, Cd. Subj., Cd. D.O., Cd. Subj. – Cd. Verb,* and *Cd. Sen.*

About the *Reminder:*

1. A true "introductory" *there* has no definite grammatical connection to the rest of the sentence:

    There *were* several *students leaving* the building.

    There *could be* other *ideas suggested* tonight.

    There *was* not a single *crumb left.*

2. *There* at the beginning of a sentence may be an adverb indicating a definite place:

    There, on the step, *lay* my *wallet.*

    There, in the wastebasket, *is* my homework *paper.*

3. Part II, sentence 1:

    There may be considered an adverb, or a simple introductory word. In either case, the point to make to the students is that *there* is not the subject of the sentence.

1. The sun was shining [brightly], but clouds cover it [now]. *(D.O.)*

2. Our players must settle [down], or they might lose the game. *(D.O.)*

3. Todd must study, or he might fail the test. *(D.O.)*

4. (You) finish your homework, so you can play tennis. *(D.O. / D.O.)*

1. [There] sat my little sister and her dog.

2. Dad washed and ironed [today]. *Cd. Subj. / Cd. verb*

3. Bob has [not] written his report, but Jared has written his. *D.O. / D.O. / Cd. Sen.*

4. Many teenagers like name-brand jeans and sneakers. *D.O. / D.O. / Cd. D.O.*

5. Water filled the boat, but it didn't sink. *D.O. / Cd. Sen.*

6. [Yesterday], Amy and Jen cleaned their rooms and [then] went to the mall. *D.O. / Cd. Subj. and Cd. verb.*

WRITTEN EXPRESSION

FINAL DRILL
Writing Compound Sentences

Instructions: Find the sentence in the right-hand column below that makes sense when added to a sentence in the left-hand column. On the lines, write each compound sentence, using an appropriate conjunction — *and, but, or, so* — and punctuating correctly. In your sentences, mark/label sentence parts.

1. The sun was shining brightly.	He might fail the test.
2. Our players must settle down.	You can play tennis.
3. Todd must study.	Clouds cover it now.
4. Finish your homework.	They might lose the game.

1. _____

2. _____

3. _____

4. _____

Distinguishing Between Compound Sentences and Sentences with Compound Parts

Instructions: Mark: verbs, subjects, adjectives, adverbs; label **D.O.** At the end of the sentence, where appropriate, write **Cd. Verb, Cd. Subj., Cd. D.O., Cd. Subj.–Cd. Verb,** or **Cd. Sen.** Insert commas where necessary.

1. There sat my little sister and her dog. ⟶ | **Reminder:** The introductory word, *There,* is not the subject; *sat* is the verb; the subject tells *who sat.*

2. Dad washed and ironed today.

3. Bob has not written his report but Jared has written his.

4. Many teenagers like name-brand jeans and sneakers.

5. Water filled the boat but it didn't sink.

6. Yesterday, Amy and Jen cleaned their rooms and then went to the mall.

Steps to Good Grammar

TEST

Grading suggestions:

<table>
<tr><td colspan="2" align="center">Part I</td><td colspan="2" align="center">Part II</td></tr>
<tr><td></td><td align="center">Points</td><td></td><td align="center">Points</td></tr>
<tr><td>Identification symbols</td><td align="center">30</td><td>Identification symbols</td><td align="center">36</td></tr>
<tr><td>Compound labels</td><td align="center">5</td><td>Correctly joined sentences,
1 point each</td><td align="center">10</td></tr>
<tr><td>Commas, sentences 2 and 5</td><td align="center">2
37</td><td>Each comma, 1 point*</td><td align="center">4</td></tr>
<tr><td></td><td></td><td>Each conjunction, 1 point</td><td align="center">5
55</td></tr>
</table>

$$\begin{array}{r} 37 \\ 55 \\ \hline 92 \end{array}$$

Subtract 1 point for each incorrect item.

*Comma is omitted in sentence 5, but including it is not grammatically incorrect—no point awarded either way.

1. Paula and Frances should arrive soon. *Cd. Subj.*

2. You may not know that boy but Pete does. *Cd. Sen.*

3. Did the girls watch *Second Noah* and *Spin City?* *Cd. D.O.*

4. The pears have been picked, boxed, and shipped. *Cd. Verb.*

5. Fortunately, Dad stopped the car, or we would have rammed the bus. *Cd. Sen.*

1. *Betsy saw the game, but Mary stayed [home].*

2. *I must pass this test, or my parents might ground me.*

3. *It might rain, so (you) take your raincoat.*

4. *Our players must settle [down], or they might lose the game.*

5. *I mowed the lawn and Jane helped me.*

WRITTEN EXPRESSION

TEST

Distinguishing Between Compound Sentences and Sentences with Compound Parts

Instructions: In the sentences below, mark: verbs, subjects, adjectives, adverbs, label **D.O.** At the end of each sentence, label correctly: **Cd. Verb, Cd. Subj., Cd. D.O.,** or **Cd. Sen.** Insert needed commas.

1. Paula and Frances should arrive soon.

2. You may not know that boy but Pete does.

3. Did the girls watch *Second Noah* and *Spin City?*

4. The pears have been picked, boxed, and shipped.

5. Fortunately, Dad stopped the car or we would have rammed the bus.

Forming Compound Sentences by Joining Two Simple Sentences

Instructions: Find the sentence in the right-hand column below that makes sense when added to a sentence in the left-hand column. On the lines provided, write each compound sentence, using appropriate conjunctions — *and, but, or, so* — and punctuating correctly. Mark and label sentence parts in each sentence you write.

1. Betsy saw the game.	Take your raincoat.
2. I must pass this test.	They might lose the game.
3. It might rain.	Mary stayed home.
4. Our players must settle down.	Jose helped me.
5. I mowed the lawn.	My parents might ground me.

1. _____

_____

2. _____

_____

3. _____

_____

4. _____

_____

5. _____

_____

Steps to Good Grammar

RECOGNIZING PRONOUNS USED AS DIRECT OBJECTS

This page is similar to page 61, which introduced nominative pronouns.

1. Read and simultaneously quiz students about each item in **Know**.

2. Instruct students to memorize the list of pronouns used in object positions in sentences.

3. Note to students that nominative *(subjective)* pronouns — *I, he, she, we, they* — are never used as direct objects.

4. Have students orally select correct pronouns and identify sentence parts.

Impose a 5% penalty for each uncorrected error when papers are turned in.

5. You can simplify paper correcting by selecting one section of the sentences as being representative of the entire page.

6. Sentence 10: Note to students that *boys* is an appositive, while the pronoun *us* is the direct object. Tell students to label *boys appos.*

1. May I call ___*you*___ and ___*her*___ [tomorrow? (you) (her, she)

2. Did you choose ___*him*___ and ___*me*___? (he, him) (me, I)

3. Kay must have seen ___*them*___ and ___*us*___. (we, us) (them, they)

4. Did the principal believe ___*you*___ and ___*him*___? (he, him) (you)

5. The club members have elected ___*her*___ and ___*him*___. (she, her) (him, he)

6. Dad just phoned ___*you*___ and ___*me*___. (I, me) (you)

7. David saw ___*her*___ and ___*me*___. (me, I) (she, her)

8. Dad will help ___*you*___ and ___*them*___. (they, them) (you)

9. Our elderly neighbor did not recognize ___*Mom*___ and ___*me*___. (I, me) (Mom)

10. The principal helped ___*us*___ boys. (we, us)

DIRECT OBJECTS—PRONOUNS

Recognizing Pronouns Used as Direct Objects

KNOW:

1. The **objective** personal pronouns are:

   Memorize

   ### ME, YOU, HIM, HER, US, THEM

   They are correct in the **direct object** position (abbreviated **D.O.**).

   Simple direct object: Dad saw **you.** Dad saw **me.**
   Compound direct object: Dad saw **you** and **me.**

2. To use the correct pronouns in a compound direct object, say each pronoun by itself after the verb:

   Is Sue inviting (they, them) and (we, us)?

   Obviously incorrect: Is Sue inviting *they*? Is Sue inviting *we*?

   Obviously correct: Is Sue inviting **them**? Is Sue inviting **us**?

3. Use **polite order** of pronouns in the direct object position:

   First: **you,** the person *to whom* you are talking.

   Second: **her, him, them,** or *nouns,* persons *about whom* you are talking.

   Third: **me** and **us.**

PRACTICE: In each sentence below, mark: verbs, subjects, adjectives, adverbs. From the sets of words in parentheses, write, in polite order, the correct direct objects in the blanks; label them **D.O.**

Example: Coach has chosen __*you*__, __*him*__, and __*me*__. (you) (me, I) (he, him)

1. May I call _____ and _____ tomorrow? (you) (her, she)

2. Did you choose _____ and _____? (he, him) (me, I)

3. Kay must have seen _____ and _____. (we, us) (them, they)

4. Did the principal believe _____ and _____? (he, him) (you)

5. The club members have elected _____ and _____. (she, her) (him, he)

6. Dad just phoned _____ and _____. (I, me) (you)

7. David saw _____ and _____. (me, I) (she, her)

8. Dad will help _____ and _____. (they, them) (you)

9. Our elderly neighbor did not recognize _____ and _____. (I, me) (Mom)

10. The principal helped _____ boys. (we, us)

© 1988, 1997 J. Weston Walch, Publisher

Steps to Good Grammar

DRILL

After checking a student's work, have the student read the sentences aloud again to establish the correct "sound."

1. Did Jo call ___*you*___ or ___*her*___ [yesterday]? (her, she) (you)

2. Aunt Susie took ___*Mom*___ and ___*me*___ [there]. (me, I) (Mom)

3. (The) nurse will check ___*them*___ and ___*us*___ [today]. (us, we) (they, them)

4. Lu invited ___*us*___ girls. (us, we)

5. Mom will meet ___*Dad*___ and ___*me*___ . (I, me) (Dad)

6. Ellie saw ___*him*___ and ___*me*___ . (he, him) (I, me)

7. (Our) dad disciplines (my) brother and ___*me*___ [quite][fairly]. (me, I) (my brother)

8. [Today] or [tomorrow], (the) teacher will coach ___*you*___ , ___*Cathy*___ , and ___*me*___ . (Cathy) (I, me) (you)

9. (Our) parents [usually] understand (my) sister and ___*me*___ . (I, me) (my sister)

10. Has Coach chosen ___*you*___ , ___*him*___ , and ___*her*___ ? (him, he) (you) (she, her)

11. (The) principal's decision surprised ___*us*___ students. (we, us)

12. (Our) very strict teacher didn't excuse either ___*him*___ or ___*her*___ . (him, he) (she, her)

13. Mom expects (my) sisters and ___*me*___ [home][early]. (me, I) (my sisters)

14. (The) school librarian [often] helps ___*them*___ and ___*us*___ . (us, we) (they, them)

15. Do (your) parents [usually] trust ___*you*___ and ___*her*___ ? (her, she) (you)

16. Should we meet ___*her*___ and ___*them*___ [there]? (her, she) (them, they)

17. Could you and she see ___*them*___ and ___*me*___ ? (they, them) (I, me)

18. Did you and Ken [actually] see ___*us*___ girls? (us, we)

19. (Some) (unnecessary) rules [really] annoy ___*us*___ students. (we, us)

20. Eileen and she have invited ___*them*___ and ___*us*___ . (we, us) (them, they)

DIRECT OBJECTS — PRONOUNS

DRILL: Using Pronouns as Direct Objects

REMEMBER: The objective personal pronouns are **ME, YOU, HIM, HER, US,** and **THEM.**

Instructions: Mark: verbs, subjects, adjectives, adverbs. From the sets of words at the end of each sentence, write, in polite order, the correct direct objects in the blanks; label them **D.O.** Label appositives **appos.**

1. Did Jo call _____ or _____ yesterday? (her, she) (you)

2. Aunt Susie took _____ and _____ there. (me, I) (Mom)

3. The nurse will check _____ and _____ today. (us, we) (they, them)

4. Lu invited _____ girls. (us, we)

5. Mom will meet _____ and _____ . (I, me) (Dad)

6. Ellie saw _____ and _____ . (he, him) (I, me)

7. Our dad disciplines _____ and _____ quite fairly. (me, I) (my brother)

8. Today or tomorrow, the teacher will coach _____, _____, and _____ . (Cathy) (I, me) (you)

9. Our parents usually understand _____ and _____ . (I, me) (my sister)

10. Has Coach chosen _____, _____, and _____ ? (him, he) (you) (she, her)

11. The principal's decision surprised _____ students. (we, us)

12. Our very strict teacher didn't excuse either _____ or _____ . (him, he) (she, her)

13. Mom expects _____ and _____ home early. (me, I) (my sisters)

14. The school librarian often helps _____ and _____ . (us, we) (they, them)

15. Do your parents usually trust _____ and _____ ? (her, she) (you)

16. Should we meet _____ and _____ there? (her, she) (them, they)

17. Could you and she see _____ and _____ ? (they, them) (I, me)

18. Did you and Ken actually see _____ girls? (us, we)

19. Some unnecessary rules really annoy _____ students. (we, us)

20. Eileen and she have invited _____ and _____ . (we, us) (them, they)

Steps to Good Grammar

FINAL DRILL AND TEST

You will need one copy of this page for each student. The top half is the final drill; the bottom half is the test.

The sentences in the final drill are designed to emphasize the "sound" difference between subject pronouns and object pronouns.

Test:

Details for grading (Direct object write-ins)

Sentence	Points	Grading Scale
1. 0 choice, 1 correct order	1	-1, 95
2. 2 choices, 1 correct order	3	-2, 91
3. 1 choice, 1 correct order	2	-3, 86
4. 1 choice	1	-4, 82
5. 1 choice, 1 order	2	-5, 77
6. 2 choices, order no concern	2	-6, 73
7. 1 choice, 1 order	2	-7, 68
8. 2 choices, order no concern	2	-8, 64
9. 1 choice, 3 correct order	4	-9, 59
10. 2 choices, 1 correct order	3	-10, 55

22

Identification symbols:

Count 1 point for each compound direct object — total points: 45. Use grading scale on page 22.

1. Mary Beth and I are expecting _____*you* and _____*her*_____. (her, she) (you)

2. Did you and Felipe [actually] report _____*John* and _____*me*_____? (I, me) (John)

3. He or she appointed _____*them* and _____*us*_____. (us, we) (they, them)

4. You and I could have helped _____*her* and _____*him*_____. (her, she) (he, him)

5. They or we can take _____*you* and _____*Kurt*_____. (Kurt) (you)

6. Could we boys help _____*you* and _____*her* [now]? (you) (she, her)

7. Did you and they [really] remember _____*him* and _____*me*_____? (he, him) (I, me)

8. She and Mark should [certainly] have told _____*you*, _____*Lana*_____, and _____*me*_____. (Lana) (I, me) (you)

9. You and Marlene must have heard _____*him* and _____*us*_____. (we, us) (him, he)

10. The principal has chosen _____*you* and _____*me*_____. (me, I) (you)

---

1. She and I were watching _____*you* and _____*Tom*_____. (Tom) (you)

2. [Tomorrow] Mom and she will take _____*them* and _____*us*_____. (they, them) (we, us)

3. Should David and I call _____*you* and _____*him* [tonight]? (he, him) (you)

4. You and he [really] surprised _____*us* girls. (we, us)

5. Aunt Susie took _____*Mom* and _____*me* [there]. (me, I) (Mom)

6. Our [very] [strict] teacher didn't excuse _____*her* or _____*him*_____. (he, him) (her, she)

7. Dad and she have challenged _____*you* and _____*me*_____. (I, me) (you)

8. Should we meet _____*her* and _____*them* [there]? (her, she) (they, them)

9. [Today] the teacher will coach _____*you*, _____*Cathy*, and _____*me*_____. (I, me) (Cathy) (you)

10. The school librarian [often] helps _____*them* and _____*us*_____. (us, we) (they, them)

DIRECT OBJECTS — PRONOUNS

FINAL DRILL: Using Pronouns as Direct Objects

Instructions: Mark: <u>verbs</u>, <u>subjects</u>, (adjectives) [adverbs]. From the sets of words at the end of each sentence, write, in polite order, the correct direct objects in the blanks; label them **D.O.** Label appositives **appos.**

1. Mary Beth and I are expecting _____ and _____. (her, she) (you)

2. Did you and Felipe actually report _____ and _____? (I, me) (John)

3. He or she appointed _____ and _____. (us, we) (they, them)

4. You and I could have helped _____ and _____. (her, she) (he, him)

5. They or we can take _____ and _____. (Kurt) (you)

6. Could we boys help _____ and _____ now? (you) (she, her)

7. Did you and they really remember _____ and _____? (he, him) (I, me)

8. She and Mark should certainly have told _____, _____, and _____. (Lana) (I, me) (you)

9. You and Marlene must have heard _____ and _____. (we, us) (him, he)

10. The principal has chosen _____ and _____. (me, I) (you)

DIRECT OBJECTS — PRONOUNS

TEST: Using Pronouns as Direct Objects

Instructions: Mark: <u>verbs</u>, <u>subjects</u>, (adjectives) [adverbs]. From the sets of words at the end of each sentence, write, in polite order, the correct direct objects in the blanks; label them **D.O.** Label appositives **appos.**

1. She and I were watching _____ and _____. (Tom) (you)

2. Tomorrow Mom and she will take _____ and _____. (they, them) (we, us)

3. Should David and I call _____ and _____ tonight? (he, him) (you)

4. You and he really surprised _____ girls. (we, us)

5. Aunt Susie took _____ and _____ there. (me, I) (Mom)

6. Our very strict teacher didn't excuse _____ or _____. (he, him) (her, she)

7. Dad and she have challenged _____ and _____. (I, me) (you)

8. Should we meet _____ and _____ there? (her, she) (they, them)

9. Today the teacher will coach _____, _____, and _____. (I, me) (Cathy) (you)

10. The school librarian often helps _____ and _____. (us, we) (they, them)

© 1988, 1997 J. Weston Walch, Publisher   *Steps to Good Grammar*

RECOGNIZING PREPOSITIONAL PHRASES

Emphasize the abbreviations:

prep. = preposition

O.P. = object of the preposition

A prepositional phrase used as an adjective tells *which one, what kind, how many,* or *whose* about the noun or pronoun it modifies:

apples (from Washington state) — what kind

pen (in my drawer) — which one

groups (of three) — how many

gift (for me) — whose

A prepositional phrase used as an adverb tells *how, when, where, how much,* or *why* about the word it modifies:

rode (on her bike) — how

must be completed (by Friday) — when

came (into the room) — where

lost (by a single point) — how much

cried (over the spilled milk) — why

Memorizing the list of prepositions may be helpful. This course of study doesn't require students to memorize the list because the words are not always used as prepositions.

Heather ran out into the rain.

Here, *out* is an adverb, not a preposition. It is sufficient for students to understand the common-sense relationship of *position* between the object of the pre*position* and the word the phrase modifies.

Read the list and select various prepositions to demonstrate *position* indicated by the pre*position:*

cat (under the tree);   danced (in the cafeteria); etc.

As students analyze the sentences, emphasize drawing the arrow from the phrase to the word that is modified.

1. The girls (in the hall) left [quietly]

2. Ramona has a dress (like that one)

3. Theo left his history book (on his desk)

4. Steve's dad will travel (by car) (to Denver).

5. Many students (in the hall) had come (from the auditorium)

PREPOSITIONAL PHRASES

Recognizing Prepositional Phrases

LEARN:

1. A **prepositional phrase** is used to describe (modify) another word in a sentence just as an adjective or an adverb is used.

2. A prepositional phrase begins with a **preposition (prep.)** and ends with a noun or pronoun **object (O.P.)**

3. A **preposition** shows a relationship of **position** between the object of the preposition and the word it modifies.

   Examples:

   a. Used as an adjective to modify a noun:
      rug (from India); pencil (on the desk); quart (of milk)

   b. Used as an adverb to modify a verb:
      sat (in a chair); arrive (on time); called (about her order)

LEARN TO RECOGNIZE: Words Frequently Used as Prepositions

about	at	beyond	from	on	toward
above	before	but (except)	in	out	under
across	behind	by	inside	outside	until
after	below	concerning	into	over	up
against	beneath	down	like	past	upon
along	beside	during	near	since	with
among	besides	except	of	through	within
around	between	for	off	to	without

DIAGRAMMING: The old man in the ragged coat sat down suddenly in the chair.

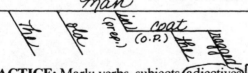

PRACTICE: Mark: verbs, subjects, adjectives, adverbs; label **D.O., prep., O.P.** Put parentheses around a prepositional phrase and draw an arrow to the word it modifies. On the reverse side of this page, diagram sentences 1, 2, 4, and 5.

1. The girls in the hall left quietly.

2. Ramona has a dress like that one.

3. Theo left his history book on his desk.

4. Steve's dad will travel by car to Denver.

5. Many students in the hall had come from the auditorium.

Steps to Good Grammar

PREPOSITIONS AND PREPOSITIONAL PHRASES

Work carefully with the students through this initial practice page dealing with prepositional phrases.

For students' understanding: A prepositional phrase that modifies a noun helps the reader to see the noun more clearly — the phrase describes the noun.

Sample sentence in Part II:

The phrase *for her birthday* doesn't modify *stereo*.

It doesn't help the reader to see the stereo more clearly. The phrase tells *why* about the verb *was given*.

Part II, sentence 4:

The phrase *in her locker* doesn't help the reader to see the *contest* or her *essay* more clearly. It is an adverb phrase that tells *where* about the verb *left*.

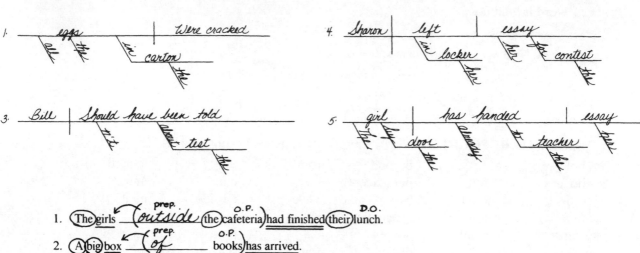

1. The girls *outside* the cafeteria had finished their lunch.
2. A big box *of* books has arrived.
3. The chorus sang several songs *during* the concert.
4. The boys *near* the gym shouted *at* us.
5. The small cat *beside* the barn ran *under* the tree.

1. Were all the eggs in the carton cracked?
2. The road to our farm is being repaired.
3. Shouldn't Bill have been told about the test?
4. Sharon left her essay for the contest in her locker.
5. The girl by the door has already handed her essay to the teacher.
6. The telephone in the office hasn't rung in the last hour.
7. The picture in that frame was painted by my grandfather.
8. A whole crowd of students came up the street to the stadium.
9. The shipment of new books arrived in the morning mail.
10. The box of grapes fell to the floor.

PREPOSITIONAL PHRASES

Prepositions and Prepositional Phrases

Using Prepositions

Instructions: Write an appropriate preposition in each blank below. Mark: <u>verbs</u>, <u>subjects</u>, (adjectives) [adverbs] label: **D.O., prep., O.P.** Put parentheses around the prepositional phrase; draw an arrow to the word it modifies.

Example: (The) child (*beside* (the) swing) was crying (*for* (his) mother)

1. The girls _____ the cafeteria had finished their lunch.

2. A big box _____ of books has arrived.

3. The chorus sang several songs _____ the concert.

4. The boys _____ the gym shouted _____ us.

5. The small cat _____ the barn ran _____ the tree.

Recognizing Prepositional Phrases

Instructions: In each sentence below, mark and label the sentence parts as in the example. Diagram sentences 1, 3, 4, and 5.

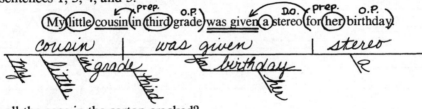

1. Were all the eggs in the carton cracked?

2. The road to our farm is being repaired.

3. Shouldn't Bill have been told about the test?

4. Sharon left her essay for the contest in her locker.

5. The girl by the door has already handed her essay to the teacher.

6. The telephone in the office hasn't rung in the last hour.

7. The picture in that frame was painted by my grandfather.

8. A whole crowd of students came up the street to the stadium.

9. The shipment of new books arrived in the morning mail.

10. The box of grapes fell to the floor.

  Steps to Good Grammar

DRILL

Opinions may differ on sentence 2 —

in Yosemite could be an adverb phrase that tells *where* about the verb *will spend, or*

in Yosemite could be an adjective phrase that tells *what kind* about the direct object, *vacation.*

Sentence 13 is an example of a true introductory *there* that has no grammatical connection to the rest of the sentence.

As the students analyze sentences 15, 16, and 18, call attention to the Reminder items.

Construct these diagrams on the chalkboard; instruct students to copy them:

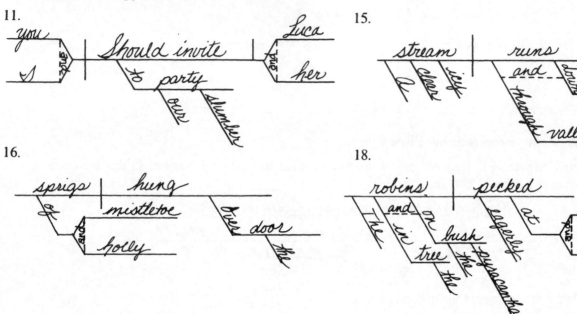

11.

15.

16.

18.

Diagrams help to point out the importance of prepositional phrases.

Students derive a visual impression from the clustering of descriptive terms under the simple subject and verb on the sentence line.

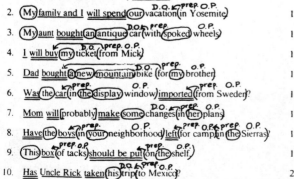

1. The first game (of (the) season) will begin soon.

2. My family and I will spend our vacation (in Yosemite)

3. My aunt bought an antique car (with spoked wheels)

4. I will buy my ticket (from Mick)

5. Dad bought a new mountain bike (for my brother)

6. Was the car (in (the) display) window imported (from Sweden)?

7. Mom will probably make some changes (in her plans)

8. Have (the) boys (in your neighborhood) left (for camping (in (the) Sierras)?

9. This box (of tacks) should be put (on (the) shelf)

10. Has Uncle Rick taken his trip (to Mexico)?

11. Should you and I invite Luca and her (to our slumber party)

12. The bake sale (for our class) will begin early (in (the) morning)

13. There have been five students chosen (for (the) committee)

14. That bowl (of flowers) will make a good centerpiece (for (the) table)

15. A clean icy stream runs (through (the) valley) and (down (the) narrow gorge)

16. (Over (the) door) hung sprigs (of mistletoe and holly)

17. Does Marlene live (beside you) (in that big white house)?

18. The robins (in (the) tree) and (on (the) pyracantha bush) pecked eagerly (at (the) fruit and berries)

19. The chimes (on (the) church) were calling (the) guests (to (the) wedding)

20. This drill (about prepositional phrases) has ended.

PREPOSITIONAL PHRASES

DRILL: Recognizing Prepositional Phrases

Instructions: Mark: <u>verbs</u>, <u>subjects</u>, (adjectives), [adverbs] label: **D.O., prep., O.P.** Put parentheses around each prepositional phrase; draw an arrow to the word modified.

1. The first game of the season will begin soon.

2. My family and I will spend our vacation in Yosemite.

3. My aunt bought an antique car with spoked wheels.

4. I will buy my ticket from Mick.

5. Dad bought a new mountain bike for my brother.

6. Was the car in the display window imported from Sweden?

7. Mom will probably make some changes in her plans.

8. Have the boys in your neighborhood left for camp in the Sierras?

9. This box of tacks should be put on the shelf.

10. Has Uncle Rick taken his trip to Mexico?

11. Should you and I invite Luca and her to our slumber party?

12. The bake sale for our class will begin early in the morning.

13. There have been five students chosen for the committee.

14. That bowl of flowers will make a good centerpiece for the table.

15. A clear, icy stream runs through the valley and down the narrow gorge.

16. Over the door hung sprigs of mistletoe and holly.

17. Does Marlene live beside you in that big white house?

18. The robins in the tree and on the pyracantha bush pecked eagerly at the fruit and berries.

19. The chimes on the church were calling the guests to the wedding.

20. This drill about prepositional phrases has ended.

8.

boys | Have left
the neighborhood camp
your the Sierras
the

Reminder: One preposition may have more than one object (sentences 16 and 18).	**Reminder:** One word may be modified by more than one prepositional phrase (sentences 15 and 18).

Steps to Good Grammar

FINAL DRILL AND TEST

You will need one copy of this page for each student. The top half is the final drill; the bottom half is the test.

Sentence 10, Final Drill: Emphasize the fact that the object of a preposition may be modified by a prepositional phrase that follows it:

in the convalescent hospital modifies *patients.*

Sentence 6 in the Test has another example of this:

beside yours modifies *house.*

Grading suggestions for the Test:

1. Count each parentheses with arrow as 1 point; if either is wrong, deduct ½ point.

2. As usual, the complete verb has a 1-point value.

3. There are 80 items in the test. Grading scale:

-1, 99	-9, 89	-17, 79	-25, 69
-2, 98	-10, 87	-18, 77	-26, 67
-3, 96	-11, 86	-19, 76	-27, 66
-4, 95	-12, 85	-20, 75	-28, 65
-5, 94	-13, 84	-21, 74	-29, 64
-6, 92	-14, 82	-22, 72	-30, 62
-7, 91	-15, 81	-23, 71	-31, 61
-8, 90	-16, 80	-24, 70	-32, 60

FINAL DRILL

1. The man in the gray suit stood up suddenly.
2. The gallon of milk was put in the refrigerator.
3. The puppy was sitting on the porch in the shade.
4. On our trip, we crossed the Sierras.
5. Does the van in your driveway belong to your brother?
6. The frightened child was calling for her father.
7. After school will you and Eric play tennis with Julio and me?
8. A can of paint had been spilled on the car.
9. My mom wants a car like that one.
10. Three girls in band uniforms performed for the patients in the Children's Hospital.

TEST

1. Have the boys in that row already finished their report on the Civil War?
2. On the six o'clock flight, Grandfather will leave for New Mexico.
3. Your large order of new books will probably be delivered in the morning.
4. The tall girl beside the door is wearing jeans like mine.
5. The sound of a gunshot frightened the herd of deer.
6. Does Marlene live in that big white house beside yours?
7. You have finished this test about prepositional phrases.

PREPOSITIONAL PHRASES

FINAL DRILL: Recognizing Prepositional Phrases

Instructions: Mark: <u>verbs</u>, <u>subjects,</u> adjectives, adverbs; label: **D.O., prep., O.P.** Put parentheses around each prepositional phrase, and draw an arrow to the word modified.

1. The man in the gray suit stood up suddenly.

2. The gallon of milk was put in the refrigerator.

3. The puppy was sitting on the porch in the shade.

4. On our trip, we crossed the Sierras.

5. Does the van in your driveway belong to your brother?

6. The frightened child was calling for her father.

7. After school, will you and Eric play tennis with Julio and me?

8. A can of paint had been spilled on the car.

9. My mom wants a car like that one.

10. Three girls in band uniforms performed for the patients in the Children's Hospital.

PREPOSITIONAL PHRASES

TEST: Recognizing Prepositional Phrases

Instructions: Mark: <u>verbs</u>, <u>subjects,</u> adjectives, adverbs; label: **D.O., prep., O.P.** Put parentheses around each prepositional phrase, and draw an arrow to the word modified.

1. Have the boys in that row already finished their report on the Civil War?

2. On the six o'clock flight, Grandfather will leave for New Mexico.

3. Your large order of new books will probably be delivered in the morning.

4. The tall girl beside the door is wearing jeans like mine.

5. The sound of a gunshot frightened the herd of deer.

6. Does Marlene live in that big white house beside yours?

7. You have finished this test about prepositional phrases.

© 1988, 1997 J. Weston Walch, Publisher

Steps to Good Grammar

RECOGNIZING PRONOUNS USED AS OBJECTS OF PREPOSITIONS

Students should recognize that this list of pronouns contains the same words they used as direct objects. *Object*ive pronouns are used in *object* positions; *object* of the preposition is an *object* position.

1.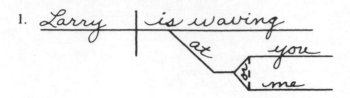

2.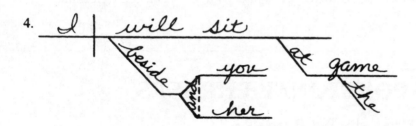

4.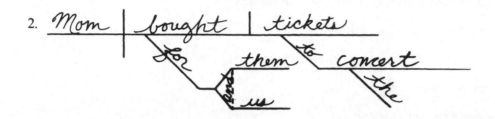

5.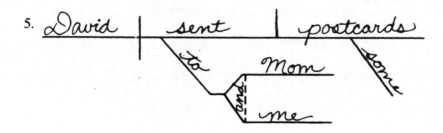

1. <u>Is Larry</u> <u>waving</u> at _____ you _____ or _____ me) _____ ? (I, me) (you)

2. <u>Mom</u> <u>bought</u> tickets to (the) concert (for _____ them and us _____). (we, us) (them, they)

3. <u>Mrs. Greene</u> <u>will give</u> a ride to _____ you _____ and him _____]. (he, him) (you)

4. <u>I</u> <u>will sit</u> beside _____ you _____ and her _____) at (the) game) (you) (her, she)

5. <u>David</u> <u>sent</u> (some) postcards (to _____ Mom _____ and me _____) . (me, I) (Mom)

PRONOUNS AS OBJECTS OF PREPOSITIONS

Recognizing Pronouns Used as Objects of Prepositions

KNOW: 1. **Objective** personal pronouns:

ME, YOU, HIM, HER, US, THEM

are used as **objects of a preposition** (abbreviated **O.P.**).

Simple O.P.: Dad called to **her**. Dad called to **me**.
Compound O.P.: Dad called to **her** and **me**.

2. To use the correct pronouns as compound objects of a preposition, say each pronoun by itself with the preposition:

Dad called to (she, her) and (me, I).

Obviously incorrect: Dad called to *she*. Dad called to *I*.
Obviously correct: Dad called to **her**. Dad called to **me**.

3. Use polite order of pronouns as objects of a preposition (first — *you*; second — *her, him, them,* nouns; last — *me, us*).

4. Diagramming:
Dad called (to her and me)

PRACTICE: Mark: verbs, subjects, adjectives, adverbs; label: **D.O., prep., O.P.** Put parentheses around each prepositional phrase and draw an arrow from the phrase to the word it modifies. From the sets of words in parentheses, write, in polite order, the correct words in the blanks. Diagram sentences 1, 2, 4, and 5.

Example: Did your brother get the tickets (to the game) (for ___you___ and ___me___)?

1. Is Larry waving at _____ or _____ ? (I, me) (you)

2. Mom bought tickets to the concert for _____ and _____. (we, us) (them, they)

3. Mrs. Greene will give a ride to _____ and _____ . (he, him) (you)

4. I will sit beside _____ and _____ at the game. (you) (her, she)

5. David sent some postcards to _____ and _____ . (me, I) (Mom)

DRILL

We hope students had expected to use *objec*tive pronouns as *objects* of prepositions and need minimal drill; hence, this is the only full practice page.

Notice: In sentence 9, *boys* is an appositive; tell students to label it *appos.*

[Sentence diagrams, handwritten]

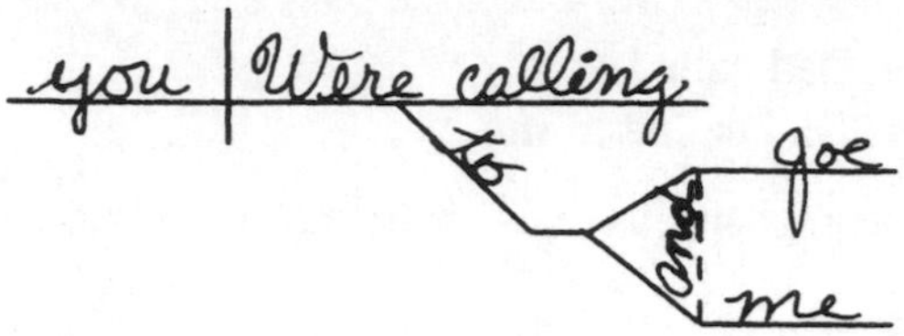

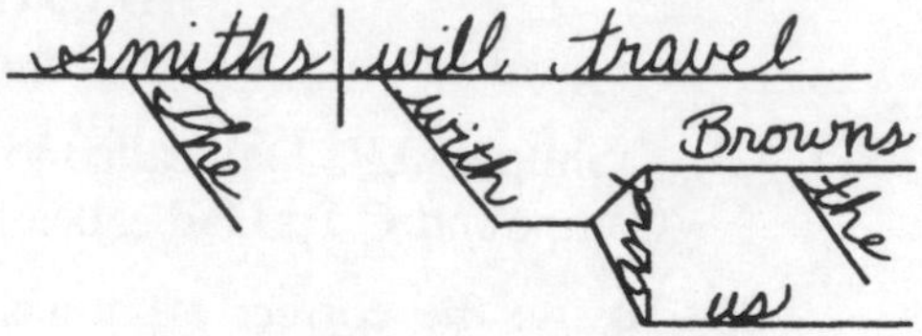

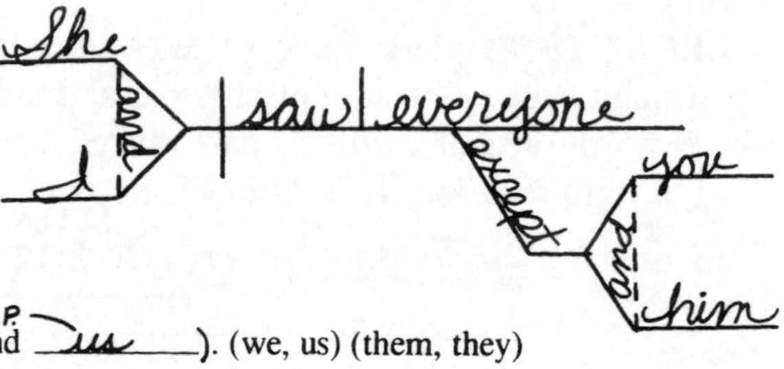

1. You and she can ride to school with *them* and *us*). (we, us) (them, they)
2. Were you calling to *Joe* and *me*)? (me, I) (Joe)
3. Alicia and I have been walking behind *you* and *your friend*)(your friend) (you)
4. You and she will be working with *him* and *me*). (I, me) (him, he)
5. The Smiths will travel with *the Browns* and *us*). (the Browns) (us, we)
6. Why were you and they looking at *him* and *her*)? (he, him) (she, her)
7. Did you get that valentine from *Chris* or *him* ? (Chris) (he, him)
8. Was the teacher signalling to *you* , *them* , or *us* ? (them, they) (we, us) (you)
9. When will Coach have the awards for *us*) boys? (us, we)
10. My little sister could sit between *you* and *me* . (you) (me, I)
11. At the assembly, were you and Jess sitting near *Dean* and *them* ? (Dean) (them, they)
12. Actually, he wasn't referring to *you* and *Mom* . (Mom) (you)
13. Will you and he leave without *Clair* and *me* ? (me, I) (Clair)
14. Your brother just hurried past *them* and *her* . (they, them) (her, she)
15. She and I saw everyone except *you* and *him* . (he, him) (you)

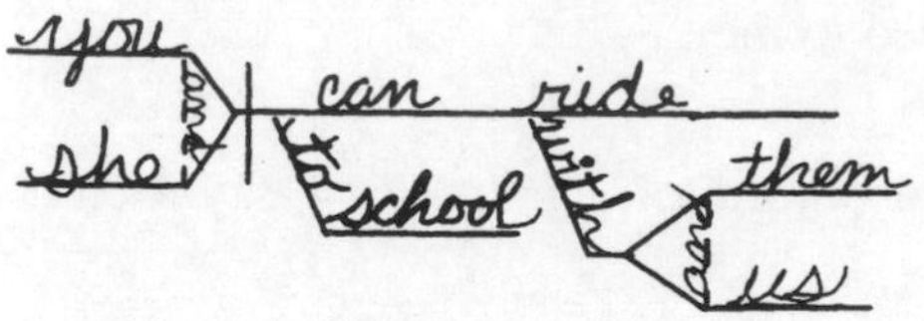

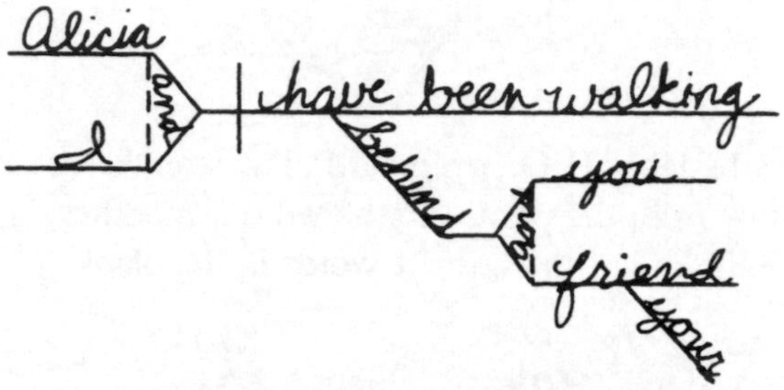

PRONOUNS AS OBJECTS OF PREPOSITIONS

DRILL: Pronouns As Objects of Prepositions

REMEMBER: Objective personal pronouns—*ME, YOU, HIM, HER, US, THEM*—are used as **objects of prepositions.**

Instructions: Mark: <u>verbs</u>, <u>subjects</u>, (adjectives) [adverbs] label: **D.O., prep., O.P.** Put parentheses around each prepositional phrase and draw an arrow from the phrase to the word it modifies. From the sets of words in parentheses, write, in polite order, the correct words in the blanks. Diagram sentences 1, 8, and 9 below and 2, 3, 5, and 15 on the back of this page.

Example: [Probably] <u>all</u> (of the students) <u>are going</u> (except ___*you*___ , ___*her*___ and ___*me*___).
(me, I) (she, her) (you)

1. You and she can ride to school with _____ and _____ . (we, us) (them, they)

2. Were you calling to _____ and _____ ? (me, I) (Joe)

3. Alicia and I have been walking behind _____ and _____ . (your friend) (you)

4. You and she will be working with _____ and _____ . (I, me) (him, he)

5. The Smiths will travel with _____ and _____ . (the Browns) (us, we)

6. Why were you and they looking at _____ and _____ ? (he, him) (she, her)

7. Did you get that valentine from _____ or _____ ? (Chris) (he, him)

8. Was the teacher signalling to _____ , _____ ,
   or _____ ? (them, they) (we, us) (you)

9. When will Coach have the awards for _____ boys? (us, we)

10. My little sister could sit between _____ and _____ . (you) (me, I)

11. At the assembly, were you and Jess sitting near _____ and _____ ?
    (Dean) (them, they)

12. Actually, he wasn't referring to _____ and _____ . (Mom) (you)

13. Will you and he leave without _____ and _____ ? (me, I) (Clair)

14. Your brother just hurried past _____ and _____ . (they, them) (her, she)

15. She and I saw everyone except _____ and _____ . (he, him) (you)

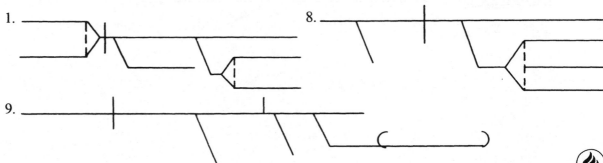

TEST

This reproducible page contains two copies of one half-page drill/test. Cut each duplicated page in half; give each student one half-page.

This test determines the student's understanding of the use of objective pronouns as objects of prepositions. Record a separate grade for this.

Grading suggestions:

Choice of pronouns:

Sentence	Items to Consider	Points	Grading Scale
1.	1 choice, 1 correct order	2	-1, 94
2.	2 choices, 1 correct order	3	-2, 89
3.	1 choice, 1 correct order	2	-3, 83
4.	2 choices, order no concern	2	-4, 78
5.	1 choice, 1 correct order	2	-5, 72
6.	1 choice, 1 correct order	2	-6, 67
7.	1 choice, 1 correct order	2	-7, 61
8.	2 choices, 1 correct order	3	-8, 56
		18	

Sentence part identification — 56 points

1 point given each parentheses with arrow.
1 point given each label for compound object of preposition.

-1, 98	-6, 89	-11, 80	-16, 71	-21, 63
-2, 96	-7, 87	-12, 78	-17, 69	-22, 61
-3, 95	-8, 85	-13, 76	-18, 67	-23, 59
-4, 93	-9, 84	-14, 75	-19, 65	-24, 57
-5, 91	-10, 82	-15, 73	-20, 64	-25, 55

1. Is Larry waving (at _____ you _____ and _____ me _____)? (you) (I, me)

2. Mom bought tickets (to the concert) (for _____ them _____ and _____ us _____). (we, us) (them, they)

3. Mrs. Greene will give a ride [home] (to _____ you _____ and _____ me _____). (you) (me, I)

4. Is this assignment (for _____ him _____ or _____ her _____)? (he, him) (her, she)

5. This note must have been written (by _____ you _____ or _____ her _____). (she, her) (you)

6. May we go (with _____ you _____ and _____ them _____) (to the game? (you) (they, them)

7. David sent some postcards (to _____ Mom _____ and _____ me _____). (me, I) (Mom)

8. Was Simone talking (about _____ them _____ and _____ us _____)? (they, them) (we, us)

PRONOUNS AS OBJECTS OF PREPOSITIONS

TEST

Instructions: Mark: <u>verbs</u>, <u>subjects</u>, adjectives, adverbs label: **D.O., prep., O.P.** Put parentheses around each prepositional phrase and draw an arrow from the phrase to the word it modifies. From the sets of words at the end of each sentence, write, in polite order, the correct words in the blanks.

1. Is Larry waving at _____ and _____ ? (you) (I, me)

2. Mom bought tickets to the concert for _____ and _____. (we, us) (them, they)

3. Mrs. Greene will give a ride home to _____ and _____ . (you) (me, I)

4. Is this assignment for _____ or _____ ? (he, him) (her, she)

5. This note must have been written by _____ or _____ . (she, her) (you)

6. May we go with _____ and _____ to the game? (you) (they, them)

7. David sent some postcards to _____ and _____ . (me, I) (Mom)

8. Was Simone talking about _____ and _____ ? (they, them) (we, us)

NAME _____ DATE _____ 117

PRONOUNS AS OBJECTS OF PREPOSITIONS

TEST

Instructions: Mark: <u>verbs</u>, <u>subjects</u>, adjectives, adverbs label: **D.O., prep., O.P.** Put parentheses around each prepositional phrase and draw an arrow from the phrase to the word it modifies. From the sets of words at the end of each sentence, write, in polite order, the correct words in the blanks.

1. Is Larry waving at _____ and _____ ? (you) (I, me)

2. Mom bought tickets to the concert for _____ and _____. (we, us) (them, they)

3. Mrs. Greene will give a ride home to _____ and _____ . (you) (me, I)

4. Is this assignment for _____ or _____ ? (he, him) (her, she)

5. This note must have been written by _____ or _____ . (she, her) (you)

6. May we go with _____ and _____ to the game? (you) (they, them)

7. David sent some postcards to _____ and _____ . (me, I) (Mom)

8. Was Simone talking about _____ and _____ ? (they, them) (we, us)

Steps to Good Grammar

RECOGNIZING NOUNS USED AS INDIRECT OBJECTS

Read the introductory material aloud. Quiz students after reading each item to establish their understanding.

The simple "ask and say" system for locating the indirect object is an almost fail-proof method by which students establish an understanding.

In analyzing the first example, ask: "Mom has bought what object?"

Then ask, "Who got it?"

As students identify the sentence parts in the Practice sentences, instruct them to follow the "ask and say" system.

1. Gil threw Pam the ball.
2. Should Randy buy his friends some tickets?
3. Earlier the teacher had asked John that same question.
4. Has Dad already made Mom some sandwiches?
5. The secretary (in the office) will lend Judy some lunch money.
6. Mom did not give Mary her permission.
7. Dad gave Grandfather a plant (for Christmas)
8. Didn't your uncle recently build his family a cabin (in the mountains)?
9. The girl (in the front seat) lent Tom a pencil.
10. Yesterday at the Mall Dad bought my little sister a new football.

INDIRECT OBJECTS — NOUNS

Recognizing Nouns Used as Indirect Objects

LEARN: 1. An **indirect object (I.O.)** is a special kind of prepositional phrase. With an I.O., a preposition is *not* used, but its meaning is understood.

Example: Mom bought my sister new shoes. (*For* is understood — "for my sister.")

2. An **indirect object (I.O.)** modifies the verb and comes between the verb and the direct object (D.O.).

3. The sentence must have a direct object in order for it to have an indirect object. The **I.O.** gets, or receives, the **D.O.**

Example: Ted had given Ron the dollar. (*To* is understood — "to Ron.")

Ask: "Ted had given what object?" Answer: "The dollar."
Ask: "Who got it?" Answer: "Ron" (the **indirect object**).

4. In diagramming, an *x* takes the place of the understood preposition. Indirect objects may be compound (more than one).

Example: Mom has bought my sister and my brother some new shoes.

PRACTICE: Mark: verbs, subjects, adjectives, adverbs (prep. phrases) label: **D.O., prep., O.P., I.O.** Draw an arrow from each prep. phrase to the word it modifies. Diagram sentences 1, 4, 6, 8, and 10.

1. Gil threw Pam the ball.

2. Should Randy buy his friends some tickets?

3. Earlier the teacher had asked John that same question.

4. Has Dad already made Mom some sandwiches?

5. The secretary in the office will lend Judy some lunch money.

6. Mom did not give Mary her permission.

7. Dad gave Grandfather a plant for Christmas.

8. Didn't your uncle recently build his family a cabin in the mountains?

9. The girl in the front seat lent Tom a pencil.

10. Yesterday at the Mall, Dad bought my little sister a new football.

Steps to Good Grammar

DRILL

As students develop an understanding of all sentence parts, they learn that they have choices in ways to express their ideas.

As you analyze the sample sentences, point out that the word immediately following the verb receives strong emphasis. In the first example, *compliment* is stressed; in the second, *students*, the receivers of the compliment, is stressed.

Establish this fact in the students' minds as they complete the practice sentences.

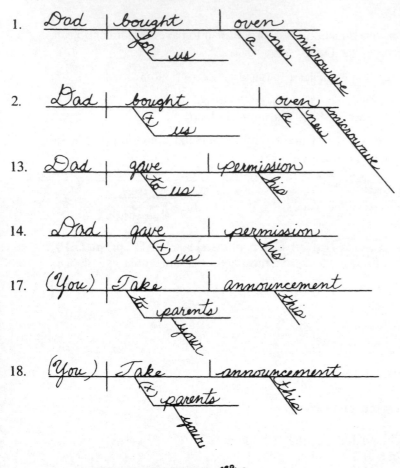

1. Dad bought a new microwave oven (for us).
2. Dad bought us a new microwave oven.
3. Aunt Ruth brought a present (for me).
4. Aunt Ruth brought me a present.
5. My sister read a story (to the little girl).
6. My sister read the little girl a story.
7. The librarian hasn't yet sent an overdue notice (to Tricia).
8. The librarian hasn't yet sent Tricia an overdue notice.
9. Did the teacher give the notebook (to Dom)?
10. Did the teacher give Dom the notebook?
11. My cousin told the truth (to his parents).
12. My cousin told his parents the truth.
13. Dad gave his permission (to us).
14. Dad gave us his permission.
15. Uncle Marty bought a Schwinn ten-speed (for me).
16. Uncle Marty bought me a Schwinn ten-speed.
17. (You) Take this announcement (to your parents).
18. (You) Take your parents this announcement.
19. Will you or she lend a dollar (to me)?
20. Will you or she lend me a dollar?

INDIRECT OBJECTS — NOUNS

DRILL: Recognizing Similarity Between Prepositional Phrases and Indirect Objects

Instructions: Mark: <u>verbs</u>, <u>subjects</u>, adjectives, adverbs, prep. phrases label: **D.O., prep., O.P., I.O.** Draw an arrow from each prep. phrase to the word it modifies. Diagram sentences 1, 2, 13, 14, 17, and 18.

Examples: The principal gave a compliment to all the students.
The principal gave all the students a compliment.

1. Dad bought a new microwave oven for us.

2. Dad bought us a new microwave oven.

3. Aunt Ruth brought a present for me.

4. Aunt Ruth brought me a present.

5. My sister read a story to the little girl.

6. My sister read the little girl a story.

7. The librarian hasn't yet sent an overdue notice to Tricia.

8. The librarian hasn't yet sent Tricia an overdue notice.

9. Did the teacher give the notebook to Dom?

10. Did the teacher give Dom the notebook?

11. My cousin told the truth to his parents.

12. My cousin told his parents the truth.

13. Dad gave his permission to us.

14. Dad gave us his permission.

15. Uncle Marty bought a Schwinn ten-speed for me.

16. Uncle Marty bought me a Schwinn ten-speed.

17.   Take this announcement to your parents.

18.   Take your parents this announcement.

19. Will you or she lend a dollar to me?

20. Will you or she lend me a dollar?

> **Reminder:** In a request or command, the subject, *You,* is frequently not spoken.
> Write *You* in parentheses before the verb in sentences 17 and 18.

Steps to Good Grammar

FINAL DRILL

Sentence 25: Challenge a student to identify the sentence parts and to diagram the sentence on the chalkboard.

Tell students this is a final drill; they should be sure their papers are correct.

Announce that a test is being given the next day.

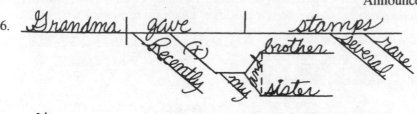

6. Gale handed Rico *her* homework paper. [I.O., D.O.]
2. Rico handed *his* homework paper (to Gale). [D.O., prep., O.P.]
3. Kathy gave Nan a present. [I.O., D.O.]
4. Did Jennifer send Liz and Megan some postcards? [I.O., I.O., D.O.]
5. Coach awarded Holly a trophy. [I.O., D.O.]
6. Recently, Grandma gave my brother and sister several rare stamps. [I.O., D.O.]
7. Recently, Grandma gave several rare stamps (to my brother and sister). [D.O., prep., O.P.]
8. The Stantons give their children generous allowances. [I.O., D.O.]
9. Mrs. Woodside made her daughter some lovely clothes. [I.O., D.O.]
10. (You) Take Mom the morning paper. [I.O., D.O.]
11. (You) Take the morning paper (to Mom). [D.O., prep., O.P.]
12. Several (of the rose bushes) (in our yard) are blooming. [prep., O.P., prep., O.P.]
13. The clerk sold my uncle a defective battery. [I.O., D.O.]
14. That man bought a brand-new car (for his daughter). [D.O., prep., O.P.]
15. That man bought his daughter a brand-new car. [I.O., D.O.]
16. The street (past our house) has been repaired. [prep., O.P.]
17. The apartment owner paid the plumber sixty dollars. [I.O., D.O.]
18. The trees were casting long shadows (across our lawn). [D.O., prep., O.P.]
19. (You) Tell Doug and Glenn your plan. [I.O., D.O.]
20. (You) Tell your plan (to Doug and Glenn). [D.O., prep., O.P.]
21. Did Marie ask her parents (for permission)? [D.O., prep., O.P.]
22. Should those two books (on the table) be mended? [prep., O.P.]
23. Grandpa gave the waitress a generous tip. [I.O., D.O.]
24. The rear tires (on that car) (in the driveway) have been slashed. [prep., O.P., prep., O.P.]
25. The list (of names) (of students) (with all A's) has been published (in the newspaper). [prep., O.P., prep., O.P., prep., O.P., prep., O.P.]

INDIRECT OBJECTS — NOUNS

FINAL DRILL: Recognizing Indirect Objects and All Other Sentence Parts

Instructions: Mark: verbs, subjects, adjectives, adverbs, prep. phrases; label: **D.O., prep., O.P., I.O.** Draw an arrow from each prep. phrase to the word it modifies. Diagram sentences 6, 7, 10, and 11.

1. Gale handed Rico her homework paper.

2. Rico handed his homework paper to Gale.

3. Kathy gave Nan a present.

4. Did Jennifer send Liz and Megan some postcards?

5. Coach awarded Holly a trophy.

6. Recently, Grandma gave my brother and sister several rare stamps.

7. Recently, Grandma gave several rare stamps to my brother and sister.

8. The Stantons give their children generous allowances.

9. Mrs. Woodside made her daughter some lovely clothes.

10. Take Mom the morning paper.

11. Take the morning paper to Mom.

12. Several of the rose bushes in our yard are blooming.

13. The clerk sold my uncle a defective battery.

14. That man bought a brand-new car for his daughter.

15. That man bought his daughter a brand-new car.

16. The street past our house has been repaired.

17. The apartment owner paid the plumber sixty dollars.

18. The trees were casting long shadows across our lawn.

19. Tell Doug and Glenn your plan.

20. Tell your plan to Doug and Glenn.

21. Did Marie ask her parents for permission?

22. Should those two books on the table be mended?

23. Grandpa gave the waitress a generous tip.

24. The rear tires on that car in the driveway have been slashed.

25. The list of names of students with all *A*'s has been published in the newspaper.

Steps to Good Grammar

TEST

This reproducible page contains two copies of one half-page drill/test. Cut each duplicated page in half; give each student one half-page.

Grading scale for 68 points:

-1, 99	-6, 91	-11, 84	-16, 77	-21, 70	-26, 62
-2, 97	-7, 90	-12, 83	-17, 75	-22, 68	-27, 61
-3, 96	-8, 88	-13, 81	-18, 74	-23, 67	-28, 59
-4, 94	-9, 87	-14, 80	-19, 72	-24, 65	-29, 58
-5, 93	-10, 85	-15, 78	-20, 71	-25, 64	-30, 56

Suggested grading:

1 point for each parentheses plus arrow
1 point for each label of a compound object of the preposition

1. Did (the) principal give (all) (the) students a compliment?

2. (You) Take (this) announcement (to (your) parents)

3. Did Coach award John a letter?

4. [Yesterday (the) (rear) tires (on (that) car (in (the) driveway) were slashed.

5. Is Grandmother giving (some) (rare) stamps (to you and Jeanne)

6. (The) (apartment) owner paid (the) plumber (sixty) dollars.

7. (That) man bought (a) brand-new car (for (his) daughter)

8. Mrs. Woodside has made (her) daughter (some) (really (lovely) clothes.

INDIRECT OBJECTS — NOUNS

TEST: Recognizing Indirect Objects and All Other Sentence Parts

Instructions: Really think! Mark: <u>verbs</u>, <u>subjects</u>, adjectives, adverbs, prep. phrases, label: **D.O.,** **prep., O.P., I.O.** Draw an arrow from each prep. phrase to the word it modifies.

1. Did the principal give all the students a compliment?

2. Take this announcement to your parents.

3. Did Coach award John a letter?

4. Yesterday the rear tires on that car in the driveway were slashed.

5. Is Grandmother giving some rare stamps to you and Jeanne?

6. The apartment owner paid the plumber sixty dollars.

7. That man bought a brand-new car for his daughter.

8. Mrs. Woodside has made her daughter some really lovely clothes.

NAME _____ DATE _____ 125

INDIRECT OBJECTS — NOUNS

TEST: Recognizing Indirect Objects and All Other Sentence Parts

Instructions: Really think! Mark: <u>verbs</u>, <u>subjects</u>, adjectives, adverbs, prep. phrases, label: **D.O.,** **prep., O.P., I.O.** Draw an arrow from each prep. phrase to the word it modifies.

1. Did the principal give all the students a compliment?

2. Take this announcement to your parents.

3. Did Coach award John a letter?

4. Yesterday the rear tires on that car in the driveway were slashed.

5. Is Grandmother giving some rare stamps to you and Jeanne?

6. The apartment owner paid the plumber sixty dollars.

7. That man bought a brand-new car for his daughter.

8. Mrs. Woodside has made her daughter some really lovely clothes.

© 1988, 1997 J. Weston Walch, Publisher

Steps to Good Grammar

REDRILL

This reproducible page contains two copies of one half-page drill/test. Cut each duplicated page in half; give each student one half-page.

This is a redrill for students who need special help. It includes several of the forms that students have studied.

Advise students who need this drill to give it their best concentrated effort. Several sentences from this page will be included in the test they take the next day.

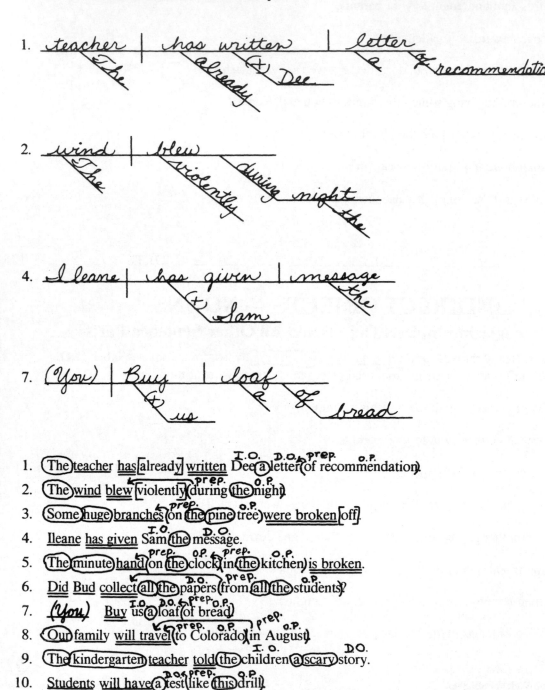

1. The teacher has [already] written Dee a letter (of recommendation).
2. The wind blew [violently] (during the night).
3. Some huge branches (on the pine tree) were broken [off].
4. Ileane has given Sam the message.
5. The minute hand (on the clock) (in the kitchen) is broken.
6. Did Bud collect all the papers (from all the students)?
7. (You) Buy us a loaf (of bread).
8. Our family will travel (to Colorado) (in August).
9. The kindergarten teacher told the children a scary story.
10. Students will have a test (like this drill).

INDIRECT OBJECTS — NOUNS

REDRILL: Recognizing Indirect Objects and All Other Sentence Parts

Instructions: Mark: verbs, subjects, adjectives, adverbs, (prep. phrases) label: **D.O., prep., O.P., I.O.** Draw an arrow from each prep. phrase to the word it modifies. Diagram sentences 1, 2, 4, and 7.

1. The teacher has already written Dee a letter of recommendation.
2. The wind blew violently during the night.
3. Some huge branches on the pine tree were broken off.
4. Ileane has given Sam the message.
5. The minute hand on the clock in the kitchen is broken.
6. Did Bud collect all the papers from all the students?
7. Buy us a loaf of bread.
8. Our family will travel to Colorado in August.
9. The kindergarten teacher told the children a scary story.
10. Students will have a test like this drill.

NAME _____ DATE _____ 127

INDIRECT OBJECTS — NOUNS

REDRILL: Recognizing Indirect Objects and All Other Sentence Parts

Instructions: Mark: verbs, subjects, adjectives, adverbs, (prep. phrases) label: **D.O., prep., O.P., I.O.** Draw an arrow from each prep. phrase to the word it modifies. Diagram sentences 1, 2, 4, and 7.

1. The teacher has already written Dee a letter of recommendation.
2. The wind blew violently during the night.
3. Some huge branches on the pine tree were broken off.
4. Ileane has given Sam the message.
5. The minute hand on the clock in the kitchen is broken.
6. Did Bud collect all the papers from all the students?
7. Buy us a loaf of bread.
8. Our family will travel to Colorado in August.
9. The kindergarten teacher told the children a scary story.
10. Students will have a test like this drill.

© 1988, 1997 J. Weston Walch, Publisher

Steps to Good Grammar

RETEST

This reproducible page contains two copies of
one half-page drill/test. Cut each duplicated page
in half; give each student one half-page.

Grading scale: Total—66 points. All identification
symbols, 1 point, including 1 point for parentheses
plus arrow.

-1, 98	-6, 91	-11, 83	-16, 76	-21, 68
-2, 97	-7, 89	-12, 82	-17, 74	-22, 67
-3, 95	-8, 88	-13, 80	-18, 73	-23, 65
-4, 94	-9, 86	-14, 79	-19, 71	-24, 64
-5, 92	-10, 85	-15, 77	-20, 70	-25, 62

This test purposely includes several sentences
from the previous drill, to help students realize that
concentrated effort on the drill has paid off.

1. Today the teacher is giving the students a test (like yesterday's drill).

2. His best friend gave my uncle that antique gun.

3. (You) Buy us a loaf of bread.

4. Did Mr. Hall ask both boys that same question?

5. The wind blew violently (during the night).

6. The kindergarten teacher told the children a scary story.

7. The minute hand on the clock in the kitchen was broken recently.

INDIRECT OBJECTS — NOUNS

RETEST: Recognizing Indirect Objects and All Other Sentence Parts

Instructions: Mark: <u>verbs</u>, <u>subjects</u>, (adjectives) [adverbs] (prep. phrases) label: **D.O., prep., O.P., I.O.** Draw an arrow from each prep. phrase to the word it modifies.

1. Today the teacher is giving the students a test like yesterday's drill.

2. His best friend gave my uncle that antique gun.

3. Buy us a loaf of bread.

4. Did Mr. Hall ask both boys that same question?

5. The wind blew violently during the night.

6. The kindergarten teacher told the children a scary story.

7. The minute hand on the clock in the kitchen was broken recently.

NAME _____ DATE _____ 129

INDIRECT OBJECTS — NOUNS

RETEST: Recognizing Indirect Objects and All Other Sentence Parts

Instructions: Mark: <u>verbs</u>, <u>subjects</u>, (adjectives) [adverbs] (prep. phrases) label: **D.O., prep., O.P., I.O.** Draw an arrow from each prep. phrase to the word it modifies.

1. Today the teacher is giving the students a test like yesterday's drill.

2. His best friend gave my uncle that antique gun.

3. Buy us a loaf of bread.

4. Did Mr. Hall ask both boys that same question?

5. The wind blew violently during the night.

6. The kindergarten teacher told the children a scary story.

7. The minute hand on the clock in the kitchen was broken recently.

Steps to Good Grammar

RECOGNIZING PRONOUNS USED AS INDIRECT OBJECTS

Read and simultaneously quiz students concerning each item in **Learn.** Ask:

1. What are the objective pronouns? In what sentence parts are they used?

2. What part of the sentence do indirect objects always modify?

3. Recite polite order in the use of objective pronouns.

Notice:

Tell students they no longer need to draw an arrow from a prepositional phrase to the word it modifies. In later worksheets, the arrow will be used for a different purpose.

Note to students that the subjective (nominative) pronouns — *I, he, she, we, they* — are never used as indirect objects.

1.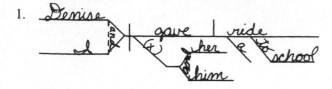

5.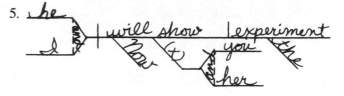

2.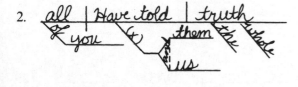

4.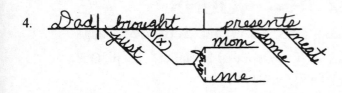

1. <u>Denise and I gave</u> *her* and *him* a ride to school. (she, her) (him, he)

2. <u>Have all of you told</u> *them* and *us* the whole truth? (we, us) (they, them)

3. <u>Someone should have told</u> *you* and *them* the plan. (they, them) (you)

4. <u>Dad just brought</u> *Mom* and *me* some neat presents. (I, me) (Mom)

5. Now, he and I <u>will show</u> *you* and *her* the experiment. (you) (her, she)

6. Did your cousin <u>send</u> *you* and *your sister* those beautiful sweaters? (your sister) (you)

7. Could <u>you tell</u> *us* students our grades? (us, we)

8. Why was Larry <u>asking</u> *them* and *us* those questions? (we, us) (they, them)

9. Our <u>parents give</u> *Tom* and *me* generous allowances. (Tom) (I, me)

10. <u>Sally has saved</u> *them* and *us* some seats. (us, we) (they, them)

INDIRECT OBJECTS — PRONOUNS

Recognizing Pronouns Used as Indirect Objects

LEARN: 1. **Objective** personal pronouns:
ME, YOU, HIM, HER, US, THEM
are used as **indirect objects** (abbreviated **I.O.**).

      Simple I.O.: Dad gave **me** a book.
      Compound I.O.: Dad gave **her** and **me** a book.

2. To use the correct pronouns as indirect objects, say each pronoun by itself after the verb:

      Mom gave (he, him) and (I, me) permission.

      Obviously incorrect: Mom gave *he* ... Mom gave *I* ...
      Obviously correct: Mom gave **him** ... Mom gave **me** ...

3. Use polite order of pronouns as indirect objects (first — *you*; second — *her, him, them,* **nouns**; last — *me, us*).

4. Diagram pronoun indirect objects as you do noun indirect objects:

      Mom | gave | permission
                     him
                     me

PRACTICE: Mark: <u>verbs</u>, <u>subjects</u>, (adjectives) [adverbs] (prep. phrases) label: **D.O., prep., O.P., I.O.** From the words at the end of each sentence, write the correct indirect objects in polite order in the blanks. Diagram sentences 1, 2, 4, and 5.

1. Denise and I gave _____ and _____ a ride to school. (she, her) (him, he)

2. Have all of you told _____ and _____ the whole truth? (we, us) (they, them)

3. Someone should have told _____ and _____ the plan. (they, them) (you)

4. Dad just brought _____ and _____ some neat presents. (I, me) (Mom)

5. Now, he and I will show _____ and _____ the experiment. (you) (her, she)

6. Did your cousin send _____ and _____ those beautiful sweaters? (your sister) (you)

7. Could you tell _____ students our grades? (us, we)

8. Why was Larry asking _____ and _____ those questions? (we, us) (they, them)

9. Our parents give _____ and _____ generous allowances. (Tom) (I, me)

10. Sally has saved _____ and _____ some seats. (us, we) (they, them)

Steps to Good Grammar

DRILL

This is the only full page of practice in recognizing correct pronouns used as indirect objects.

After checking students' selection of words and identification of sentence parts, instruct students to reread each sentence aloud to establish what "sounds right."

Check a representative number of sentences; deduct 5% for each uncorrected error; record score.

Announce test scheduled for the next day.

1. Dad handed _him_ and _me_ our allowances for the week. (he, him) (I, me)

2. (After school) could you or he bring _my brother_ and _me_ our homework? (me, I) (my brother)

3. The principal just told _us_ students the election results. (we, us)

4. The teacher wrote _them_ and _us_ very good recommendations. (we, us) (them, they)

5. They or we can lend _you_ and _Kim_ money for the tickets. (you) (Kim)

6. Did that child ask _you_ and _her_ the same question? (her, she) (you)

7. Will their parents give _her_ and _him_ their permission? (he, him) (she, her)

8. Didn't you promise _her_ and _me_ some prints of those snapshots? (me, I) (she, her)

9. Uncle Art bought _him_ and _me_ new dirt bikes. (him, he) (me, I)

10. Has the librarian already shown _you_ and _them_ the new books? (you) (they, them)

11. Mr. Davis will give _her_ and _us_ a ride home. (we, us) (her, she)

12. Elizabeth and I will bring _him_ and _them_ some souvenirs. (he, him) (them, they)

13. The dentist will show _Mom_ and _me_ the X-rays tomorrow. (I, me) (Mom)

14. Does your grandmother always send _you_ and _her_ so many postcards during her trips? (she, her) (you)

15. Could you and she give _them_, _him_, and _us_ rides to the game? (they, them) (him, he) (us, we)

INDIRECT OBJECTS — PRONOUNS

DRILL: Using Pronouns as Indirect Objects

Instructions: Mark: verbs, subjects, adjectives, adverbs, (prep. phrases) label: **D.O., prep., O.P., I.O., appos.** From the words at the end of each sentence, write the correct indirect objects in the blanks. Diagram sentences 2, 4, 5, 8, and 14.

1. Dad handed _____ and _____ our allowances for the week. (he, him) (I, me)

2. After school, could you or he bring _____ and _____ our homework? (me, I) (my brother)

3. The principal just told _____ students the election results. (we, us)

4. The teacher wrote _____ and _____ very good recommendations. (we, us) (them, they)

5. They or we can lend _____ and _____ money for the tickets. (you) (Kim)

6. Did that child ask _____ and _____ the same question? (her, she) (you)

7. Will their parents give _____ and _____ their permission? (he, him) (she, her)

8. Didn't you promise _____ and _____ some prints of those snapshots? (me, I) (she, her)

9. Uncle Art bought _____ and _____ new dirt bikes. (him, he) (me, I)

10. Has the librarian already shown _____ and _____ the new books? (you) (they, them)

11. Mr. Davis will give _____ and _____ a ride home. (we, us) (her, she)

12. Elizabeth and I will bring _____ and _____ some souvenirs. (he, him) (them, they)

13. The dentist will show _____ and _____ the X-rays tomorrow. (I, me) (Mom)

14. Does your grandmother always send _____ and _____ so many postcards during her trips? (she, her) (you)

15. Could you and she give _____ , _____ , and _____ rides to the game? (they, them) (him, he) (us, we)

Steps to Good Grammar

TEST

This reproducible page contains two copies of one half-page drill/test. Cut each duplicated page in half; give each student one half-page.

Sentence part identification:

1 point each parentheses around prepositional phrase	3
1 point each compound indirect object	7
All other identification symbols	42
	52 points

Subtract 2% for each incorrect identification.

At this point, it is realistic to expect that no student will score below 75% on any part of a test.

Grading pronoun choice and order:

Sentence	Pronoun choice	Order	Points	Grading scale
1	2	3	5	-1, 95
2	2	1	3	-2, 89
3	1	1	2	-3, 84
4	1	1	2	-4, 79
5	1	1	2	-5, 74
6	2	1	3	-6, 68
7	1	1	2	-7, 63
			19	-8, 58

1. Did the teacher give _____ you _____, _____ him _____, and _____ me _____ her permission? (he, him) (you) (I, me)

2. Have all of you told _____ them _____ and _____ us _____ the whole truth? (we, us) (them, they)

3. Dad and Mom give _____ Eddie _____ and _____ me _____ generous allowances. (Eddie) (I, me)

4. Didn't Julie promise _____ you _____ and _____ her _____ some prints of those snapshots? (she, her) (you)

5. The librarian will show _____ you _____ and _____ them _____ the new books. (they, them) (you)

6. Why was Larry asking _____ her _____ and _____ us _____ those questions? (we, us) (her, she)

7. After school, could you or he bring _____ my brother _____ and _____ me _____ our homework? (I, me) (my brother)

INDIRECT OBJECTS—PRONOUNS

TEST: Using Pronouns as Indirect Objects

Instructions: Mark: <u>verbs</u>, <u>subjects</u>, adjectives, adverbs (prep. phrases) label: **D.O., prep., O.P., I.O.** From the words at the end of each sentence, write the correct words in the blanks.

1. Did the teacher give _____, _____, and _____ her permission? (he, him) (you) (I, me)

2. Have all of you told _____ and _____ the whole truth? (we, us) (them, they)

3. Dad and Mom give _____ and _____ generous allowances. (Eddie) (I, me)

4. Didn't Julie promise _____ and _____ some prints of those snapshots? (she, her) (you)

5. The librarian will show _____ and _____ the new books. (they, them) (you)

6. Why was Larry asking _____ and _____ those questions? (we, us) (her, she)

7. After school, could you or he bring _____ and _____ our homework? (I, me) (my brother)

NAME _____ DATE _____ 135

INDIRECT OBJECTS—PRONOUNS

TEST: Using Pronouns as Indirect Objects

Instructions: Mark: <u>verbs</u>, <u>subjects</u>, adjectives, adverbs (prep. phrases) label: **D.O., prep., O.P., I.O.** From the words at the end of each sentence, write the correct words in the blanks.

1. Did the teacher give _____, _____, and _____ her permission? (he, him) (you) (I, me)

2. Have all of you told _____ and _____ the whole truth? (we, us) (them, they)

3. Dad and Mom give _____ and _____ generous allowances. (Eddie) (I, me)

4. Didn't Julie promise _____ and _____ some prints of those snapshots? (she, her) (you)

5. The librarian will show _____ and _____ the new books. (they, them) (you)

6. Why was Larry asking _____ and _____ those questions? (we, us) (her, she)

7. After school, could you or he bring _____ and _____ our homework? (I, me) (my brother)

Steps to Good Grammar

RECOGNIZING NOUNS USED AS APPOSITIVES

Have students memorize the definition of an appositive.

Discuss the use of commas with appositives:

Usually an appositive is set off with commas.

Occasionally when the appositive is restrictive, or closely related to the preceding word, the comma is not needed (as in examples students have already encountered in this book):

My brother Tim. Our dog Sparky. We girls.

Notice: In the first diagram, the forked lines for the compound appositive return to the sentence line in order to show the closing parenthesis.

Practice sentences:

1. Remind students to set off appositives with commas.

2. Sentence 5: The word group that identifies *José* extends through the prepositional phrase; therefore, the comma is placed after *from Mexico.*

3. Sentence 6: *Fourth of July* is a special noun; *of July* is not labeled as a prepositional phrase.

4. Sentences 6 and 10: *Independence Day, Nancy Boyd Park,* and *Church Street* are proper nouns; *Independence, Nancy Boyd,* and *Church* are not marked as adjectives.

5. Sentence 10: The period at the end of the sentence takes the place of the commas that would otherwise close the appositive.

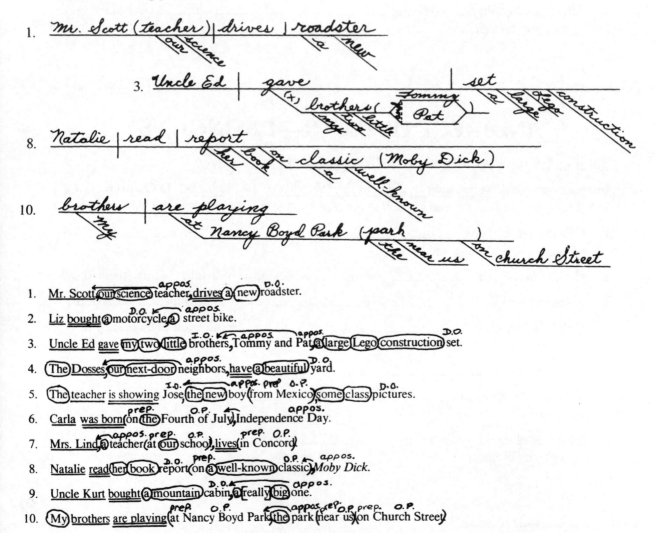

1. Mr. Scott, our science teacher, drives a new roadster.
2. Liz bought a motorcycle, a street bike.
3. Uncle Ed gave my two little brothers, Tommy and Pat, a large Lego construction set.
4. The Dosses, our next-door neighbors, have a beautiful yard.
5. The teacher is showing Jose, the new boy from Mexico, some class pictures.
6. Carla was born on the Fourth of July, Independence Day.
7. Mrs. Lind, a teacher at our school, lives in Concord.
8. Natalie read her book report on a well-known classic, Moby Dick.
9. Uncle Kurt bought a mountain cabin, a really big one.
10. My brothers are playing at Nancy Boyd Park, the park near us on Church Street.

APPOSITIVES

Recognizing Nouns Used as Appositives

LEARN: 1. An **appositive**, abbreviated **appos.**, is a noun (or pronoun) that identifies or renames the noun it follows.

2. An appositive, or a word group containing the appositive, is usually set off from the rest of the sentence by a comma or commas.

3. An appositive may be used to identify a subject, a direct object, the object of a preposition, or an indirect object.

4. An appositive may be compound.

5. In diagramming, an appositive is shown in parentheses immediately following the word it identifies.

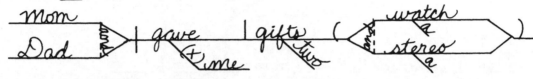

Mom and Dad gave me two gifts, a watch and a stereo.

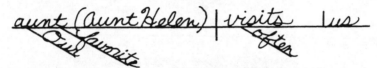

Our favorite aunt, Aunt Helen, visits us often.

PRACTICE: Mark: verbs, subjects, adjectives, adverbs, prep. phrases; label: **D.O., prep., O.P., I.O., appos.** Draw an arrow from the appositive to the word it identifies; insert commas. Diagram sentences 1, 3, 8, and 10.

1. Mr. Scott our science teacher drives a new roadster.

2. Liz bought a motorcycle a street bike.

3. Uncle Ed gave my two little brothers Tommy and Pat a large Lego construction set.

4. The Dosses our next-door neighbors have a beautiful yard.

5. The teacher is showing Jose the new boy from Mexico some class pictures.

6. Carla was born on the Fourth of July Independence Day.

7. Mrs. Lind a teacher at our school lives in Concord.

8. Natalie read her book report on a well-known classic *Moby Dick.*

9. Uncle Kurt bought a mountain cabin a really big one.

10. My brothers are playing at Nancy Boyd Park the park near us on Church Street.

© 1988, 1997 J. Weston Walch, Publisher

Steps to Good Grammar

USING NOUNS AS APPOSITIVES

Understanding the use of appositives is important in helping students to develop variety in their own original sentences.

Identifying sentence parts in the given short sentences is purposely avoided, since the second and third sentences contain linking verbs. The study of linking verbs begins on page 152.

Examine carefully with the students the introductory material:

1. In the sample sentence, *my little sister* identifies

Ileane; sister is the appositive to *Ileane; a Cabbage Patch Preemie* identifies *doll* and is written as an appositive to it.

2. Commas are used to set off the appositives.
3. In diagramming, an appositive is shown in parentheses following the word it identifies.

In the Practice work, help students identify words in the second and third sentences that can be written as appositives into the first sentences. Emphasize the placement of commas.

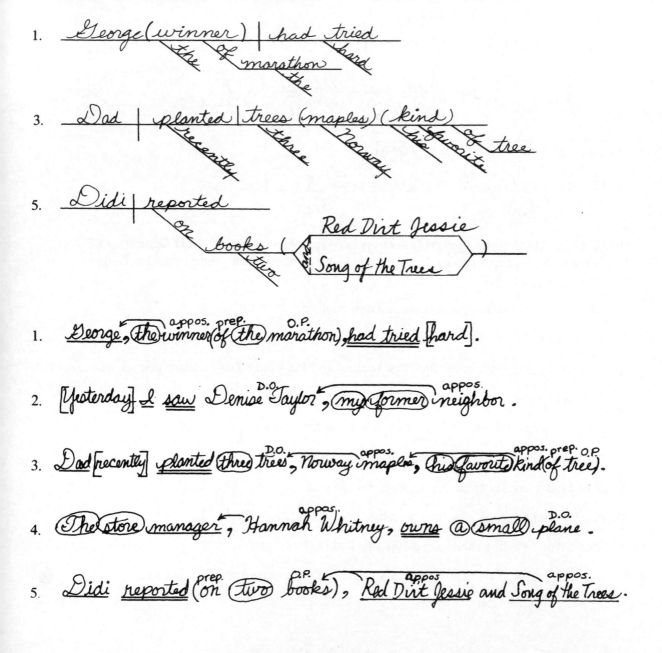

APPOSITIVES

Using Nouns as Appositives

Using appositives is one way to combine two or more short sentences into one. Improve your writing style by using appositives!

Example: Aunt Julie gave Ileane a new doll. Ileane is my little sister. The doll is a Cabbage Patch Preemie.

METHOD: Use *sister* in the second sentence as an appositive to *Ileane* in the first sentence. Use *Cabbage Patch Preemie* in the third sentence as an appositive to *doll* in the first sentence.

Aunt Julie gave Ileane, my little sister, a new doll, a Cabbage Patch Preemie.

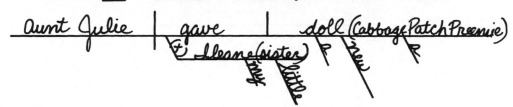

PRACTICE: Rewrite each of the following short sentences into one. Use the first sentence as the main idea. Expand it by writing related words from the next sentence(s) as appositives.

In the sentences you write, mark: verbs, subjects, adjectives, adverbs, prep. phrases, label: **D.O., prep., O.P., I.O., appos.** Draw an arrow from the appositive to the word it identifies; insert commas. Diagram sentences 1, 3, and 5.

1. George had tried hard. He was the winner of the marathon.

2. Yesterday I saw Denise Taylor. She is my former neighbor.

3. Dad recently planted three trees. They are Norway maples. They are his favorite kind of tree.

4. The store manager owns a small plane. Her name is Hannah Whitney.

5. Didi reported on two books. They were *Red Dirt Jessie* and *Song of the Trees*.

Steps to Good Grammar

DRILL

The sentences in the top half of this page illustrate that all parts of sentences in which nouns are used can have appositives. Sentences 1 and 3 have appositives to the subject, sentence 2 to the direct object, sentence 4 to the indirect object, and sentence 5 to the object of a preposition and to another appositive.

Construct the blank diagram on the chalkboard; help students write the words in the correct spaces.

Students may need help in rewriting the short sentences. Guide them to:

Sentence 2: Write one appositive to the subject and another appositive to the direct object.

Sentence 5: Write one appositive to the subject and another appositive to *that* appositive.

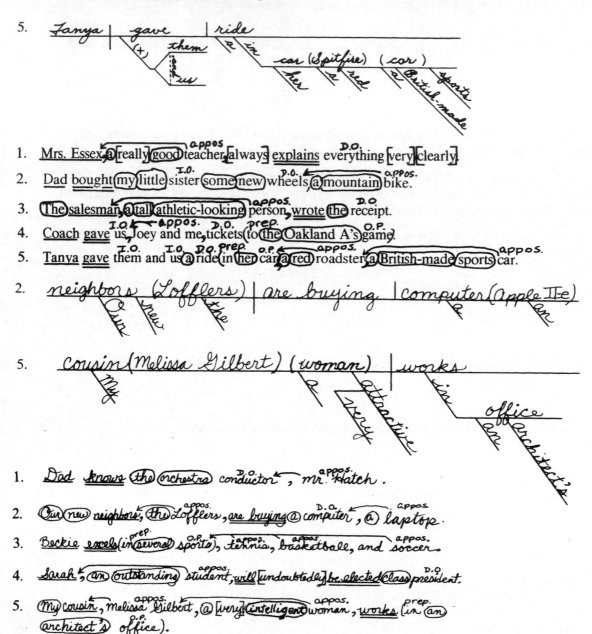

1. Mrs. Essex, a really good teacher, always explains everything very clearly.
2. Dad bought my little sister some new wheels, a mountain bike.
3. The salesman, a tall athletic-looking person, wrote the receipt.
4. Coach gave us, Joey and me, tickets to the Oakland A's game.
5. Tanya gave them and us a ride in her car, a red roadster, a British-made sports car.

1. Dad knows the orchestra conductor, Mr. Hatch.
2. Our new neighbors, the Lofflers, are buying a computer, a laptop.
3. Beckie excels in several sports, tennis, basketball, and soccer.
4. Sarah, an outstanding student, will undoubtedly be elected class president.
5. My cousin, Melissa Gilbert, a very intelligent woman, works in an architect's office.

APPOSITIVES

DRILL: Recognizing and Using Nouns as Appositives

Recognizing Noun Appositives

Instructions: Mark: <u>verbs</u>, <u>subjects</u>, adjectives, adverbs, (prep. phrases), label **D.O., prep., O.P., I.O., appos.** Draw an arrow from the appositive to the word it identifies; insert commas. Diagram sentence 5 on the given outline.

1. Mrs. Essex a really good teacher always explains everything very clearly.

2. Dad bought my little sister some new wheels a mountain bike.

3. The salesman a tall athletic-looking person wrote the receipt.

4. Coach gave us Joey and me tickets to the Oakland A's game.

5. Tanya gave them and us a ride in her car a red roadster a British-made sports car.

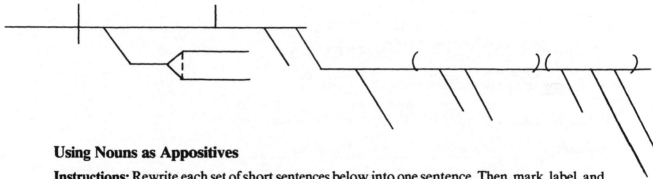

Using Nouns as Appositives

Instructions: Rewrite each set of short sentences below into one sentence. Then, mark, label, and punctuate the sentences you write as you did above. Diagram sentences 2 and 5.

1. Dad knows the orchestra conductor. He is Mr. Hatch.

2. Our new neighbors are buying a computer. It is a laptop. Our new neighbors are the Lofflers.

3. Beckie excels in several sports. She excels in tennis, baseball, and soccer.

4. Sarah will undoubtedly be elected class president. She is an outstanding student.

5. My cousin works in an architect's office. My cousin is Melissa Gilbert. Melissa is a very intelligent woman.

Steps to Good Grammar

FINAL DRILL

This page provides further practice in recognizing and using appositives for students who need it.

Remind students to set off appositives with commas; this is the instruction they most often forget.

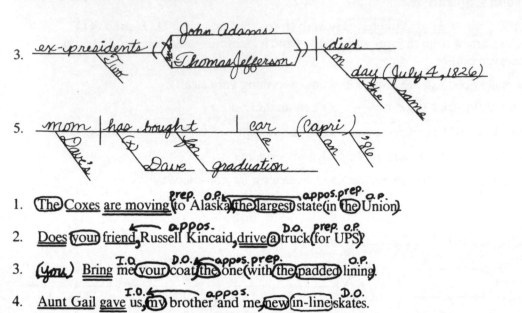

1. (The) Coxes are moving (to Alaska) the largest state (in the Union)

2. Does (your) friend, Russell Kincaid, drive (a) truck (for UPS)

3. (You) Bring me (your) coat (the) one (with the padded lining)

4. Aunt Gail gave us, (my) brother and me, new in-line skates.

5. (The) counselor handed Trish, (the) new girl (from Boston) (her) class schedule.

1. Uncle Fred has (a) dog, (a) (Scottish) terrier.

2. We took (a) trip (down (the) Nile), (the) longest river (in the world).

3. (Two) ex-presidents, John Adams and Thomas Jefferson, died (on (the) same) day), July 4, 1826.

4. Mr. and Mrs. Watson, residents (of San Francisco), adopted (two) (stray) dogs, (German) shepherds.

5. (Dave's) mom has bought Dave (a) car, (a) ('97) (sports) car (for graduation).

APPOSITIVES

FINAL DRILL: Recognizing and Using Nouns as Appositives

Recognizing Noun Appositives

Instructions: Mark: verbs, subjects, adjectives, adverbs, (prep. phrases); label: **D.O., prep., O.P., I.O., appos.** Draw an arrow from the appositive to the word it identifies; insert commas. Diagram sentence 5 on the outline given.

1. The Coxes are moving to Alaska the largest state in the Union.

2. Does your friend Russell Kincaid drive a truck for UPS?

3.   Bring me your coat the one with the padded lining.

4. Aunt Gail gave us my brother and me new in-line skates.

5. The counselor handed Trish the new girl from Boston her class schedule.

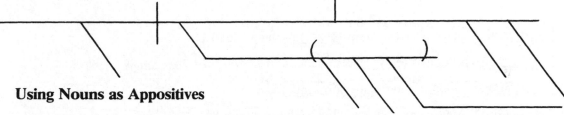

Using Nouns as Appositives

Instructions: Use the first sentence in each group below as the main idea. Then expand it by writing related words from the next sentence(s) as appositives. As usual, mark and label all sentence parts; draw an arrow from the appositive to the word it identifies; insert commas. Diagram sentences 3 and 5.

1. Uncle Fred has a dog. It is a Scottish terrier.

2. We took a trip down the Nile. It is the longest river in the world.

3. Two ex-presidents died on the same day. The day was July 4, 1826. The ex-presidents were John Adams and Thomas Jefferson.

4. Mr. and Mrs. Watson adopted two stray dogs. The Watsons are residents of San Francisco. The dogs were German Shepherds.

5. Dave's mom has bought Dave a car for graduation. It is a '97 sports car.

Steps to Good Grammar

TEST 1

This reproducible page contains two copies of one half-page drill/test. Cut each duplicated page in half; give each student one half-page.

Both tests, pages 145 and 147, are composed of sentences students have analyzed in the unit. This offers students the reward of earning a high grade for having paid attention in class during practice work; it can help them to a realization that effort, understanding, and memory are basic factors in achievement.

The test on page 147 includes combining sentences by using appositives.

Grading suggestions:

Point value

1 point each comma	13
1 point each prepositional phrase in parentheses	6
All other underlinings and labels	90
	109

Deduct 1% for each error.

1. Mrs. Essex, a really good teacher in Antioch, explains things clearly.
2. Natalie wrote her report on a well-known classic, The Adventures of Tom Sawyer.
3. The Dosses, our next-door neighbors, have a beautiful yard.
4. Dad promised my little sister some new wheels, a mountain bike.
5. Liz is buying a motorcycle, a street bike.
6. Uncle Kurt has bought a mountain cabin, a really nice one.
7. The teacher showed José, the new boy from Mexico, class pictures.
8. Clark was born on the Fourth of July, Independence Day.
9. Dad and Mom gave me two gifts, a watch and a stereo.
10. The Coxes have moved to Alaska, the largest state in the Union.

APPOSITIVES

TEST 1: Recognizing Noun Appositives and All Other Sentence Parts

Instructions: Mark: verbs, subjects, adjectives, adverbs, prep. phrases, label: **D.O., prep., O.P., I.O., appos.** Insert commas.

1. Mrs. Essex a really good teacher in Antioch explains things clearly.

2. Natalie wrote her report on a well-known classic *The Adventures of Tom Sawyer*.

3. The Dosses our next-door neighbors have a beautiful yard.

4. Dad promised my little sister a new bike a mountain bike.

5. Liz is buying a motorcycle a street bike.

6. Uncle Kurt has bought a mountain cabin a really nice one.

7. The teacher showed José the new boy from Mexico class pictures.

8. Clark was born on the Fourth of July Independence Day.

9. Dad and Mom gave me two gifts a watch and a stereo.

10. The Coxes have moved to Alaska the largest state in the Union.

NAME _____ DATE _____ 145

APPOSITIVES

TEST 1: Recognizing Noun Appositives and All Other Sentence Parts

Instructions: Mark: verbs, subjects, adjectives, adverbs, prep. phrases, label: **D.O., prep., O.P., I.O., appos.** Insert commas.

1. Mrs. Essex a really good teacher in Antioch explains things clearly.

2. Natalie wrote her report on a well-known classic *The Adventures of Tom Sawyer*.

3. The Dosses our next-door neighbors have a beautiful yard.

4. Dad promised my little sister a new bike a mountain bike.

5. Liz is buying a motorcycle a street bike.

6. Uncle Kurt has bought a mountain cabin a really nice one.

7. The teacher showed José the new boy from Mexico class pictures.

8. Clark was born on the Fourth of July Independence Day.

9. Dad and Mom gave me two gifts a watch and a stereo.

10. The Coxes have moved to Alaska the largest state in the Union.

© 1988, 1997 J. Weston Walch, Publisher

Steps to Good Grammar

TEST 2

This test is more indicative than the test on page 145 of the students' complete understanding, since it includes combining sentences by using appositives. The test on page 145 could be used as a make-up test for absentees.

Grading suggestions:

Point value

Part I:		
1 point each comma		9
1 point each arrow		6
1 point each prepositional phrase in parentheses		1
All other symbols		44
		60

Part II:		
1 point each comma		12
1 point each arrow		9
1 point each prepositional phrase in parentheses		3
All other symbols		48
		72

Deduct 1 point for each incorrect symbol.

1. Our favorite aunt, Aunt Helen, visits us [often].

2. His sister bought a motorcycle, a street bike

3. The teacher is showing José the new boy (from Mexico), some class pictures

4. Dad [recently] planted three trees, Norway maples, his favorite tree.

5. Sarah, an outstanding student, will [undoubtedly] be elected class president.

1. Our new neighbors, the Lofflers, are buying a computer, a PC.

2. My cousin, Melissa Gilbert, a [very] intelligent woman, works (in an architect's office).

3. Didi reported (on two books), Red Dirt Jessie and Song of the Trees.

4. Aunt Julie gave Ileana, my little sister, a new doll, a Cabbage Patch Preemie.

5. George, the winner (of the marathon), had tried [hard].

APPOSITIVES

TEST 2: Recognizing and Using Noun Appositives

Recognizing Noun Appositives and Other Sentence Parts

Instructions: Mark: <u>verbs</u>, <u>subjects</u>, (adjectives), [adverbs], (prep. phrase); label: **D.O., prep., O.P., I.O., appos.** Draw an arrow from the appositive to the word it identifies. Insert commas.

1. Our favorite aunt Aunt Helen visits us often.

2. His sister bought a motorcyle a street bike.

3. The teacher is showing José the new boy from Mexico some class pictures.

4. Dad recently planted three trees Norway maples his favorite tree.

5. Sarah an outstanding student will undoubtedly be elected class president.

Using Noun Appositives

Instructions: Using appositives, rewrite each set of short sentences below into one sentence. Then mark, label, and punctuate the sentences you write, as you did above.

1. Our new neighbors are buying a computer. It is a PC. Our new neighbors are the Lofflers.

2. My cousin works in an architect's office. She is Melissa Gilbert. Melissa is a very intelligent woman.

3. Didi reported on two books. They were *Red Dirt Jessie* and *Song of the Trees*.

4. Aunt Julie gave Ileane a new doll. Ileane is my little sister. The doll is a Cabbage Patch Preemie.

5. George had tried hard. He was the winner of the marathon.

Steps to Good Grammar

RECOGNIZING NOUNS OF DIRECT ADDRESS

The noun of direct address is the last sentence part we will study in which nouns are used. Tell students that a test is scheduled after only one page of practice.

Instruct students to memorize the definition of a noun in direct address.

The drill actually furnishes a final practice in recognizing all the sentence parts the students have studied so far.

1. As students analyze the sentences, point out that the noun of direct address (N.A.) may be used at the beginning, in the middle, or at the end of a sentence.

2. Remind students that the N.A. is set off from the rest of the sentence by a comma or commas.

3. Sentences 3 and 10 use a true "introductory" *there*. Point out this fact when students diagram the sentences.

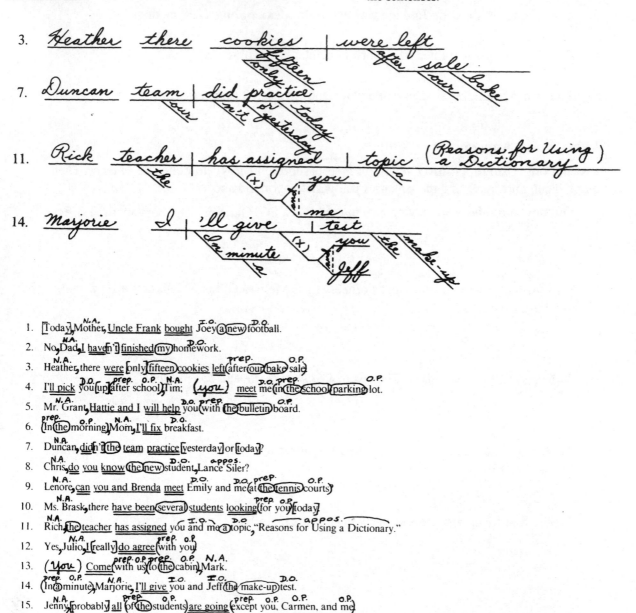

1. [Today,] Mother, Uncle Frank bought Joey a new football.
2. No, Dad, I haven't finished my homework.
3. Heather, there were only fifteen cookies left after our bake sale.
4. I'll pick you up after school, Tim; (you) meet me in the school parking lot.
5. Mr. Grant, Hattie and I will help you with the bulletin board.
6. In the morning, Mom, I'll fix breakfast.
7. Duncan, didn't the team practice yesterday or today?
8. Chris, do you know the new student, Lance Siler?
9. Lenore, can you and Brenda meet Emily and me at the tennis courts?
10. Ms. Brask, there have been several students looking for you today.
11. Rich, the teacher has assigned you and me a topic, "Reasons for Using a Dictionary."
12. Yes, Julio, I really do agree with you.
13. (You) Come with us to the cabin, Mark.
14. In a minute, Marjorie, I'll give you and Jeff the make-up test.
15. Jenny, probably all of the students are going except you, Carmen, and me.

NOUN OF DIRECT ADDRESS

Recognizing Nouns of Direct Address

DEFINITION: A **noun of direct address** is a person's name written as though the writer were speaking to the person, addressing him or her directly.

LEARN:

1. A **noun of direct address,** abbreviated **N.A.,** is set off from the rest of the sentence by a comma or commas.

2. A noun of address has no grammatical connection to the rest of the sentence.

3. In diagramming, no matter where the **N.A.** appears in the sentence, it is diagrammed ahead of the sentence, as are the introductory words: *yes, no, well, oh,* and *there.*

Example: Well, Kay, will you be visiting us soon?

PRACTICE/DRILL: Mark: verbs, subjects, adjectives, adverbs, (prep. phrases) label: **D.O., prep., O.P.; I.O., appos.** Insert commas. Diagram sentences 3, 7, 11, and 14.

1. Today Mother Uncle Frank bought Joey a new football.

2. No Dad I haven't finished my homework.

3. Heather there were only fifteen cookies left after our bake sale.

4. I'll pick you up after school Tim; meet me in the school parking lot.

5. Mr. Grant Hattie and I will help you with the bulletin board.

6. In the morning Mom I'll fix breakfast.

7. Duncan didn't the team practice yesterday or today?

8. Chris do you know the new student Lance Siler?

9. Lenore can you and Brenda meet Emily and me at the tennis courts?

10. Ms. Brask there have been several students looking for you today.

11. Rich the teacher has assigned you and me a topic "Reasons for Using a Dictionary."

12. Yes Julio I really do agree with you.

13. Come with us to the cabin Mark.

14. In a minute Marjorie I'll give you and Jeff the make-up test.

15. Jenny probably all of the students are going except you, Carmen, and me.

Steps to Good Grammar

TEST

This reproducible page contains two copies of one half-page drill/test. Cut each duplicated page in half; give each student one half-page.

To most students, the noun of address is an obvious concept. One page of practice in recognizing it is sufficient.

Grading suggestions:

Point Value

1 point each inserted comma	7
1 point each prepositional phrase in parentheses	6
All other identification symbols	55
	68

Use the grading scale on page 124.

Probably no student will score lower than 80%.

1. Lenore, can you and Brenda meet Emily and me (at the tennis courts)?

2. Rich, the teacher has assigned you and me a topic, "Reasons for Using a Dictionary."

3. Meet me (in the school parking lot) (after school), Tim.

4. Jenny, probably all (of the students) are going (except you, Carmen, and me).

5. Ms. Brask, there have been several students looking (for you) [today].

6. Didn't the team practice [yesterday] or [today], Duncan?

NOUN OF DIRECT ADDRESS

TEST: Recognizing Nouns of Direct Address and All Other Sentence Parts

Instructions: Mark: <u>verbs</u>, <u>subjects</u>, adjectives, adverbs (prep. phrases) label: **D.O., prep., O.P., I.O., appos., N.A.** Insert commas.

1. Lenore can you and Brenda meet Emily and me at the tennis courts?

2. Rich the teacher has assigned you and me a topic "Reasons for Using a Dictionary."

3. Meet me in the school parking lot after school Tim.

4. Jenny probably all of the students are going except you, Carmen, and me.

5. Ms. Brask there have been several students looking for you today.

6. Didn't the team practice yesterday or today Duncan?

NAME _____ DATE _____ 151

NOUN OF DIRECT ADDRESS

TEST: Recognizing Nouns of Direct Address and All Other Sentence Parts

Instructions: Mark: <u>verbs</u>, <u>subjects</u>, adjectives, adverbs (prep. phrases) label: **D.O., prep., O.P., I.O., appos., N.A.** Insert commas.

1. Lenore can you and Brenda meet Emily and me at the tennis courts?

2. Rich the teacher has assigned you and me a topic "Reasons for Using a Dictionary."

3. Meet me in the school parking lot after school Tim.

4. Jenny probably all of the students are going except you, Carmen, and me.

5. Ms. Brask there have been several students looking for you today.

6. Didn't the team practice yesterday or today Duncan?

© 1988, 1997 J. Weston Walch, Publisher

Steps to Good Grammar

RECOGNIZING LINKING VERBS

Read aloud the introductory material as the students read silently.

Cover the following points with your students:

1. So far, students have studied sentences containing only "doing" verbs and "helping" verbs (the verbs that "help" or give added meaning to "doing" verbs). Now they are going to study the other main verb type, **linking verbs.**

2. Tell students they are to memorize:
   - the list of seventeen linking verbs;
   - this definition: A linking verb links the subject and the linking verb complement.

3. Point out that the first eight words in the linking verb list are the same as the first eight "helping" verbs. Stress that the rest of the twenty-three helping verbs are *never* linking verbs.

4. In other courses of study, the LVC-N is called a predicate nominative; the LVC-A is called a predicate adjective.

5. Emphasize the point made in **Understand** and carefully examine the sample sentences that illustrate the concept.

6. Work with the students in identifying the sentence parts in the Practice section.

1. Laurie is my niece.
2. We are teenagers.
3. I am a student.
4. I am interested.
5. Lucy was the winner.
6. Vic was excited.
7. The men were successful.
8. Luke will be a doctor.
9. Al is being a problem.
10. Mom had been a pilot.

LINKING VERBS

Recognizing Linking Verbs

DEFINITION:

A **linking verb** links, or joins, the subject and the linking verb **complement** — the word that follows the linking verb. *Complement* means "completer." The completer may be either a noun or an adjective.

You will use these labels: Linking Verb = **LV**

                        Noun Linking Verb Complement = **LVC-N**

                        Adjective Linking Verb Complement = **LVC-A**

MEMORIZE: Words frequently used as **linking verbs** are:

> **IS AM ARE WAS WERE BE BEING BEEN BECOME**
> **SEEM APPEAR FEEL TASTE SMELL SOUND GROW LOOK**

> *Examples:* Sue is. Without a complement, the sentence lacks meaning.
> Sue is my cousin. The noun *cousin* — the LVC-N — identifies
>   Sue and completes the meaning.
> Sue is popular. The adjective *popular* — the LVC-A —
>   describes Sue and completes the meaning.

UNDERSTAND: A linking verb expresses no action; the subject *doesn't do anything,* and *nothing is done* to the subject.

> *Examples:* Sue is my cousin.   Sue isn't *doing* anything. She *is* what the
>   She is popular.   sentences say, a *cousin, popular.*
> Jack was feeling better. Jack wasn't *doing* anything. The sentence simply
>   reports his condition.

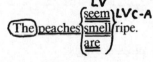

> The peaches smell ripe.   The peaches aren't *doing* anything.
>   The sentence simply reports the peaches'
>   condition — *ripe.*

PRACTICE: Mark and label all sentence parts below, including **LV, LVC-N,** and **LVC-A.**

1. Laurie is my niece.

2. We are teenagers.

3. I am a student.

4. I am interested.

5. Lucy was the winner.

6. Vic was excited.

7. The men were successful.

8. Luke will be a doctor.

9. Al is being a problem.

10. Mom had been a pilot.

Steps to Good Grammar

USING *TO BE* AS A LINKING VERB

As you read the four introductory items aloud, quiz the students to establish their understanding.

The first three Practice sentences make very clear the uses of *be* as a linking verb and as a helping verb.

Emphasize the differences in use in the rest of the sentences; remind students that they *can do* "doing" verbs; they cannot *do* LVC-As or LVC-Ns!

1. My brother should be the winner.
    <small>LV   LVC-N</small>
2. My brother should be excited.
    <small>LV LVC-A</small>
3. My brother should be sleeping.
4. The dog was a spaniel.
    <small>LV   LVC-N</small>
5. The dog was old.
    <small>LV LVC-A</small>
6. The dog was barking.
7. Cathy is an outstanding student.
    <small>LV   LVC-N</small>
8. I am an American citizen.
    <small>LV   LVC-N</small>
9. Those boys are star basketball players.
    <small>LV   LVC-N</small>
10. Those boys are practicing.
11. Was your dad an army officer?
    <small>LV   LVC-N</small>
12. Was Dawn really trying?
13. The boys were cooperating.

14. Our team had been winning.
15. Our team had been the winners.
    <small>LV   LVC-N</small>
16. Sean should have been studying.
17. Was the man being impatient?
    <small>LV LVC-A</small>
18. The man was being questioned.
19. Have she and he been good assistants?
    <small>LV   LVC-N</small>
20. Will your dad be late?
    <small>LV LVC-A</small>
21. He is coming now.
22. Those carpenters are very capable.
    <small>LV   LVC-A</small>
23. The cat was being a pest.
    <small>LV   LVC-N</small>
24. The cat was being clever.
    <small>LV LVC-A</small>
25. The team and the students had
    been discouraged.
    <small>LV LVC-A</small>

LINKING VERBS

Using *TO BE* as a Linking Verb

These are all forms of the verb *to be:*

IS   AM   ARE   WAS   WERE   BE   BEING   BEEN

1. When *is, am, are, was,* or *were* is the *only* verb word in the sentence, it is *always* a **linking verb (LV).**

2. When *be, being,* or *been* is the *last* verb word in the sentence, it is *always* a **linking verb (LV).** (Use "helping" verbs with these three words.)

3. When those eight words are *followed by doing verbs, they are "helping" verbs,* not "linking" verbs. They should *not* be labeled LV.

4. Be sure to recognize an adjective following a linking verb. Adjectives in the LVC-A position sometimes seem like verb words.

Example: (The huge) audience was [really] excited and noisy.

> Realize that *excited* and *noisy* are not verbs. You cannot do *excited* or *do noisy.* Therefore, *was* is the only verb word. The adjectives *excited* and *noisy* describe *audience.*

PRACTICE: Distinguishing Linking Verbs from "Helpers"

Instructions: Mark: verbs, subjects, adjectives (except LVC-A), adverbs label **LV, LVC-N, LVC-A.**

1. My brother should be the winner.

2. My brother should be excited.

3. My brother should be sleeping.

4. The dog was a spaniel.

5. The dog was old.

6. The dog was barking.

7. Cathy is an outstanding student.

8. I am an American citizen.

9. Those boys are star basketball players.

10. Those boys are practicing.

11. Was your dad an army officer?

12. Was Dawn really trying?

13. The boys were cooperating.

14. Our team had been winning.

15. Our team had been the winners.

16. Sean should have been studying.

17. Was the man being impatient?

18. The man was being questioned.

19. Have she and he been good assistants?

20. Will your dad be late?

21. He is coming now.

22. Those carpenters are very capable.

23. The cat was being a pest.

24. The cat was being clever.

25. The team and the students had been discouraged.

Steps to Good Grammar

RECOGNIZING LINKING VERBS

The objective of this page is to establish a firm understanding of linking verbs based upon recognizing them in these sentences.

Tell students that no "doing" verbs are used in this drill. Reinforce frequently the fact that in none of these sentences does the subject *do* anything.

Ask volunteers to recite the list of seventeen linking verbs.

1. Those girls are star basketball players. [LV, LVC-N]
2. Was Dad an army captain? [LV, LVC-N]
3. Uncle Harold and Dad were officers in the army. [LV, LVC-N, prep, O.P.]
4. My cousin will be a pediatrician. [LV, LVC-N]
5. The little boy was being a fair player. [LV, LVC-N]
6. I am quite hopeful. [LV, LVC-A]
7. The roofers are certainly well-trained. [LV, LVC-A]
8. Emma and she were very cautious. [LV, LVC-A]
9. The people on the tour were being very observant. [prep, O.P., LV, LVC-A]
10. The team had been overconfident. [LV, LVC-A]
11. Mom and I were becoming very concerned. [LV, LVC-A]
12. Alex has become an expert water-skier. [LV, LVC-N]
13. Our neighbor surely seems very energetic. [LV, LVC-A]
14. Studying should seem both desirable and rewarding. [LV, LVC-A, LVC-A]
15. The librarian appears preoccupied. [LV, LVC-A]
16. The driver certainly had appeared confused. [LV, LVC-A]
17. I am feeling quite determined. [LV, LVC-A]
18. Has Grandmother felt better today? [LV, LVC-A]
19. This orange certainly tastes good. [LV, LVC-A]
20. That roasting turkey is smelling perfectly delicious! [LV, LVC-A]
21. The dog's bark sounded very threatening to me. [LV, LVC-A, prep, O.P.]
22. The students were growing more enthusiastic. [LV, LVC-A]
23. The passengers must have grown annoyed with the delay. [LV, LVC-A, prep, O.P.]
24. The clouds have been looking very ominous. [LV, LVC-A]
25. Don't the kindergarteners look excited and happy? [LV, LVC-A, LVC-A]

LINKING VERBS

Recognizing Linking Verbs — Practice

Memorize the **linking verbs:**

**IS   AM   ARE   WAS   WERE   BE   BEING   BEEN   BECOME   SEEM
APPEAR   FEEL   TASTE   SMELL   SOUND   GROW   LOOK**

Instructions: Mark: complete <u>verbs</u>, <u>subjects</u>, adjectives (except LVC-A), adverbs (prep. phrases), label: **prep., O.P., LVC-N, LVC-A, LV.**

His mother has been a practicing lawyer for several years.
    LV   LVC-N prep.   O.P.

The huge audience was becoming extremely excited and noisy.
             LV   LVC-A LVC-A

1. Those girls are star basketball players.

2. Was Dad an army captain?

3. Uncle Harold and Dad were officers in the army.

4. My cousin will be a pediatrician.

5. The little boy was being a fair player.

6. I am quite hopeful.

7. The roofers are certainly well-trained.

8. Emma and she were very cautious.

9. The people on the tour were being very observant.

10. The team had been overconfident.

11. Mom and I were becoming very concerned.

12. Alex has become an expert water-skier.

13. Our neighbor surely seems very energetic.

14. Studying should seem both desirable and rewarding.

15. The librarian appears preoccupied.

16. The driver certainly had appeared confused.

17. I am feeling quite determined.

18. Has Grandmother felt better today?

19. This orange certainly tastes good.

20. That roasting turkey is smelling perfectly delicious!

21. The dog's bark sounded very threatening to me!

22. The students were growing more enthusiastic.

23. The passengers must have grown annoyed with the delay.

24. The clouds have been looking very ominous.

25. Don't the kindergarteners look excited and happy?

Steps to Good Grammar

DISTINGUISHING BETWEEN LINKING
AND "DOING" VERBS

Quiz students on the Remember items.

Examine with the students the sample sentences and the diagrams.

Sample sentence 1: The slanted line following a linking verb shows that the LVC is linked or related to the subject. Students do not need to use the dotted arrow.

Sample sentence 2: The comma after *director* is essential to show that the word is, indeed, an appositive to *Aunt Helen*.

Sample sentences 2 and 3: Compare the two uses of *been* in these sentences.

Work with the students in analyzing and diagramming the Practice sentences.

1.

2.

3.

6.

9.

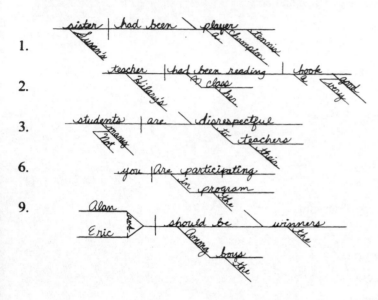

1. (Susan's) sister had been (a) champion (tennis) player.

2. (Hilary's) teacher had been reading (her) class (a) (very) (good) book.

3. (Not) (many) students are disrespectful (to) (their) teachers).

4. (A) (good) (awards) program has been set (up) recently).

5. Students are enthusiastic (about it).

6. Are you participating (in (the) program)?

7. I am working (on it).

8. (My) (best) friend, Amy, (will) (probably) be (the) winner.

9. (Among (the) boys), Alan and Eric should be (the) winners.

10. (Alicia's) idea sounds excellent.

LINKING VERBS

Distinguishing Between Linking and "Doing" Verbs

REMEMBER:

A **linking verb** expresses no action. It is followed by an LVC that either identifies or describes the subject.

A **doing verb** tells what is being done in the sentence. It may or may not have a direct object.

DIAGRAMMING is an aid to understanding sentence structure.

Study these examples to understand linking verb diagramming and to refresh your memory about all other sentence parts.

The director of our camp is my Aunt Helen.

Use a slanted line after the linking verb to show that the linking verb complement, in this sentence, *identifies* the subject.

Aunt Helen, the director, has very patiently been teaching us girls the rules.   (Here, *been* is a "helper.")

Yes, Aunt Helen has purposely been very patient!   (Here, *been* is a linking verb.)

PRACTICE: Mark and label all sentence parts below as in the sentences above. Diagram sentences 1, 2, 3, 6, and 9.

1. Susan's sister had been a champion tennis player.

2. Hilary's teacher had been reading her class a very good book.

3. Not many students are disrespectful to their teachers.

4. A good awards program has been set up recently.

5. Students are enthusiastic about it.

6. Are you participating in the program?

7. I am working on it.

8. My best friend, Amy, will probably be the winner.

9. Among the boys, Alan and Eric should be the winners.

10. Alicia's idea sounds excellent.

Steps to Good Grammar

DRILL 1

In the first part of this practice page, students recognize linking verbs: *become, seem, appear, feel, taste, smell, sound, grow, look.*

In the second part they distinguish between the use of those words as linking verbs and as doing verbs. Point out to students that *seem* is always used as a linking verb.

1. (My)(little)sister becomes angry [quite][easily].
   LV   LVC-A

2. (The)audience was becoming restless.
   LV   LVC-A

3. Uncle Lars will become (a)pilot.
   LV   LVC-N

4. (Our)neighbor [surely] seems energetic.
   LV   LVC-A

5. Mario had seemed happy and excited.
   LV   LVC-A   LVC-A

6. (The)librarian appears preoccupied.
   LV   LVC-A

7. (The)driver appeared confused.
   LV   LVC-A

8. I am feeling [rather] discouraged.
   LV   LVC-A

9. Has Grandmother felt better [today]?
   LV   LVC-A

10. Does(that)orange taste good?
    LV   LVC-A

11. (The)roasting turkey is smelling delicious!
    LV   LVC-A

12. (The)big(dog's)bark sounded threatening.
    LV   LVC-A

13. Maria [certainly] sounds determined.
    LV   LVC-A

14. (The)teacher is growing annoyed.
    LV   LVC-A

15. [Why]are you looking [so]suspicious?
    LV   LVC-A

1. Dad was looking [at(the)clouds]. (The)clouds were looking [very] threatening.
   prep.   O.P.   LV   LVC-A

2. (That)dress [really] becomes Sharon. Sharon could become(a)model.
         D.O.   LV   LVC-N

3. Felix appeared [constantly(on stage)]. Felix appeared tired.
            prep. O.P.   LV   LVC-A

4. (You) Feel(the)sandpaper. (The)sandpaper feels [so]scratchy.
         D.O.   LV   LVC-A

5. May I taste(the)frosting? (The)frosting tastes good.
            D.O.   LV   LVC-A

6. I did smell(fresh)cinnamon)rolls! (The)cinnamon)rolls smell delicious.
              D.O.   LV   LVC-A

7. (Our)camp)cook sounded(the)dinner)gong. (The)cook sounded impatient.
                    D.O.   LV   LVC-A

8. (My)brother is growing pumpkins. (My)brother is growing excited.
              D.O.   LV   LVC-A

9. [Before(the)reception], Mom looked us [over] [carefully]. [Apparently], we looked satisfactory.
   prep.   O.P.   D.O.   LV   LVC-A

LINKING VERBS

DRILL 1

Recognizing Linking Verbs

BECOME SEEM APPEAR FEEL TASTE SMELL SOUND GROW LOOK

REMEMBER:

In sentences with linking verbs, the subject is *not doing* anything. The sentences simply report a condition or ask a question about a condition.

Instructions: Mark and label sentence parts as in sentence 1 below.

1. My little sister becomes angry quite easily.

2. The audience was becoming restless.

3. Uncle Lars will become a pilot.

4. Our neighbor surely seems energetic.

5. Mario had seemed happy and excited.

6. The librarian appears preoccupied.

7. The driver appeared confused.

8. I am feeling rather discouraged.

9. Has Grandmother felt better today?

10. Does that orange taste good?

11. The roasting turkey is smelling delicious!

12. The big dog's bark sounded threatening.

13. Maria certainly sounds determined.

14. The teacher is growing annoyed.

15. Why are you looking so suspicious?

Recognizing Differences in Verb Use

Instructions: Mark and label sentence parts as in sentence 1 below.

1. Dad was looking at the clouds. The clouds were looking very threatening.

2. That dress really becomes Sharon. Sharon could become a model.

3. Felix appeared constantly on stage. Felix appeared tired.

4. Feel the sandpaper. The sandpaper feels so scratchy.

5. May I taste the frosting? The frosting tastes good.

6. I did smell fresh cinnamon rolls! The cinnamon rolls smell delicious.

7. Our camp cook sounded the dinner gong. The cook sounded impatient.

8. My brother is growing pumpkins. My brother is growing excited.

9. Before the reception, Mom looked us over carefully. Apparently, we looked satisfactory.

Steps to Good Grammar

DRILL 2

The objective: By analyzing the sentences in the four separate groupings, the students will be able to understand clearly the differences in the use of linking and "doing" verbs.

This is the last practice sheet in the unit.

Announce a test for the next day.

LVC-N:

1. You or Donn should be the winner.
2. Warren's brother has become a salesman for that company.
3. The Smiths have been very good neighbors.
4. Was your grandfather really a college professor?
5. Ten dollars will be the prize.

LVC-A:

1. The children were being very well-behaved.
2. The students must have been quite disappointed.
3. He and she really could be more considerate.
4. Lenore is very creative and industrious.
5. Dinner should be ready.
6. Your cousin seems rather shy.
7. Don't those children look excited and happy?
8. Mom surely sounded annoyed.
9. Some of the students appear slightly bored.
10. The boys felt very confused.

"DOING" VERBS WITH D.O.:

1. The rowdy student was disturbing the whole class.
2. Several students were being given library passes.
3. Have you and he been cleaning the garage?
4. The actors were practicing their parts.
5. The wind is blowing all the leaves off the tree.

"DOING" VERBS WITHOUT D.O.:

1. Uncle Ken was driving very slowly.
2. Sue and he will not be arriving soon.
3. The carpenter had been working carefully.
4. Our team is winning easily.
5. The package should be delivered today.

* * * * * * *

1. Those girls are good tennis players.
2. The man must have been driving carelessly.
3. The big barking dog looked and sounded vicious.
4. The team was being given final instructions.
5. This drill sheet should have been completed carefully.

LINKING VERBS

DRILL 2

Instructions: Mark: complete <u>verbs</u>, <u>subjects</u>, (adjectives) (except LVC-A), [adverbs] (prep. phrases), label: **D.O., prep., O.P., LV, LVC-N, LVC-A.**

LVC-N:

1. You or Donn should be the winner.
2. Warren's brother has become a salesman for that company.
3. The Smiths have been very good neighbors.
4. Was your grandfather really a college professor?
5. Ten dollars will be the prize.

LVC-A:

1. The children were being very well-behaved.
2. The students must have been quite disappointed.
3. He and she really could be more considerate.
4. Lenore is very creative and industrious.
5. Dinner should be ready.
6. Your cousin seems rather shy.
7. Don't those children look excited and happy?
8. Mom surely sounded annoyed.
9. Some of the students appear slightly bored.
10. The boys felt very confused.

"DOING" VERBS WITH D.O.:

1. The rowdy student was disturbing the whole class.
2. Several students were being given library passes.
3. Have you and he been cleaning the garage?
4. The actors were practicing their parts.
5. The wind is blowing all the leaves off the tree.

"DOING" VERBS WITHOUT D.O.:

1. Uncle Ken was driving very slowly.
2. Sue and he will not be arriving soon.
3. The carpenter had been working carefully.
4. Our team is winning easily.
5. The package should be delivered today.

* * * * * * *

1. Those girls are good tennis players.
2. The man must have been driving carelessly.
3. The big barking dog looked and sounded vicious.
4. The team was being given final instructions.
5. This drill sheet should have been completed carefully.

© 1988, 1997 J. Weston Walch, Publisher

Steps to Good Grammar

TEST

This reproducible page contains two copies of one half-page drill/test. Cut each duplicated page in half; give each student one half-page.

In sentence 8, *student body* may be considered a two-word noun, or *student* may be circled as an adjective.

Grading suggestions:

In sentences with linking verbs, give 1 point for underlining the complete verb and one point for the LV label.

Give 1 point for each set of parentheses around a prepositional phrase.

Complete verbs	11
Linking verbs	7
Sets of parentheses	3
Other identification symbols	49
Total	70

1. Alison obviously has been very careful.
2. The teacher is reading a good book to us.
3. The cake looked and tasted delicious.
4. This assignment must be finished promptly.
5. Josie will probably become an architect or a carpenter.
6. Most students seem quite respectful to teachers.
7. Surely the package will be delivered today.
8. Amanda's brother had been the president of the student body.
9. Did the principal appear very upset?
10. The three students are being given another chance.

LINKING VERBS

TEST: Distinguishing Between Linking and "Doing" Verbs

Instructions: Mark: complete verbs, subjects, adjectives (except LVC-A), adverbs (prep. phrases); label: **D.O., prep., O.P., LV, LVC-N, LVC-A.**

1. Alison obviously has been very careful.

2. The teacher is reading a good book to us.

3. The cake looked and tasted delicious.

4. This assignment must be finished promptly.

5. Josie will probably become an architect or a carpenter.

6. Most students seem quite respectful to teachers.

7. Surely the package will be delivered today.

8. Amanda's brother had been the president of the student body.

9. Did the principal appear very upset?

10. The three students are being given another chance.

LINKING VERBS

TEST: Distinguishing Between Linking and "Doing" Verbs

Instructions: Mark: complete verbs, subjects, adjectives (except LVC-A), adverbs (prep. phrases); label: **D.O., prep., O.P., LV, LVC-N, LVC-A.**

1. Alison obviously has been very careful.

2. The teacher is reading a good book to us.

3. The cake looked and tasted delicious.

4. This assignment must be finished promptly.

5. Josie will probably become an architect or a carpenter.

6. Most students seem quite respectful to teachers.

7. Surely the package will be delivered today.

8. Amanda's brother had been the president of the student body.

9. Did the principal appear very upset?

10. The three students are being given another chance.

Steps to Good Grammar

RETEST

Grading suggestions:

Every sentence part symbol is given 1 point, including 1 point for underlining a complete verb and 1 point for labeling a linking verb; 56 points in all.

This retest is provided in case you need one.

Use the grading scale for sentence part identification on page 116.

1. Carrie has been giving him and me some extra help.

2. The trail seems rather treacherous.

3. Zeke's sister is a successful electronics salesperson.

4. Matt will probably become a dentist.

5. Is Grandfather feeling better today?

6. All the students were finishing their reports.

7. Chan and I have been helping the librarian.

8. Dinner should be ready soon.

9. Several students were given passes.

10. Rico must have been very late.

LINKING VERBS

RETEST: Distinguishing Between Linking and "Doing" Verbs

Instructions: Mark: complete <u>verbs</u>, <u>subjects</u>, (adjectives) (except LVC-A, [adverbs] label: **D.O., I.O., LV, LVC-N, LVC-A.**

1. Carrie has been giving him and me some extra help.

2. The trail seems rather treacherous.

3. Zeke's sister is a successful electronics salesperson.

4. Matt will probably become a dentist.

5. Is Grandfather feeling better today?

6. All the students were finishing their reports.

7. Chan and I have been helping the librarian.

8. Dinner should be ready soon.

9. Several students were given passes.

10. Rico must have been very late.

NAME _____ DATE _____ 167

LINKING VERBS

RETEST: Distinguishing Between Linking and "Doing" Verbs

Instructions: Mark: complete <u>verbs</u>, <u>subjects</u>, (adjectives) (except LVC-A) [adverbs] label: **D.O., I.O., LV, LVC-N, LVC-A.**

1. Carrie has been giving him and me some extra help.

2. The trail seems rather treacherous.

3. Zeke's sister is a successful electronics salesperson.

4. Matt will probably become a dentist.

5. Is Grandfather feeling better today?

6. All the students were finishing their reports.

7. Chan and I have been helping the librarian.

8. Dinner should be ready soon.

9. Several students were given passes.

10. Rico must have been very late.

Steps to Good Grammar

PRONOUNS USED AS LINKING VERB COMPLEMENTS

Nominative pronouns are grammatically prescribed, especially in formal writing, after forms of the verb *be: is, am, are, was, were, be, being, been:*

This is she. It was I. It must have been they.

About this usage of pronouns, more than any other, students will say, "It doesn't sound right!" So when working through this page with your class, be sure to have students read the sample and drill sentences aloud to reinforce the sound of correct usage.

The word *nominative* implies "has to do with the subject." Nominative pronouns used as LVCs "have to do" with the subject in that they refer back to the subject — can be used in place of the subject.

Emphasize item 3 in Remember; remind students about 4 and 5.

Work with the students as they rewrite the Practice sentences. Have students read correctly completed sentences aloud.

1. Ronnie was a winner. He was a winner. The winners were _Ronnie_ and _he_ .

2. We couldn't be the losers. They couldn't be the losers. The losers couldn't be _they_ or _we_ .

3. You and they were top scorers. Top scorers were _you_ and _they_ .

4. He was a guard. I was a guard. The guards were _he_ and _I_ .

5. Ellen and she were probably the noisiest. The noisiest were probably _Ellen_ and _she_ .

PRONOUN LINKING VERB COMPLEMENTS

Pronouns Used as Linking Verb Complements

KNOW:

1. **Linking Verbs (LVs)** are:

    IS   AM   ARE   WAS   WERE   BE   BEING   BEEN

2. A sentence with an LV requires a **linking verb complement (LVC).**

3. In a sentence with an LV, the subject and the LVC can trade places and the meaning remains the same:

    Joey was the winner.   The winner was Joey.

    He was the winner.   The winner was he.   (Label pronouns LVCs **LVC-N.**)

4. *Subject*ive (nominative) pronouns are used as LVCs and as subjects:

    I   YOU   HE   SHE   WE   THEY

5. Remember **polite order** in using pronouns in compound LVCs: (first — *you*; second — *he, she, they,* or **nouns;** last — *I, we*).

TO BE SURE that you are using the correct pronoun in the LVC position, turn the sentence around, as in the examples above, and say the pronouns separately with the verb:

> The captains will be (he, him) and (me, I).

> Obviously incorrect: *Him* will be . . . *Me* will be . . .

> Obviously correct: **He** will be . . .I will be . . .

> The captains will be he and I.

PRACTICE: In the sentences below, mark: complete verbs, subjects, adjectives, adverbs, label: **LV, LVC-N.** In the blanks, write the nouns and/or pronouns to form the linking verb complement.

1. Ronnie was a winner. He was a winner. The winners were _____ and _____.

2. We couldn't be the losers. They couldn't be the losers. The losers couldn't be _____ or

    _____.

3. You and they were top scorers. Top scorers were _____ and _____.

4. He was a guard. I was a guard. The guards were _____ and _____.

5. Ellen and she were probably the noisiest. The noisiest were probably _____ and

    _____.

USING PRONOUNS AS LVCs — PRACTICE

Occasionally, as students are selecting the correct LVC pronouns, instruct them to reverse the sentence, using the pronouns as the subject. This may help to establish the "right sound."

Also, as in the previous introductory drill, be sure to have students read correctly completed sentences aloud to reinforce the sound of correct usage.

1. The most surprised people were __they__ and __we__ . (them, they) (us, we)

2. The best players have always been __you__ and __he__ . (he, him) (you)

3. The pranksters might have been __they__ . (them, they)

4. The team's captain is __he__ . (him, he)

5. Could the winner be __she__ ? (her, she)

6. The new assistants will be __Trish__ or __I__ . (I, me) (Trish)

7. The Most Valuable Player will probably be __you__ or __Lex__ . (Lex) (you)

8. Are the only guests __they__ and __we__ ? (we, us) (they, them)

9. The newly elected officers are __you__ , __Sherry__ , and __I__ . (me, I) (Sherry) (you)

10. The contest winners were __he__ and __she__ . (he, him) (her, she)

11. The doubles finalists were __they__ and __we__ . (us, we) (them, they)

12. The last three speakers will be __you__ , __Jean__ , and __I__ . (Jean) (me, I) (you)

13. The noisy students certainly weren't __he__ and __I__ . (me, I) (he, him)

14. The only volunteers were __she__ , __Mike__ , and __I__ . (her, she) (Mike) (me, I).

15. Could the mystery person be __he__ ? (him, he)

16. Was the principal's choice __they__ or __we__ ? (we, us) (them, they)

17. Aren't the best students __she__ and __he__ ? (her, she) (him, he)

18. Three lucky teenagers are __you__ , __Lynn__ , and __I__ . (Lynn) (me, I) (you)

19. Unfortunately, the loser was __I__ ! (me, I)

20. Were the award recipients __you__ , __Lars__ , and __I__ ? (me, I) (Lars) (you)

PRONOUN LINKING VERB COMPLEMENTS

Using pronouns as LVCs — Practice

Instructions: Mark: complete <u>verbs</u>, <u>subjects</u>, (adjectives) [adverbs] label: **LV, LVC-N.** In the blanks, using the words in parentheses, write the correct LVC pronouns in polite order.

1. The most surprised people were _____ and _____. (them, they) (us, we)

2. The best players have always been _____ and _____. (he, him) (you)

3. The pranksters might have been _____. (them, they)

4. The team's captain is _____. (him, he)

5. Could the winner be _____? (her, she)

6. The new assistants will be _____ or _____. (I, me) (Trish)

7. The Most Valuable Player will probably be _____ or _____. (Lex) (you)

8. Are the only guests _____ and _____? (we, us) (they, them)

9. The newly elected officers are _____, _____, and _____. (me, I) (Sherry) (you)

10. The contest winners were _____ and _____. (he, him) (her, she)

11. The doubles finalists were _____ and _____. (us, we) (them, they)

12. The last three speakers will be _____, _____, and _____. (Jean) (me, I) (you)

13. The noisy students certainly weren't _____ and _____. (me, I) (he, him)

14. The only volunteers were _____, _____, and _____. (her, she) (Mike) (me, I).

15. Could the mystery person be _____? (him, he)

16. Was the principal's choice _____ or _____? (we, us) (them, they)

17. Aren't the best students _____ and _____? (her, she) (him, he)

18. Three lucky teenagers are _____, _____, and _____. (Lynn) (me, I) (you)

19. Unfortunately, the loser was _____! (me, I)

20. Were the award recipients _____, _____, and _____? (me, I) (Lars) (you)

Steps to Good Grammar

REVIEW DRILL AND FINAL DRILL

You will need one copy of this page for each student. The top half is a review drill; the bottom half is a final drill.

The test on the next page includes nominative pronouns used as subjects and as linking verb complements. Therefore, this review drill allows students to review subject pronouns.

The final drill requires students to recognize and use nominative pronouns in both subject and LVC-N positions.

1. *Melinda* and *I* were [there][early]. (me, I) (Melinda)
2. Could *they* and *we* stay [here]? (we, us) (they, them)
3. *You*, *he*, and *I* should listen [more][carefully]. (me, I) (he, him) (you)
4. [Frequently] *my brother* and *I* arrive [early]. (me, I) (my brother)
5. *They* and *we* were appointed. (them, they) (we, us)
6. *She* and *I* have been excused. (I, me) (her, she)
7. Can *you* and *she* leave [right][now]? (you) (her, she)
8. *Sara*, *he*, and *I* have agreed [completely]. (Sara) (him, he) (me, I)
9. Have *you* and *they* volunteered? (them, they) (you)
10. [Suddenly] *he* and *she* ran [in] and sat [down]. (he, him) (her, she)

1. [Why] must *you* and *I* leave [so][soon]? (me, I) (you)
2. Are the new officers *you*, *Paul*, and *I*? (me, I) (Paul) (you)
3. The doubles finalists are *they* and *we*. (them, they) (us, we)
4. *They* and *we* have been working [very][hard]. (us, we) (they, them)
5. [Actually] *we* students seldom work [too][hard]. (us, we)
6. (As usual) the only volunteers were *he*, *she*, and *I*. (me, I) (he, him) (her, she)
7. Neither *you* nor *he* were winners. (he, him) (you)
8. The noisy students weren't *she* and *he*. (him, he) (she, her)
9. Will *they* or *he* be working? (them, they) (he, him)
10. [Probably] *you*, *she*, and *I* should leave [soon]. (she, her) (you) (me, I)

PRONOUN LINKING VERB COMPLEMENTS

REVIEW DRILL: Pronouns Used As Subjects

Instructions: Mark: <u>verbs</u>, [adverbs] In the blanks, using the words in parentheses, write the correct subject words in polite order. Remember, subject pronouns are the same as LVC pronouns.

1. _____ and _____ were there early. (me, I) (Melinda)

2. Could _____ and _____ stay here? (we, us) (they, them)

3. _____, _____, and _____ should listen more carefully. (me, I) (he, him) (you)

4. Frequently _____ and _____ arrive early. (me, I) (my brother)

5. _____ and _____ were appointed. (them, they) (we, us)

6. _____ and _____ have been excused. (I, me) (her, she)

7. Can _____ and _____ leave right now? (you) (her, she)

8. _____, _____, and _____ have agreed completely. (Sara) (him, he) (me, I)

9. Have _____ and _____ volunteered? (them, they) (you)

10. Suddenly, _____ and _____ ran in and sat down. (he, him) (her, she)

PRONOUN LINKING VERB COMPLEMENTS

FINAL DRILL: Pronouns Used As Subjects and LVCs

Instructions: Mark: complete <u>verbs</u>, (adjectives) [adverbs] (prep. phrases) label: **LV, LVC-N, prep., O.P., appos.** In the blanks, using the words in parentheses, write the correct subject/LVC words in polite order.

1. Why must _____ and _____ leave so soon? (me, I) (you)

2. Are the new officers _____, _____, and _____? (me, I) (Paul) (you)

3. The doubles finalists are _____ and _____. (them, they) (us, we)

4. _____ and _____ have been working very hard. (us, we) (they, them)

5. Actually, _____ students seldom work too hard. (us, we)

6. As usual, the only volunteers were _____, _____, and _____. (me, I) (he, him) (her, she)

7. Neither _____ nor _____ were winners. (he, him) (you)

8. The noisy students weren't _____ and _____. (him, he) (she, her)

9. Will _____ or _____ be working? (them, they) (he, him)

10. Probably _____, _____, and _____ should leave soon. (she, her) (you) (me, I)

Steps to Good Grammar

TEST

This reproducible page contains two copies of one half-page drill/test. Cut each duplicated page in half; give each student one half-page.

Suggested grading:

Grading pronoun choice and order:

Sentence	Choice	Order	Points
1	2	1	3
2	2	1	3
3	2	1	3
4	2	1	3
5	1	0	1
6	1	1	2
7	1	3	4
8	2	0	2
9	2	3	5
10	1	3	4
			30

Grading scale

-1, 97	-7, 77
-2, 93	-8, 73
-3, 90	-9, 70
-4, 87	-10, 67
-5, 83	-11, 63
-6, 80	-12, 60

Sentence part identification:

1 point for each label above compound LVC-N
1 point for underlining each compound subject
1 point for underlining each complete verb
1 point for labeling each linking verb

Total points 55

See page 116 for grading scale.

1. The (doubles) finalists will [probably] be **they** and **we**. (us, we) (they, them)
2. **You**, **he**, and **she** are [never] tardy. (he, him) (her, she) (you)
3. The newly (elected) officers are **he** and **I**. (I, me) (he, him)
4. **They** and **we** have been swimming. (us, we) (them, they)
5. Do **we** students [ever] work [too] hard? (we, us)
6. The losers were **you** and **they**. (you) (them, they)
7. Are (the squad) captains **you**, **Paul**, and **I**? (Paul) (I, me) (you)
8. The most (accomplished) students are **he** and **she**. (he, him) (her, she)
9. [Probably] **you**, **he**, and **I** should leave [soon]. (me, I) (he, him) (you)
10. [Incidentally] **you**, **Amy**, and **I** are (the) (contest) winners! (Amy) (you) (me, I)

PRONOUN LINKING VERB COMPLEMENTS

TEST: Pronouns Used As Subjects and LVCs

Instructions: Mark: complete <u>verbs</u>, <u>subjects</u>, (adjectives) [adverbs] label: **LV, LVC-N, LVC-A, appos.** In the blanks, using the words in parentheses, write the correct subject/LVC pronouns in polite order.

1. The doubles finalists will probably be _____ and _____. (us, we) (they, them)

2. _____, _____, and _____ are never tardy. (he, him) (her, she) (you)

3. The newly elected officers are _____ and _____. (I, me) (he, him)

4. _____ and _____ have been swimming. (us, we) (them, they)

5. Do _____ students ever work too hard? (we, us)

6. The losers were _____ and _____. (you) (them, they)

7. Are the squad captains _____, _____, and _____? (Paul) (I, me) (you)

8. The most accomplished students are _____ and _____. (he, him) (her, she)

9. Probably _____, _____, and _____ should leave soon. (me, I) (he, him) (you)

10. Incidentally, _____, _____, and _____ are the contest winners! (Amy) (you) (me, I)

NAME _____ DATE _____ 175

PRONOUN LINKING VERB COMPLEMENTS

TEST: Pronouns Used As Subjects and LVCs

Instructions: Mark: complete <u>verbs</u>, <u>subjects</u>, (adjectives) [adverbs] label: **LV, LVC-N, LVC-A, appos.** In the blanks, using the words in parentheses, write the correct subject/LVC pronouns in polite order.

1. The doubles finalists will probably be _____ and _____. (us, we) (they, them)

2. _____, _____, and _____ are never tardy. (he, him) (her, she) (you)

3. The newly elected officers are _____ and _____. (I, me) (he, him)

4. _____ and _____ have been swimming. (us, we) (them, they)

5. Do _____ students ever work too hard? (we, us)

6. The losers were _____ and _____. (you) (them, they)

7. Are the squad captains _____, _____, and _____? (Paul) (I, me) (you)

8. The most accomplished students are _____ and _____. (he, him) (her, she)

9. Probably _____, _____, and _____ should leave soon. (me, I) (he, him) (you)

10. Incidentally, _____, _____, and _____ are the contest winners! (Amy) (you) (me, I)

© 1988, 1997 J. Weston Walch, Publisher

Steps to Good Grammar

PRONOUN REVIEW

* * * * *

Instruct students to *save* page 177 for reference as they complete pages 179 through 185.

PRONOUN REVIEW

Nominative and Objective Personal Pronouns

Nominative *(Subjective)* Pronouns: I YOU SHE HE WE THEY

1. Polite order: First — *you;* next—*she, he, they,* **nouns;** last — *I, we.*

2. To hear the correct pronouns to use, say each pronoun separately *before* the verb.

3. Used as **subject:** You, she, and I should leave now.

   They and we have a good idea.

   We students like our school.

4. Used as **LVC:** The new officers are they and we.

   The winner will surely be she or he.

   The first students in line were we girls.

Objective Pronouns: ME YOU HER HIM US THEM

1. Polite order: First — *you;* next — *her, him, them,* **nouns;** last — *me, us.*

2. Used as **D.O.:** To hear the correct pronouns to use, say each pronoun separately *after* the verb:

   Mom will take them and us.

   Dad watched her and me.

   The principal chose us boys.

3. Used as **O.P.:** To hear the correct pronouns to use in a compound object of a preposition, say each pronoun separately *after* the preposition:

   Was Marcie waving at you, Lynn, and me?

   The superintendent talked to them and us.

   Most teachers care about us students.

4. Used as **I.O.:** To hear the correct pronouns to use as a compound indirect object, say each pronoun separately *after* the verb:

   Ms. O'Brien gave her and him the make-up test.

   Marjorie sent my sister and me an invitation.

   Coach gave us players a compliment.

Steps to Good Grammar

NOMINATIVE AND OBJECTIVE PRONOUNS

1. [Undoubtedly] *you* and *he* are (the)(best) athletes. (you) (him, he)

2. [Undoubtedly (the)(best) athletes are *you* and *he*. (he, him) (you)

3. Will *you* or *Roberto* be (the)(office) assistant? (Roberto) (you)

4. Will (the)(office) assistant be *you* or *Roberto*? (you) (Roberto)

5. [Perhaps] *you*, *she*, and *I* will be (the)(new) officers. (her, she) (you) (me, I)

6. [Perhaps (the)(new) officers will be *you*, *she*, and *I*. (I, me) (she, her) (you)

7. *They* and *we* were (the)(last) contestants. (we, us) (them, they)

8. (The)(last) contestants were *they* and *we*. (us, we) (they, them)

1. Did Joel call *you* or *her* [yesterday]? (she, her) (you)

2. Lucy saw *him* and *me*. (he, him) (I, me)

3. (Our) dad disciplines (my brother) and *me* [quite][fairly]. (me, I) (my brother)

4. [Tomorrow] (the) teacher will coach *you*, *Candy*, and *me*. (Candy) (I, me) (you)

5. (Mr. Adams's) decision surprised *us* students. (we, us)

6. Could you and she see *them* and *me*? (they, them) (I, me)

7. (Our)[very] (strict) teacher didn't excuse *him* or *her*. (him, he) (she, her)

8. Rosa and she have invited *them* and *us*. (us, we) (them, they)

PRONOUN REVIEW

Nominative and Objective Pronouns

Nominative Pronouns Used as Subjects or LVCs

Instructions: Mark: complete <u>verbs</u>, <u>subjects</u>, adjectives, adverbs label: **LV, LVC-N**. In the blanks, using the words in parentheses, write the correct subject/LVC pronouns in polite order.

1. Undoubtedly _____ and _____ are the best athletes. (you) (him, he)

2. Undoubtedly the best athletes are _____ and _____ . (he, him) (you)

3. Will _____ or _____ be the office assistant? (Roberto) (you)

4. Will the office assistant be _____ or _____? (you) (Roberto)

5. Perhaps _____, _____, and _____ will be the new officers. (her, she) (you) (me, I)

6. Perhaps the new officers will be _____, _____, and _____ . (I, me) (she, her) (you)

7. _____ and _____ were the last contestants. (we, us) (them, they)

8. The last contestants were _____ and _____ . (us, we) (they, them)

Objective Pronouns Used as Direct Objects

Instructions: Mark: complete <u>verbs</u>, <u>subjects</u>, adjectives, adverbs label: **D.O., appos.** In the blanks, using the words in parentheses, write the correct direct object words in polite order.

1. Did Joel call _____ or _____ yesterday? (she, her) (you)

2. Lucy saw _____ and _____ . (he, him) (I, me)

3. Our dad disciplines _____ and _____ quite fairly. (me, I) (my brother)

4. Tomorrow, the teacher will coach _____ , _____ , and _____ . (Candy) (I, me) (you)

5. Mr. Adams's decision surprised _____ students. (we, us)

6. Could you and she see _____ and _____? (they, them) (I, me)

7. Our very strict teacher didn't excuse _____ or _____ . (him, he) (she, her)

8. Rosa and she have invited _____ and _____ . (us, we) (them, they)

Steps to Good Grammar

OBJECTIVE PRONOUNS

1. Everyone is going (except _**you**_, _**her**_, and _**me**_. (I, me) (you) (she, her)

2. Were you calling (to _**Walt**_ and _**me**_)? (me, I) (Walt)

3. Alix and I were walking (behind _**you**_ and _**your friend**_) (your friend) (you)

4. You and she may go (with _**him**_ and _**me**_). (I, me) (him, he)

5. [When] will Coach have (the awards (for _**us**_) players? (we, us)

6. My little sister could sit (between _**you**_ and _**me**_). (you) (I, me)

7. (At the assembly) were you and Jared sitting near _**them**_ and _**us**_)? (us, we) (they, them)

8. Will you and he leave (without **my sister** and _**me**_)? (my sister) (I, me)

9. Mom was looking (for _**you**_ and _**them**_). (them, they) (you)

10. (The) principal was talking (in a [very] complimentary way) (about _**you**_, _**her**_, and _**him**_). (him, he) (you) (she, her)

1. Could you or he bring **my brother** and _**me**_ (our) homework? (my brother) (I, me)

2. (The) principal told _**us**_ students (the test) results. (we, us)

3. He wrote _**you**_, _**Chas**_, and _**me**_ (good) recommendations. (Chas) (I, me) (you)

4. Do (your) parents give _**you**_ and (your) sister (weekly) allowances? (your sister) (you)

5. Mrs. Talt gave _**her**_ and _**me**_ (a list (of mystery) books) (she, her) (me, I)

6. I will lend _**you**_ and _**Anna**_ (the) money. (Anna) (you)

7. Will (their) parents give _**him**_ and _**her**_ (their) permission? (he, him) (her, she)

8. Could you give _**her**_, _**him**_, and _**me**_ (a ride to (the game)? (me, I) (she, her) (he, him)

9. Aunt Louise has brought _**you**_ and _**me**_ (some) souvenirs. (me, I) (you)

10. Cousin Dan has lent _**us**_ boys (his (new) VCR. (we, us)

PRONOUN REVIEW

Objective Pronouns

Objective Pronouns Used as Objects of Prepositions

Instructions: Mark: <u>verbs</u>, <u>subjects</u>, (adjectives) [adverbs] (prep. phrases) label: **D.O., prep., O.P., appos.** In the blanks, using the words in parentheses, write the correct words in polite order.

1. Everyone is going except _____, _____, and _____. (I, me) (you) (she, her)

2. Were you calling to _____ and _____? (me, I) (Walt)

3. Alix and I were walking behind _____ and _____. (your friend) (you)

4. You and she may go with _____ and _____. (I, me) (him, he)

5. When will Coach have the awards for _____ players? (we, us)

6. My little sister could sit between _____ and _____. (you) (I, me)

7. At the assembly, were you and Jared sitting near _____ and _____? (us, we) (they, them)

8. Will you and he leave without _____ and _____? (my sister) (I, me)

9. Mom was looking for _____ and _____. (them, they) (you)

10. The principal was talking in a very complimentary way about _____, _____, and _____. (him, he) (you) (she, her)

Objective Pronouns Used as Indirect Objects

Instructions: Mark: <u>verbs</u>, <u>subjects</u>, (adjectives) [adverbs] (prep. phrases) label: **D.O., prep., O.P., I.O., appos.** In the blanks, using the words in parentheses, write the correct words in polite order.

1. Could you or he bring _____ and _____ our homework? (my brother) (I, me)

2. The principal told _____ students the test results. (we, us)

3. He wrote _____, _____, and _____ good recommendations. (Chas) (I, me) (you)

4. Do your parents give _____ and _____ weekly allowances? (your sister) (you)

5. Mrs. Talt gave _____ and _____ a list of mystery books. (she, her) (me, I)

6. I will lend _____ and _____ the money. (Anna) (you)

7. Will their parents give _____ and _____ their permission? (he, him) (her, she)

8. Could you give _____, _____, and _____ a ride to the game? (me, I) (she, her) (he, him)

9. Aunt Louise has brought _____ and _____ some souvenirs. (me, I) (you)

10. Cousin Dan has lent _____ boys his new VCR. (we, us)

Steps to Good Grammar

DRILL

1. ___*You*___, ___*Pete*___, and ___*I*___ (Pete) (I, me) (you) will go (to (the) cabin)
   (with ___*her*___ and ___*them*___). (she, her) (they, them)

2. Ms. Johnston and ___*I*___ (me, I) have chosen ___*you*___ and ___*him*___.
   (he, him) (you)

3. [Surely] (the (new) officers will be ___*he*___ and ___*she*___. (he, him) (she, her)

4. Were ___*she*___ and ___*he*___ (him, he) (she, her) signaling (to ___*them*___ or
   ___*us*___? (we, us) (they, them)

5. ___*You*___ and ___*he*___ (he, him) (you) could have told ___*them*___ and
   ___*us*___ (we, us) (them, they) (about (the) plan).

6. ___*They*___ and ___*we*___ (we, us) (them, they) must have gotten (the (highest) grades.

7. Coach handed ___*us*___ (us, we) boys (our) trophies.

8. Will ___*Sally*___ and ___*I*___ (me, I) (Sally) be (the (office) assistants?

9. (The) teacher will give (the (test (to ___*you*___, ___*him*___, and ___*me*___). (me, I)
   (he, him) (you)

10. ___*We*___ (we, us) girls played (a (really (good) game.

11. May ___*he*___ and ___*I*___ (I, me) (he, him) ride (with ___*you*___ and
    ___*them*___? (you) (they, them)

12. (The (lucky) winners were ___*Pat*___ and ___*I*___. (me, I) (Pat)

13. Most (of ___*us*___) (we, us) students have learned (about pronouns)

14. Are ___*you*___ and ___*she*___ (she, her) (you) going (with ___*them*___ and
    ___*me*___? (I, me) (they, them)

15. (The (contest) winners could be ___*she*___ and ___*he*___. (she, her) (him, he)

16. ___*You*___, ___*Jane*___, and ___*I*___ have been chosen. (Jane) (me, I) (you)

17. ___*Mom*___ and ___*I*___ (me, I) (Mom) were looking (for ___*you*___ and
    ___*him*___). (you) (he, him)

18. (The (teacher handed ___*her*___ and ___*me*___ (me, I) (she, her) (our (corrected (test
    papers.

19. Did ___*you*___ and ___*she*___ (she, her) (you) ask (your) parents (for permission?

20. ___*You*___ and ___*she*___ (she, her) (you) should look (for ___*them*___ or
    ___*us*___) (they, them) (we, us) (after school).

PRONOUN REVIEW

DRILL: Using Both Nominative and Objective Personal Pronouns

Instructions: Mark: complete <u>verbs</u>, <u>subjects</u>, (adjectives) [adverbs] (prep. phrases); label: **D.O.,
prep., O.P., I.O., appos., LV, LVC-N.** In the blanks, using the words in parentheses, write the
correct words in polite order.

1. _____, _____, and _____ (Pete) (I, me) (you) will go to the cabin
   with _____ and _____. (she, her) (they, them)

2. Ms. Johnston and _____ (me, I) have chosen _____ and _____.
   (he, him) (you)

3. Surely the new officers will be _____ and _____. (he, him) (she, her)

4. Were _____ and _____ (him, he) (she, her) signaling to _____ or
   _____? (we, us) (they, them)

5. _____ and _____ (he, him) (you) could have told _____ and
   _____ (we, us) (them, they) about the plan.

6. _____ and _____ (we, us) (them, they) must have gotten the highest grades.

7. Coach handed _____ (us, we) boys our trophies.

8. Will _____ and _____ (me, I) (Sally) be the office assistants?

9. The teacher will give the test to _____, _____, and _____. (me, I)
   (he, him) (you)

10. _____ (we, us) girls played a really good game.

11. May _____ and _____ (I, me) (he, him) ride with _____ and
    _____? (you) (they, them)

12. The lucky winners were _____ and _____. (me, I) (Pat)

13. Most of _____ (we, us) students have learned about pronouns.

14. Are _____ and _____ (she, her) (you) going with _____ and
    _____? (I, me) (they, them)

15. The contest winners could be _____ and _____. (she, her) (him, he)

16. _____, _____, and _____ have been chosen. (Jane) (me, I) (you)

17. _____ and _____ (me, I) (Mom) were looking for _____ and
    _____. (you) (he, him)

18. The teacher handed _____ and _____ (me, I) (she, her) our corrected test
    papers.

19. Did _____ and _____ (she, her) (you) ask your parents for permission?

20. _____ and _____ (she, her) (you) should look for _____ or
    _____ (they, them) (we, us) after school.

Steps to Good Grammar

TEST

This reproducible page contains two copies of
one half-page drill/test. Cut each duplicated page
in half; give each student one half-page.

Grading scale

-1, 96	-5, 81	-9, 67
-2, 93	-6, 78	-10, 63
-3, 89	-7, 74	-11, 59
-4, 85	-8, 70	-12, 56

Suggested grading:

Pronoun choice and order:

Sentence	Choice	Order	Points
1	1	1	2
2	2	1	3
3	1	1	2
4	3	2	5
5	2	0	2
6	2	1	3
7	1	1	2
8	1	3	4
9	1	0	1
10	2	0	2
			26

Sentence part identification:

1 point each set of parentheses for prepositional
phrases
1 point labeling each linking verb
1 point each label of compound: subject, linking verb
complement, direct object, object of a preposition,
indirect object
1 point each complete verb underlining

Total points: 62

-1, 98	-6, 90	-11, 82	-16, 74	-21, 66
-2, 97	-7, 89	-12, 81	-17, 73	-22, 65
-3, 95	-8, 87	-13, 79	-18, 71	-23, 63
-4, 94	-9, 86	-14, 77	-19, 69	-24, 61
-5, 92	-10, 84	-15, 76	-20, 68	-25, 60

1. The first students in the room were _Jesse_ and _I_. (Jesse) (me, I)
2. Cyndy has already told _them_ and _us_. (we, us) (them, they)
3. Will Guido be sitting with _you_ and _me_? (me, I) (you)
4. Should _they_ or _we_ (we, us) (them, they) get _you_ and _her_ (she, her) (you) a copy of the rules?
5. It wasn't _they_ or _she_. (her, she) (them, they)
6. At noon _Erica_ and _I_ (me, I) (Erica) always watch for _Prem_ and _him_. (Prem) (he, him)
7. Mrs. Jones will call _you_ and _them_. (you) (they, them)
8. _You_, _John_, and _I_ should get library passes. (I, me) (you) (John)
9. The principal gave _us_ students a compliment. (we, us)
10. Were _he_ and _she_ the only volunteers? (him, he) (she, her)

PRONOUN REVIEW

TEST: Nominative and Objective Personal Pronoun Usage

Instructions: Mark: complete verbs, subjects, adjectives, adverbs, prep. phrases, label: **D.O.,** **prep., O.P., I.O., appos., LV, LVC-N.** In the blanks, using the words in parentheses, write the correct words in polite order.

1. The first students in the room were _____ and _____. (Jesse) (me, I)
2. Cyndy has already told _____ and _____. (we, us) (them, they)
3. Will Guido be sitting with _____ and _____? (me, I) (you)
4. Should _____ or _____ (we, us) (them, they) get _____ and _____ (she, her) (you) a copy of the rules?
5. It wasn't _____ or _____. (her, she) (them, they)
6. At noon, _____ and _____ (me, I) (Erica) always watch for _____ and _____. (Prem) (he, him)
7. Mrs. Jones will call _____ and _____. (you) (they, them)
8. _____, _____, and _____ should get library passes. (I, me) (you) (John)
9. The principal gave _____ students a compliment. (we, us)
10. Were _____ and _____ the only volunteers? (him, he) (she, her)

NAME _____ DATE _____ 185

PRONOUN REVIEW

TEST: Nominative and Objective Personal Pronoun Usage

Instructions: Mark: complete verbs, subjects, adjectives, adverbs, prep. phrases, label: **D.O.,** **prep., O.P., I.O., appos., LV, LVC-N.** In the blanks, using the words in parentheses, write the correct words in polite order.

1. The first students in the room were _____ and _____. (Jesse) (me, I)
2. Cyndy has already told _____ and _____. (we, us) (them, they)
3. Will Guido be sitting with _____ and _____? (me, I) (you)
4. Should _____ or _____ (we, us) (them, they) get _____ and _____ (she, her) (you) a copy of the rules?
5. It wasn't _____ or _____. (her, she) (them, they)
6. At noon, _____ and _____ (me, I) (Erica) always watch for _____ and _____. (Prem) (he, him)
7. Mrs. Jones will call _____ and _____. (you) (they, them)
8. _____, _____, and _____ should get library passes. (I, me) (you) (John)
9. The principal gave _____ students a compliment. (we, us)
10. Were _____ and _____ the only volunteers? (him, he) (she, her)

Steps to Good Grammar

FACTS ABOUT PRONOUNS

Help the students to establish firmly in their minds the Reminder.

You might tell students that a long time ago grammarians standardized the forms and use of pronouns. They established a certain set of pronouns to show possession. Possessive personal pronouns are complete in themselves; they need no apostrophe.

Tell students that they will use the abbreviation, **poss.** to show a possessive pronoun on the Practice sheets.

CORRECT USAGE

You have studied the English sentence from the ground up, so to speak. There isn't the slightest doubt in your mind as to what a verb word is. You can recognize verbs. You can use verbs. You know that the verb is the "alive" part of the sentences you speak and write.

You know the various uses of nouns in sentences. You are aware that nouns—the people, things, ideas you talk and write about—do not, of themselves, change or do anything. An apple is an apple is an apple!

But you know how to make nouns easier to see. You can give them personality by surrounding them with adjectives, "how much" adverbs, and phrases of various sorts. Using your imagination, you could write: "The velvet-smooth, enticingly polished red apple in the cut-glass fruit bowl on the dining room table…" That would be a one-of-a-kind apple! However, you would know that you had to give the apple a verb in order for it to be the subject of your sentence. So you might add "…. beckoned to me, yielded to my grasp, and crunched juicily between my teeth."

Well, yes—that's a bit much! But the verbs certainly make the sentence, and the apple, come alive!

For really effective expression, knowing sentence parts and how to combine them into interesting, complete sentences isn't quite enough. To this understanding we must add the element of correctness.

You will now study "correct," currently acceptable usage within the various sentence parts. Don't *let* this phase of study be boring! Practice and understand each item of correctness so thoroughly that it becomes a natural part of your thinking, speaking, and writing. Use your language effectively.

CORRECT USAGE — PRONOUNS

Facts About Pronouns

You have already learned the correct use of nominative and objective personal pronouns. Here are a few more facts about pronoun usage you should remember.

Possessive pronouns show that something belongs to, or is owned by, a particular person or persons:

my, mine; your, yours; his; her, hers; its; our, ours; their, theirs

1. Possessive pronouns used as adjectives before a noun:

   my, your ⎫
   her, his, its ⎬ **house**
   our, their ⎭

   Example: Behind our house sat our dog beside its house.

2. Possessive pronouns that show ownership of nouns they follow:

   This house is ⎰ **mine, yours,**
   ⎱ **hers, his, its**
   ⎰ **ours, theirs**

   Example: Is that house yours, hers, his, or theirs?

> **Reminder:** *Never* use an apostrophe with a possessive personal pronoun.

Steps to Good Grammar

FACTS ABOUT PRONOUNS (continued)

This page contains a great deal of information for the students to absorb. Work slowly with them to assure that they comprehend each item.

Indefinite Pronouns

We use indefinite pronouns when we don't know, or for some reason do not choose to use, a person's name.

Give students this definition: Indefinite pronouns refer to an unknown or purposely unnamed person: use *'s* to form the possessive.

If students express interest in *else* in Practice sentence 5, point out that, as it is used here, it means "in addition/additional" or "different":

"... that one is a different unnamed person's."

Verb Contractions with Pronouns

1. Only helping verbs are used in the subject-verb contractions.

2. Nominative pronouns are the usual subject.

3. Students *know* helping verbs; they *know* subject pronouns. Use this knowledge to help students understand exactly how contractions are formed as you duplicate the examples on the chalkboard.

4. Tell students they will use the label **contrac.** to identify a contraction on the Practice sheets.

Compound Pronouns

1. It seems logical that "hisself" and "theirselves" would be correct, since possessive pronouns are the root of *myself, yourself, yourselves, herself,* and *ourselves.* But objective pronouns are the root of *himself* and *themselves.*

   Impossible to explain! Students must just remember to use *himself* and *themselves.*

   Point out that the plural of *self* is *selves.*

2. (a) Students already understand the label **appos.**, which identifies the correct use of compound pronouns for *emphasis.*

   (b) Explain that the label **reflex.** (*reflexive*) identifies the correct use of compound pronouns to *reflect* the subject.

   (c) Helpful reminders:
   - An **appositive** follows immediately the noun it emphasizes.
   - A **reflexive** compound pronoun comes after the verb.

   Emphasize this thinking-spelling problem summarized in the Reminder box.

   Demonstrate on the chalkboard that *there, they're,* and *their* begin with *the.* Never use *thier.*

1. Everybody's idea was acceptable, but hers was chosen.

2. No one's car is new except yours.

3. Not everyone's wish is always granted, but maybe ours can be!

4. Someone's book is behind the bookcase; is it his?

5. This house is ours; that one is someone else's.

CORRECT USAGE — PRONOUNS

Facts About Pronouns (continued)

Indefinite pronouns do not refer to a definite noun. Some are:

anyone, everyone, no one, someone, one, somebody, everybody

LEARN: Indefinite pronouns *do* use apostrophes to show possession:

> Is anyone's project finished?
> One's dreams sometimes come true.

PRACTICE: Insert apostrophes where necessary in these sentences.

1. Everybodys idea was acceptable, but hers was chosen.

2. No ones car is new except yours.

3. Not everyones wish is always granted, but maybe ours can be!

4. Someones book is behind the bookcase; is it his?

5. This house is ours; that one is someone elses.

Verb Contractions with Nominative Personal Pronouns

LEARN: In writing a contraction of a helping verb with a nominative pronoun, use an apostrophe where you leave out a letter or letters in the verb. There is no change in the pronoun.

Helping verbs that are shortened in a contraction are:

is, am, are, has, have, had, would, shall, will

Examples: I'm (I am) wondering. I've (I have) wondered.
She's (She is) leaving. She's (She has) left.
We're (We are) running. We'd (We had) run.
You're (You are) deciding. They'll (They will) sit.
You'd (You would) decide. They'd (They had) sat.

Compound Pronouns — Pronouns joined with *self* or *selves*:

myself, yourself, himself (never "hisself"), **herself, itself**
ourselves, yourselves, themselves (never "theirselves")

LEARN: Compound pronouns have two main uses in sentences:

1. As an appositive to a noun for *emphasis*:
    Karen herself said it.   I saw Mary herself buy the dress.

2. Used after a verb to *reflect* the subject (label: **reflex.**):
    Lisa hurt herself.   Julie is herself once again.

3. Compound pronouns are never used as regular subjects or objects:
    You and (myself, I) can go.   Jill saw Amy and (myself, me).

> **Reminder:** *their* = possessive of *they; they're* = contraction of *they are;
> there* refers to *place* or is used as an *introductory word.*

© 1988, 1997 J. Weston Walch, Publisher   *Steps to Good Grammar*

PRACTICE WITH PRONOUNS

This is a challenging page designed to encourage students to think analytically and, therefore, to firm up their understanding and retention of the information on pages 187 and 189. Help them to select and label their choices correctly.

Several pronoun choices in the Part II sentences could have additional labeling:

Sentence 1: *yours* could also be labeled *O.P.,*

object of the preposition *like.*

Sentence 3: *we* could be underlined once and labeled *subject.*

Sentence 5: *me* could be labeled *I.O.*

Sentence 10: *myself* could also be labeled *I.O.*

Sentence 14: *there* could be bracketed and labeled *adverb.*

---

1. I'd mailed (the) package (to you) yourself.
2. Sally bought herself (that) book.
3. (The) children had entertained (themselves, ~~theirselves~~).
4. (Our) parents gave Rob and (~~myself~~, me) (a) CD player; we're [really] enjoying it.
5. You've overslept [again].

---

1. (~~There~~, ~~They're~~, Their) car is in the driveway; (it's, ~~its~~) a black sedan like (~~your's~~, yours).
2. (Their, ~~They're~~) flight is overdue; (~~their~~, they're) just arriving now.
3. Our neighbors and (~~ourselves~~, we) will vacation together.
4. Dad (~~hisself~~, himself) had chosen the tie.
5. The teacher gave you and (me, ~~myself~~) a pass.
6. (~~Someones~~, Someone's) purse is in the office; Kay thinks (~~its~~, it's) (hers, ~~her's~~).
7. The boys (~~theirselves~~, themselves) said the girls had played better.
8. (Everyone's, ~~Everyones~~) report is due.
9. (~~Its~~, It's) still early; (you're, ~~your~~) not leaving now, are you?
10. I just bought (~~me~~, myself) a new pen.
11. The dog broke (its, ~~it's~~) leg.
12. The Thorps (themselves, ~~theirselves~~) parked (~~they're~~, their) car on the street.
13. Now (someone's, ~~someones~~) car has taken (its, ~~it's~~) place in the driveway.
14. Actually, (~~its~~, it's) (ours, ~~our's~~); my dad parked it (there, ~~their~~) (~~hisself~~, himself).
15. Is this wallet (~~your's~~, yours)? (~~Its~~, It's) not mine.

CORRECT USAGE — PRONOUNS

Practice With Pronouns

Compound Pronouns and Verb Contractions with Pronouns

Instructions: Mark: <u>verbs</u>, <u>subjects</u>, (adjectives) [adverbs] (prep. phrases) label: **D.O., prep., O.P., I.O.** Insert apostrophes where needed. Label compound pronouns **reflex.** or **appos.** Cross out the incorrect words.

Example: (The) Joneses <u>have bought</u> (~~theirselves~~, themselves *I.O. reflex.*) (a new) computer; (they're, ~~their~~ *D.O.*) <u>using</u> it *D.O.* [regularly].

1. Id mailed the package to you yourself.

2. Sally bought herself that book.

3. The children had entertained (themselves, theirselves).

4. Our parents gave Rob and (myself, me) a CD player. were really enjoying it.

5. Youve overslept again.

DRILL: Pronoun Facts

Instructions: Choose the correct word in the parentheses and label it **poss., contrac., reflex.,** or **appos.** where appropriate. Cross out the incorrect pronouns.

1. (There, They're, Their) car is in the driveway; (it's, its) a black sedan like (your's, yours).

2. (Their, They're) flight is overdue; (their, they're) just arriving now.

3. Our neighbors and (ourselves, we) will vacation together.

4. Dad (hisself, himself) had chosen the tie.

5. The teacher gave you and (me, myself) a pass.

6. (Someones, Someone's) purse is in the office; Kay thinks (its, it's) (hers, her's).

7. The boys (theirselves, themselves) said the girls had played better.

8. (Everyone's, Everyones) report is due.

9. (Its, It's) still early; (you're, your) not leaving now, are you?

10. I just bought (me, myself) a new pen.

11. The dog broke (its, it's) leg.

12. The Thorps (themselves, theirselves) parked (they're, their) car on the street.

13. Now (someone's, someones) car has taken (its, it's) place in the driveway.

14. Actually, (its, it's) (ours, our's); my dad parked it (there, their) (hisself, himself).

15. Is this wallet (your's, yours)? (Its, It's) not mine.

© 1988, 1997 J. Weston Walch, Publisher

Steps to Good Grammar

FINAL DRILL: PRONOUN FACTS

This page provides further practice in applying facts concerning pronouns from pages 187 and 189.

Several choices could have additional labeling:

Sentences 4, 6, 13, 17, 19: The reflexive pronouns could also be labeled *I.O.*

Sentence 5: *I* is part of the compound subject and

could be underlined once and labeled *subject.*

Sentence 8: *me* could be labeled *O.P.*

Sentence 13: *me* could be labeled *I.O.*

Sentence 14: *there* could be bracketed and labeled *adverb.*

1. The teacher (~~hisself~~, himself) gave me this book. *[appos.]*
2. Someone's book was left on my desk yesterday. *[poss.] [poss.]*
3. Apparently it's not anyone's in this class. *[contrac.] [poss.]*
4. My grandparents have bought (themselves, ~~theirselves~~) a ski chalet; (~~there~~, they're, ~~their~~) really enjoying it. *[poss.] [reflex. I.O.] [contrac.]*
5. Mom and (~~myself~~, I) went to the mall. *[subj.]*
6. Alexis and I bought (~~ourselfs~~, ourselves) new backpacks. *[reflex. I.O.]*
7. Has everyone's test paper been turned in? *[poss.]*
8. Dave sent postcards to my sister and (me, ~~myself~~). *[poss.] [O.P.]*
9. He'd arrived before we'd left. *[contrac.] [contrac.]*
10. That's (~~there~~, ~~they're~~, their) car; this is (~~our's~~, ours). *[contrac.] [poss.] [poss.]*
11. Mom herself reupholstered this chair. *[appos.]*
12. Is this book (~~your's~~, yours), (his, ~~his'~~), or (hers, her's)? *[poss.] [poss.] [poss.]*
13. My parents bought (themselves, ~~theirselves~~) and (~~myself~~, me) new bedroom sets. *[reflex. I.O.] [I.O.]*

14. [Write *there, they're,* or *their* correctly in the blanks:]

    They're using *their* old car as a down payment on that new one over *[there]*. *[contrac.] [poss.] [adverb]*

15. Surely (~~your~~, you're) coming with us; we've saved a place for you. *[contrac.] [contrac.]*
16. The librarian herself suggested this book. *[appos.]*
17. Dad has bought (~~hisself~~, himself) a new tool chest. *[reflex. I.O.]*
18. (Everybody's, ~~Everybodies~~) suggestion is good; we'll follow (~~your's~~, yours) or (~~her's~~, hers). *[poss.] [contrac.] [poss.] [poss.]*
19. I'll buy (~~me~~, myself) a new pen tomorrow. *[contrac.] [reflex. I.O.]*
20. Is (~~you're~~, your) house air-conditioned? (~~Their's~~, Theirs) isn't, and neither is (ours, ~~our's~~). *[poss.] [poss.] [poss.]*

CORRECT USAGE — PRONOUNS

FINAL DRILL: Pronoun Facts

Instructions: Draw a line through the incorrect words in parentheses. In all sentences write the correct label above pronoun forms where appropriate: **poss., contrac., reflex., appos.** Insert apostrophes where needed. Where a personal pronoun is the correct choice in parentheses, label its use in the sentence.

1. The teacher (hisself, himself) gave me this book.

2. Someones book was left on my desk yesterday.

3. Apparently its not anyones in this class.

4. My grandparents have bought (themselves, theirselves) a ski chalet; (there, they're, their) really enjoying it.

5. Mom and (myself, I) went to the mall.

6. Alexis and I bought (ourselfs, ourselves) new backpacks.

7. Has everyones test paper been turned in?

8. Dave sent postcards to my sister and (me, myself).

9. Hed arrived before wed left.

10. Thats (there, they're, their) car; this is (our's, ours).

11. Mom herself reupholstered this chair.

12. Is this book (your's, yours), (his, his'), or (hers, her's)?

13. My parents bought (themselves, theirselves) and (myself, me) new bedroom sets.

14. [Write *there, they're,* or *their* correctly in the blanks:]

_____ using _____ old car as a down payment on that new one over

_____ .

15. Surely (your, youre) coming with us; weve saved a place for you.

16. The librarian herself suggested this book.

17. Dad has bought (hisself, himself) a new tool chest.

18. (Everybodys, Everybodies) suggestion is good; well follow (your's, yours) or (her's, hers).

19. Ill buy (me, myself) a new pen tomorrow.

20. Is (you're, your) house air-conditioned? (Their's, Theirs) isn't, and neither is (ours, our's).

Steps to Good Grammar

TEST 1: PRONOUN FACTS

This reproducible page contains two copies of one half-page drill/test. Cut each duplicated page in half; give each student one half-page.

Grading suggestion:

On this, there are 21 items to check. Subtract 5% for each error.

This test and the one on page 197 are optional. This one is less exacting than the next one.

1. Is that book (~~your's~~, yours)? This one is (hers, ~~her's~~).

2. (~~Their~~, They're) not going, since (it's, ~~its~~) so late; (~~your~~, you're) not going either, are you?

3. Is (~~you're~~, your) house air-conditioned? (~~Their's~~, Theirs) isn't, and neither is (ours, ~~ours'~~).

4. John saw (~~hisself~~, himself) on the TV news tonight; I have never seen (~~me~~, myself) on TV!

5. (~~Everyones~~, Everyone's) report is due; (no one's, ~~no ones~~) name is on this one.

6. Is your horse in (~~it's~~, its) stall?

7. My uncle bought (himself, ~~hisself~~) a new car; (~~our's~~, ours) is the same old one.

8. (~~Everybodies'~~, Everybody's) plan was good, but (hers, ~~her's~~) was chosen.

9. Do you hope that (~~yourself~~, you) and Emilio will win?

10. Of all the projects, (~~our's~~, ours) was good, but we (~~ourselfs~~, ourselves) thought (~~theirs'~~, theirs) was best.

CORRECT USAGE — PRONOUNS

TEST 1: Pronoun Facts

Instructions: Draw a line through incorrect forms in parentheses.

1. Is that book (your's, yours)? This one is (hers, her's).

2. (Their, They're) not going, since (it's, its) so late; (your, you're) not going either, are you?

3. Is (you're, your) house air-conditioned? (Their's, Theirs) isn't, and neither is (ours, ours').

4. John saw (hisself, himself) on the TV news tonight; I have never seen (me, myself) on TV!

5. (Everyones, Everyone's) report is due; (no one's, no ones) name is on this one.

6. Is your horse in (it's, its) stall?

7. My uncle bought (himself, hisself) a new car; (our's, ours) is the same old one.

8. (Everybodies', Everybody's) plan was good, but (hers, her's) was chosen.

9. Do you hope that (yourself, you) and Emilio will win?

10. Of all the projects, (our's, ours) was good, but we (ourselfs, ourselves) thought (theirs', theirs) was best.

NAME _____ DATE _____ 195

CORRECT USAGE — PRONOUNS

TEST 1: Pronoun Facts

Instructions: Draw a line through incorrect forms in parentheses.

1. Is that book (your's, yours)? This one is (hers, her's).

2. (Their, They're) not going, since (it's, its) so late; (your, you're) not going either, are you?

3. Is (you're, your) house air-conditioned? (Their's, Theirs) isn't, and neither is (ours, ours').

4. John saw (hisself, himself) on the TV news tonight; I have never seen (me, myself) on TV!

5. (Everyones, Everyone's) report is due; (no one's, no ones) name is on this one.

6. Is your horse in (it's, its) stall?

7. My uncle bought (himself, hisself) a new car; (our's, ours) is the same old one.

8. (Everybodies', Everybody's) plan was good, but (hers, her's) was chosen.

9. Do you hope that (yourself, you) and Emilio will win?

10. Of all the projects, (our's, ours) was good, but we (ourselfs, ourselves) thought (theirs', theirs) was best.

Steps to Good Grammar

TEST 2: PRONOUN FACTS

Grading suggestion:

33 items — subtract 3% for each error.

1. That book is ___*hers*___ (she), this is ___*yours*___ (you), and these are ___*theirs*___ (they).

2. (Their, **They're**) not going, since (**it's**, its) so late; (your, **you're**) not going either, are you?

3. ___*Everybody's*___ (Everybody) plan was good; unfortunately, ___*no one's*___ (no one) was chosen.

4. The house with ___*its*___ (it) shutters painted green is ___*his*___ (he).

5. We girls went by (ourselfs, **ourselves**). *reflex.*

6. If (there, **their**, they're) plane is on time, (**they're**, their, there) leaving at 5:00 A.M. tomorrow.

7. Is your horse in ___*its*___ (it) stall? (Its, **It's**) in ___*its*___ (it) corral.

8. Are you (yourselfs, **yourselves**) fully prepared? *appos.*

9. Not ___*everyone's*___ (everyone) dream will come true; hopefully, ___*mine*___ (I) will.

10. The principal (hisself, **himself**) conducted the assembly. *appos.*

11. (Its, **It's**) quite possible that (**it's**, its) going to rain tomorrow.

12. For Christmas, our parents bought (theirselves, **themselves**), my brother, and (myself, **me**) new waterbeds. *reflex.*

13. ___*Everybody's*___ (Everybody) test has been handed in; ___*nobody's*___ (nobody) name is on this one.

14. Our neighbors and (ourselves, **we**) often vacation together.

15. Surely (your, **you're**) not leaving now; (**it's**, its) so early!

CORRECT USAGE — PRONOUNS

TEST 2: Pronoun Facts

Instructions: In sentences where a choice is given in parentheses, draw a circle around the correct form. Label the use of compound ("self") pronouns: **reflex.** = reflexive; **appos.** = an appositive used for emphasis. In sentences with blanks, write the possessive form of the nominative pronoun shown in parentheses after the blank.

Example: _Our_ (we) project is good, but (there's, (heirs)) is better.

1. That book is _____ (she), this is _____ (you), and these are _____ (they).

2. (Their, They're) not going, since (it's, its) so late; (your, you're) not going either, are you?

3. _____ (Everybody) plan was good; unfortunately, _____ (no one) was chosen.

4. The house with _____ (it) shutters painted green is _____ (he).

5. We girls went by (ourselfs, ourselves).

6. If (there, their, they're) plane is on time, (they're, their, there) leaving at 5:00 A.M. tomorrow.

7. Is your horse in _____ (it) stall? (Its, It's) in _____ (it) corral.

8. Are you (yourselfs, yourselves) fully prepared?

9. Not _____ (everyone) dream will come true; hopefully, _____ (I) will.

10. The principal (hisself, himself) conducted the assembly.

11. (Its, It's) quite possible that (it's, its) going to rain tomorrow.

12. For Christmas, our parents bought (theirselves, themselves), my brother, and (myself, me) new waterbeds.

13. _____ (Everybody) test has been handed in; _____ (nobody) name is on this one.

14. Our neighbors and (ourselves, we) often vacation together.

15. Surely (your, you're) not leaving now; (it's, its) so early!

© 1988, 1997 J. Weston Walch, Publisher

Steps to Good Grammar

PRONOUN SUBJECT-VERB AGREEMENT

Emphasize the learning section with students who frequently use forms such as "I is," "we was," and "they does."

This study deals with compound subjects composed of pronouns. Point out to students that the facts presented here also apply to compound subjects composed of nouns. Go over these examples on the chalkboard:

John and Sue (was, were) leaving.

(Has, Have) your dad and mom bought that car?

Because the subject determines the correct verb

to use, be sure students draw the arrow *from* the subject *to* the verb.

Compound subject with *and:* Read and demonstrate the four items presented here. This memory device is very helpful to many students.

Students may point out that the plural substitute for *she and I* in sentence 4 should be *we*. Compliment them and approve their use of *we* if they wish. However, point out that the two pronouns use the same verbs. To keep the method simple, we still suggest saying, "For *and*, think *they*."

1. (Wasn't, Weren't) she coming (with you)?
2. (Hasn't, Haven't) they arrived yet?
3. (Don't, Doesn't) she want any help?
4. We (wasn't, weren't) looking for you.
5. (Don't, Doesn't) it seem cold today?

1. (Was, Were) he and she going?
2. Joel and she (belong, belongs) to 4-H.
3. (Does, Do) he and Josh go to the school dances?
4. She and I (were, was) late.
5. Jason and she (has, have) been playing tennis.

CORRECT USAGE — PRONOUNS

Pronoun Subject-Verb Agreement

LEARN: 1. These pronoun subjects: **HE, SHE, IT** (and **singular nouns**)
use helping verbs that end in *s:* **IS, WAS, HAS, DOES**
and "doing verbs in the present tense that **end in** *s*.
These are "singular" verbs, verbs to singular subjects:

He, she, it, John: is, was, has, does, wants, uses, etc.

2. These pronoun subjects: **YOU, WE, THEY** (and **plural nouns**)
use helping verbs that do *not* end in *s:* **ARE, WERE, HAVE, DO**
and "doing" verbs in the present tense that **do *not* end in** *s*.
These are "plural" verbs, verbs to plural subjects:

You, we, they, the boys: are, were, have, do, want, use, etc.

3. The pronoun subject: **I**
uses: **AM, WAS, HAVE, DO, want, use,** etc.

PRACTICE: Using the information above, draw two lines under the correct verb in parentheses below and cross out the incorrect verb. Mark: verbs, subjects, adjectives, adverbs, prep. phrases, label: **D.O., prep., O.P., LV, LVC-A.**

1. (Wasn't, Weren't) she coming with you?

2. (Hasn't, Haven't) they arrived yet?

3. (Don't, Doesn't) she want any help?

4. We (wasn't, weren't) looking for you.

5. (Don't, Doesn't) it seem cold today?

Correct Verbs for Compound Subjects

- You know a compound subject has two or more subject words.
- Compound subjects are joined by *and* or *or*.

Compound Subject Joined by *AND*

1. *And* means two or more.
2. To say *he and she* in one word, say *they*.
3. To use the right verb for *he and she*, think *they*.
4. To help you remember, box *and* and write *they* above it: and
   Draw an arrow from *they* to the correct verb.

PRACTICE: Box and label: and ; draw an arrow to the verb. Mark and underline all sentence parts as in the drill above.

1. (Was, Were) he and she going?

2. Joel and she (belong, belongs) to 4-H.

3. (Does, Do) he and Josh go to the school dances?

4. She and I (were, was) late.

5. Jason and she (has, have) been playing tennis.

Steps to Good Grammar

CORRECT VERBS FOR COMPOUND SUBJECTS

Again, read aloud and demonstrate the items in Learn.

Make especially clear the positions of the subject words in the two examples.

When students draw the box around *or/nor*, be sure they don't write *they* above it; only *and* means "they." The arrow students draw for *or/nor* is *from* the nearest subject word *to* the correct verb.

In the rule, "the subject word nearest the verb...," *nearest* should be *nearer*, since only two words make up the compound subject in the examples. If students

point this out, compliment them! However, if there were three words in the compound subject, as is often the case, *nearest* would be right. To keep the method simple, we still suggest saying, "The subject word nearest the verb determines the correct verb to use."

Practice and Drill:

Instruct students first to locate the conjunction joining the compound subject and box it, then determine the correct verb and draw the arrow. Then they should complete the identification of the other sentence parts.

1. (Do, Does) he or the Joneses have enough insurance?
2. (Do, Does) the Joneses or he have enough insurance?
3. (Have, Has) they or she become ill?
4. (Have, Has) she or they become ill?
5. Neither he nor I (want, wants) dessert.

---

1. (Have, Has) either he or she called you?
2. (Isn't, Aren't) he and I needed? We (was, were) sent here by Ms. Lee.
3. (Was, Were) they and he riding on the subway?
4. Neither they nor he (like, likes) lemon pie; neither (do, does) she or I.
5. Yesterday they and we (was, were) at the wharf.
6. Usually he or they (gives, give) me a ride to school.
7. Neither they nor she (have, has) lived here very long.
8. She and I (wasn't, weren't) really angry with you.
9. (Isn't, Aren't) you or she entering the photography contest?
10. She and they (have, has) climbed Mount Washington.

CORRECT USAGE — PRONOUNS

Correct Verbs for Compound Subjects (continued)

Compound Subject Joined by *OR* or *NOR*

LEARN: 1.   OR/NOR indicates a choice — "either this one or that one."

2.   In a compound subject joined by *or/nor,* the subject word nearest the verb determines (chooses) the correct verb.

3.   To help you remember, draw a box around *or/nor* and draw an arrow from the subject word nearest the verb to the correct verb.

(Hasn't, Haven't) he or they arrived yet?

He, the subject word nearest the verb, uses hasn't.

Neither he nor they (have, has) arrived yet?

They, the subject word nearest the verb, uses have.

PRACTICE: Draw a box around *or;* draw an arrow from the subject word nearest the verb to the correct verb. Mark and label the rest of the sentence parts as in the drill below.

1.   (Do, Does) he or the Joneses have enough insurance?

2.   (Do, Does) the Joneses or he have enough insurance?

3.   (Have, Has) they or she become ill?

4.   (Have, Has) she or they become ill?

5.   Neither he nor I (want, wants) dessert.

DRILL: Recognizing Correct Verb Forms with Compound Subjects

Instructions: Box and label: and ; box: or , nor ; draw arrows to the correct verbs. Mark: verbs, subjects, adjectives, adverbs, (prep. phrases); label: **D.O., prep., O.P., I.O., LV, LVC-A.**

1.   (Have, Has) either he or she called you?

2.   (Isn't, Aren't) he and I needed? We (was, were) sent here by Ms. Lee.

3.   (Was, Were) they and he riding on the subway?

4.   Neither they nor he (like, likes) lemon pie; neither (do, does) she or I.

5.   Yesterday they and we (was, were) at the wharf.

6.   Usually he or they (gives, give) me a ride to school.

7.   Neither they nor she (have, has) lived here very long.

8.   She and I (wasn't, weren't) really angry with you.

9.   (Isn't, Aren't) you or she entering the photography contest?

10.   She and they (have, has) climbed Mount Washington.

FINAL DRILL: SUBJECT-VERB AGREEMENT AND PRONOUN FACTS

During class, students could do the work on this paper individually as a self-test. As you review the correct markings with them, students should correct any errors they may have made.

Students could take this paper home with them to use as a study sheet in preparation for the test scheduled the next day.

1. Either my brothers or she (~~have~~, has) forgotten the key.
   they
2. He and she (sing, ~~sings~~) very well.
   they
3. (~~Was~~, Were) he and she making arrangements?
4. Tomaso or one of those two other boys always (~~finish~~, finishes) first.
5. (Has, ~~Have~~) he or they reached a decision?
6. Neither you nor she (~~look~~, looks) very happy.
   they
7. (~~Is~~, Are) he and his brother usually ready on time?
8. (Were, ~~Was~~) they or she coming with us?
9. (~~Were~~, Was) she or they coming with us?
10. Neither his brothers nor he (~~play~~, plays) on the team.
    they
11. They and he (~~was~~, were) going into the building.
12. (~~Have~~, Has) she or they been chosen?
13. (Have, ~~Has~~) they or she been chosen?
    they
14. (Do, ~~Does~~) both you and he own mountain bikes?
15. (Is, ~~Are~~) Mom or she planning the party?

1. ~~Heres~~ my tennis racket, but where is ~~it's~~ cover?   *Here's* ... *its*
2. ~~Our's~~ is a better plan than ~~their's~~.   *Ours* ... *theirs*
3. ~~Wheres~~ ~~you're~~ bicycle? Is that one ~~your's~~?   *Where's your* ... *yours*
4. ~~There~~ exchanging ~~there~~ old car for that new one over ~~their~~.   *They're* ... *their* ... *there*
5. That coat must be ~~her's~~ or ~~your's~~.   *hers yours*
6. Do you know which book is ~~yours'~~ by ~~it's~~ cover?   *yours its*
7. ~~Its~~ too late now to give the puppy ~~it's~~ bath.   *It's* ... *its*
8. ~~Her's~~ was a good report, but ~~your's~~ was better.   *Hers* ... *yours*
9. ~~Everybodys~~ report was good, but ~~her's~~ was best.   *Everybody's* ... *hers*
10. ~~Nobodies~~ mail was delivered that day.   *Nobody's*

CORRECT USAGE — PRONOUNS

FINAL DRILL: Subject-Verb Agreement and Pronoun Facts

Part I. Instructions: Box and label: and ; box: or , nor ; draw arrows to the correct verbs. Mark: verbs, subjects. Cross out the incorrect verb in parentheses. No other labeling is necessary.

1. Either my brothers or she (have, has) forgotten the key.

2. He and she (sing, sings) very well.

3. (Was, Were) he and she making arrangements?

4. Tomaso or one of those two other boys always (finish, finishes) first.

5. (Has, Have) he or they reached a decision?

6. Neither you nor she (look, looks) very happy.

7. (Is, Are) he and his brother usually ready on time?

8. (Were, Was) they or she coming with us?

9. (Were, Was) she or they coming with us?

10. Neither his brothers nor he (play, plays) on the team.

11. They and he (was, were) going into the building.

12. (Have, Has) she or they been chosen?

13. (Have, Has) they or she been chosen?

14. (Do, Does) both you and he own mountain bikes?

15. (Is, Are) Mom or she planning the party?

Part II. Instructions: Above each error in usage, write the correct form; then cross out the errors.

1. Heres my tennis racket, but where is it's cover?

2. Our's is a better plan than their's.

3. Wheres you're bicycle? Is that one your's?

4. There exchanging there old car for that new one over their.

5. That coat must be her's or your's.

6. Do you know which book is yours' by it's cover?

7. Its too late now to give the puppy it's bath.

8. Her's was a good report, but your's was better.

9. Everybodys report was good, but her's was best.

10. Nobodies mail was delivered that day.

Steps to Good Grammar

TEST 1: SUBJECT-VERB AGREEMENT AND PRONOUN FACTS

Grading suggestions:

Part I: Count all required markings.

Point value
1 point, underlining complete verb
1 point, underlining complete subject
1 point, box around conjunction
1 point, *they* above *and*
1 point, arrow from subject to *correct* verb

Total points: 45
Use grading scale on page 22.

Part II: 24 items

-1, 96	-5, 79	-9, 62
-2, 92	-6, 75	-10, 58
-3, 87	-7, 71	
-4, 83	-8, 67	

Both parts of the test are of equal importance; average the two grades. Or use the grading scale for 68 point (total points, Parts I and II — 69) on page 124.

1. (Have, ~~Has~~) she and he returned the books?   *they*

2. Neither you nor I (was, ~~were~~) given permission.

3. Her sisters and she (~~has~~, have) been quite popular.   *they*

4. (Don't, ~~Doesn't~~) she and I play in the next game?   *they*

5. Both Hector and she (~~tries~~, try) very hard.   *they*

6. (Is, ~~Are~~) he or they in the room?

7. Neither his brothers nor he (~~practice~~, practices) regularly.

8. Either Dad or they (help, ~~helps~~) us.

9. (~~Does~~, Do) you or she want a ride?

10. (Were, ~~Was~~) you and I given parts in the play?   *they*

1. The boat in the harbor could be ~~their's~~ or ours.   *theirs*

2. Is this wallet ~~your's~~ or ~~her's~~? ~~It's~~ closing snap is broken.   *yours   hers   Its*

3. Look at that cute puppy! ~~Its~~ chasing ~~it's~~ tail!   *It's   its*

4. ~~Your~~ bringing ~~you're~~ guitar, I hope!   *you're   your*

5. ~~Somebodies~~ book is on the teacher's desk. Sara thinks ~~its her's~~, and Eileen thinks ~~its her's~~.   *Somebody's   it's hers   it's hers*

6. [In the blanks, write *their, there,* or *they're* correctly:] ___*They're*___ planning to drive

   ___*their*___ truck when they go ___*there*___ .

7. ~~Your's~~ is a much better plan than ~~our's~~.   *yours   ours*

8. ~~Everyones~~ report was turned in on time.   *Everyone's*

9. ~~Its you're~~ turn, not ~~their's~~.   *It's your   theirs*

10. ~~Their~~ not going because ~~its~~ so late.   *They're   it's*

CORRECT USAGE — PRONOUNS

TEST 1: Subject-Verb Agreement and Pronoun Facts

Part I. Instructions: Box and label: and ; box: or , nor ; draw arrows to the correct verbs. Mark: verbs, subjects. Cross out the incorrect verb in parentheses. No other labeling is necessary.

1. (Have, Has) she and he returned the books?

2. Neither you nor I (was, were) given permission.

3. Her sisters and she (has, have) been quite popular.

4. (Don't, Doesn't) she and I play in the next game?

5. Both Hector and she (tries, try) very hard.

6. (Is, Are) he or they in the room?

7. Neither his brothers nor he (practice, practices) regularly.

8. Either Dad or they (help, helps) us.

9. (Does, Do) you or she want a ride?

10. (Were, Was) you and I given parts in the play?

Part II. Instructions: Above each error in usage, write the correct form; then cross out the errors.

1. The boat in the harbor could be their's or ours.

2. Is this wallet your's or her's? It's closing snap is broken.

3. Look at that cute puppy! Its chasing it's tail!

4. Your bringing you're guitar, I hope!

5. Somebodies book is on the teacher's desk. Sara thinks its her's, and Eileen thinks its her's.

6. [In the blanks, write *their, there,* or *they're* correctly:] _____ planning to drive

   _____ truck when they go _____ .

7. Your's is a much better plan than our's.

8. Everyones report was turned in on time.

9. Its you're turn, not their's.

10. Their not going because its so late.

TEST 2: SUBJECT-VERB AGREEMENT AND PRONOUN FACTS

Grading suggestions:

Part I: Count all required markings.

Point value
1 point, underlining complete verb
1 point, underlining complete subject
1 point, box around conjunction
1 point, *they* above *and*
1 point, arrow from subject to *correct* verb

Total points: 45
Use grading scale on page 22.

Part II: 21 points — subtract 5% for each error.

Both parts of the test are of equal importance; average the two grades. Or, grade the complete test — total point value 66 — using this grading scale:

-1, 98	-7, 89	-13, 80	-19, 71	-25, 62	-31, 53
-2, 97	-8, 88	-14, 79	-20, 70	-26, 61	-32, 52
-3, 95	-9, 86	-15, 77	-21, 68	-27, 59	-33, 50
-4, 94	-10, 85	-16, 76	-22, 67	-28, 58	-34, 49
-5, 92	-11, 83	-17, 74	-23, 65	-29, 56	-35, 47
-6, 91	-12, 82	-18, 73	-24, 64	-30, 55	-36, 46

1. (Do, Does) he and she need passes? *(they)*

2. Neither you nor I (were, was) invited?

3. (Is, Are) she or he coming with us?

4. Geoff and he (has, have) practiced regularly. *(they)*

5. (Doesn't, Don't) either he or his brother play tennis?

6. He and she (read, reads) many books. *(they)*

7. He or I (are, am, is) driving to the game.

8. (Haven't, Hasn't) my sister and I been given parts in the play? *(they)*

9. She and I (was, were) only pretending. *(they)*

10. His brother or he always (deliver, delivers) our paper.

1. ~~Someones~~ *Someone's* purse is on my desk; it wasn't ~~anybodies~~ *anybody's* in the other class; is it ~~your's~~ *yours* or anyone ~~elses~~ *else's* in this class?

2. ~~There~~ *They're* sure ~~its~~ *it's* not ~~there~~ *their* turn; maybe it's ~~our's~~ *ours*.

3. ~~Shes~~ *She's* not riding her bike because its rear tire is flat.

4. Yes, your ~~reports~~ *report's* good; but so are his, ~~her's~~ *hers*, and ours.

5. Which ~~cars~~ *car's* yours? ~~Thats our's~~ *That's ours* over ~~their~~ *there*.

6. ~~Theirs~~ *There's* no way, is there, that they could prove ~~its their's~~ *it's theirs*?

7. I have ~~everyones~~ *everyone's* test paper, apparently; however, no ~~ones names~~ *one's name's* on this one.

CORRECT USAGE — PRONOUNS

TEST 2: Subject-Verb Agreement and Pronoun Facts

Part I. Instructions: Box and label: ~~and~~ *they* ; box: or , nor ; draw arrows to the correct verbs. Mark: <u>verbs</u>, <u>subjects</u>. Cross out the incorrect verb in parentheses. No other labeling is necessary.

1. (Do, Does) he and she need passes?

2. Neither you nor I (were, was) invited?

3. (Is, Are) she or he coming with us?

4. Geoff and he (has, have) practiced regularly.

5. (Doesn't, Don't) either he or his brother play tennis?

6. He and she (read, reads) many books.

7. He or I (are, am, is) driving to the game.

8. (Haven't, Hasn't) my sister and I been given parts in the play?

9. She and I (was, were) only pretending.

10. His brother or he always (deliver, delivers) our paper.

Part II. Instructions: Above each error in usage, write the correct form; then cross out the errors.

1. Someones purse is on my desk; it wasn't anybodies in the other class; is it your's or anyone elses in this class?

2. There sure its not there turn; maybe it's our's.

3. Shes not riding her bike because its rear tire is flat.

4. Yes, your reports good; but so are his, her's, and ours.

5. Which cars yours? Thats our's over their.

6. Theirs no way, is there, that they could prove its their's?

7. I have everyones test paper, apparently; however, no ones names on this one.

Steps to Good Grammar

PRINCIPAL PARTS OF VERBS

A knowledge of the principal parts of verbs prepares students for the use of advanced forms of expression including gerunds, infinitive phrases, and participial phrases.

1. Explain that the term "simple" used with the present and past principal parts indicates that no helping verbs are needed.

2. As you read the introductory material, quiz students:

   (a) What are the common words you may use to identify the principal parts? ("Today I" with the simple present; "Yesterday I" with the simple past; "Often I *have*" with the past participle.)

   (b) What ending is added to the root word *talk* to form the present participle? ("-*ing*")

   (c) What does the term "participle" mean about a verb? (The root word is only part of the expression; it uses helping verbs.)

   (d) Repeat *b* and *c* when discussing the past participle.

3. In going through the Practice sentences, emphasize the endings and the use or lack of helpers.

1. I <u>play</u> tennis every day. ___*S. Pres.*___
2. Often <u>Herb</u> <u>has played</u> tennis. ___*Past Part.*___
3. <u>Carrie</u> <u>is playing</u> tennis now. ___*Pres. Part.*___
4. Yesterday, <u>Kay and Al</u> <u>played</u> tennis. ___*S. Past*___
5. <u>They</u> <u>had liked</u> *Past Part.* apple pie; now <u>they</u> <u>like</u> cherry pie. ___*S. Pres.*___

CORRECT USAGE — REGULAR VERBS

Principal Parts of Verbs

Understanding the principal parts of verbs will strengthen your ability to express your ideas clearly and correctly. Every verb has four main parts called the principal parts: simple present, present participle, simple past, and past participle.

Simple Present: I **talk**   he **talks**   you **talk**   John **talks**

> **THINK:** "Today" I talk. "Today" he talks.

> **REMEMBER:** The subjects *he, she, it,* and singular nouns use verbs ending in an *s* in the present tense.

Present Participle: talk — **talking**   save — **saving**

> Add *-ing* to the root word; if the root word ends in an *e,* first drop the *e.*

> **LEARN:** A **participle** form of a verb is only *part* of the expression. Participle forms always use "helping" verbs.

> Present participle "helping" verbs are:

> **is   am   are   was   were   — be   — being   — been**

> The last three always use helping verbs themselves.

> I **am talking.**   They **were talking.**   She **had been talking.**

Simple Past: talk — **talked**   save — **saved**

> Add *-d* or *-ed* to the root word.

> **THINK:** "Yesterday" I talked. "Yesterday" John talked. This is simple! No special reminders? *No* helping verbs!

Past Participle: talk — **talked**   save — **saved**

> Add *-d* or *-ed* to the root word.

> **THINK:** "Often I have" talked. "Often John had" talked.

> **REMEMBER:** A **participle** is only part of the expression. The past participle uses these helping verbs:

> **have   has   had   shall/will have**

PRACTICE: Recognizing Principal Parts of Verbs

Instructions: Underline <u>verbs</u> and <u>subjects</u>. In the blank, write the principal part used in the verb: Simple = **S. Pres., S. Past;** Participle = **Pres. Part., Past Part.**

1.   I play tennis every day. _____

2.   Often Herb has played tennis. _____

3.   Carrie is playing tennis now. _____

4.   Yesterday, Kay and Al played tennis. _____

5.   They had liked _____ apple pie; now they like cherry pie. _____

Steps to Good Grammar

SIMPLE TENSES

Read the instructional material aloud and quiz students to help them retain the information.

Demonstrate how the *first, second,* and *third* persons are determined.

Clarify *singular* and *plural,* especially about *you.*

To very capable students, you might explain the use of *shall/will* in the future tense in very formal expression; in general usage, no such distinction is made.

1. With first person, singular and plural, use *shall* to make a simple statement:

    I (we) shall leave at noon.

To express determination or promise:

    I (we) *will* leave at noon.

2. The words are reversed for second and third person, singular and plural. To make a simple statement:

    You (he, she, they) will leave at noon.

To express determination or promise:

    You (he, she, they) *shall* leave at noon.

Establish the use of the common words to identify the tenses:

Present: today   Past: yesterday   Future: tomorrow

1. **use:** Present tense, second person singular ___*You use.*___
2. **look:** Past tense, first person plural ___*We looked.*___
3. **ask:** Past tense, third person singular ___*He/She/It/John asked.*___
4. **work:** Future tense, first person plural ___*We will work.*___
5. **play:** Present tense, third person plural ___*They play.*___
6. **laugh:** Past tense, second person singular ___*You laughed.*___
7. **walk:** Present tense, second person plural ___*You walk.*___
8. **cook:** Future tense, third person singular ___*He/She/It/John will cook.*___
9. **push:** Past tense, first person singular ___*I pushed.*___
10. **expect:** Future tense, first person singular ___*I will expect.*___

CORRECT USAGE — REGULAR VERBS

Simple Tenses

The word *tense* in grammar means "time." Obviously, the times you talk and write about are *present,* "today"; *past,* "yesterday"; and *future,* "tomorrow."

There are two groups of tenses — **simple tenses** and **perfect tenses.**

Tenses are arranged for understanding according to **subjective pronouns.**

SIMPLE TENSES

Singular		**Plural**	
Present "today"	*First person* (the speaker) I talk	*First person* (the speakers) We talk	
	Second person (the person spoken to) You talk	*Second person* (the persons spoken to) You talk	
	Third person (the person spoken of) He/She/It/John talks	*Third person* (the persons spoken to) They/People talk	

Past The pattern of "persons" for the Present Tense is repeated.

"yesterday" All subjects use *"talked." No* helping verb is used.

Future The pattern of "persons" is repeated.

"tomorrow" All subjects use *"talk"* and the helping verb *"will": will talk.*

PRACTICE: In the space provided, write the subject and verb tense indicated for the verbs listed.

Example: **excuse:** Past tense, third person singular *He/She/It/John excused.*

1. **use:** Present tense, second person singular _____

2. **look:** Past tense, first person plural _____

3. **ask:** Past tense, third person singular _____

4. **work:** Future tense, first person plural _____

5. **play:** Present tense, third person plural _____

6. **laugh:** Past tense, second person singular _____

7. **walk:** Present tense, second person plural _____

8. **cook:** Future tense, third person singular _____

9. **push:** Past tense, first person singular _____

10. **expect:** Future tense, first person singular _____

Steps to Good Grammar

TENSES OF THE VERB *TO HAVE*

Students should *know* the simple tenses of *to have,* since these are the required helping verbs in the perfect tenses of other verbs.

Establish these uses:

"today" with the present tense:

"Today" I *have*; "Today" he *has*.

"yesterday" with the past tense:

"Yesterday" I *had*; "Yesterday" he *had*.

"tomorrow" with the future tense:

"Tomorrow" I *shall have*;
"Tomorrow" you *will have*.

In Practice, the sample sentence uses the subject *visitors*.

Point out that plural nouns use the verb form of the third person plural pronoun, *they*.

Remind students that singular nouns use the verb form of the third person singular pronouns, *he, she, it*.

1. We had lunch [there][yesterday]. *First pers. pl., Past*

2. I will have time [tomorrow]. *First pers. sing., Fut.*

3. They had a good chance [yesterday]. *Third pers. pl., Past*

4. Good! You have your raincoat (with you)! *Second pers. sing., Pres.*

5. He will have dinner (at home). *Third pers. sing., Fut.*

6. I had my turn [yesterday]. *First pers. sing., Past*

7. Good! You all have your books! *Second pers. pl., Pres.*

8. Carrie has her book report [today]. *Third pers. sing., Pres.*

9. Our neighbors will have a vacation [soon]. *Third pers. pl., Fut.*

10. Will you students have your reports [ready][tomorrow]? *Second pers. pl., Fut.*

CORRECT USAGE — REGULAR VERBS

Tenses of the Verb *To Have*

To understand the perfect tenses, you must first know how to conjugate (join together all the tense forms of) the verb **have**.

CONJUGATION OF SIMPLE TENSES: *HAVE*

	Singular		**Plural**	
Present	*First person:*	I have	*First person:*	We have
"today"	*Second person:*	You have	*Second person*	You have
	Third person	He/She/It/ John *has*	*Third person:*	They/People have

Past "yesterday"	All subjects use *had*: I had
Future "tomorrow"	All subjects use *will have:* you will have

PRACTICE: Mark: <u>verbs</u>, <u>subjects</u>, (adjectives) [adverbs] (prep. phrases) label: **D.O., prep., O.P., appos.** In the space after each sentence, write the person and tense of the verb. Use these abbreviations: *pers.* (person), *sing.* (singular), *pl.* (plural), *Pres.* (Present), *Fut.* (Future). *Past* needs no abbreviation.

Example: (The) <u>visitors</u> <u>will have</u> (a) tour [tomorrow]. *Third pers. pl., Fut.*

1. We had lunch there yesterday._____

2. I will have time tomorrow._____

3. They had a good chance yesterday._____

4. Good! You have your raincoat with you! _____

5. He will have dinner at home._____

6. I had my turn yesterday._____

7. Good! You all have your books! _____

8. Carrie has her book report today. _____

9. Our neighbors will have a vacation soon. _____

10. Will you students have your reports ready tomorrow?_____

Steps to Good Grammar

PERFECT TENSES

Write on the chalkboard the abbreviations given in the Instructions for Practice on page 213, which students are to use for persons and tenses of each verb. Add **Perf.** to the list for *Perfect*.

To explain present perfect: *have/has* is the *present* part of present perfect; *-d* or *-ed* is the *perfect* part of present perfect. Use "today."

I *have* talk*ed* with him today.
⊤ ⊤
(present) (perfect)

To explain past perfect: *had* is the *past* part of past perfect; *-d* or *-ed* is the *perfect* part of past perfect. Use "yesterday."

I *had* talk*ed* with him yesterday.
⊤ ⊤
(past) (perfect)

To explain future perfect: *will have* is the *future* part of future perfect; *-d* or *-ed* is the perfect part of future perfect. Use "tomorrow."

I *will have* talk*ed* with him by this time tomorrow.
⊤ ⊤
(future) (perfect)

1. I have [already] played tennis [today]. *First pers. sing., Pres. Perf.*
2. (By lunch time), we will have played (for two hours) *First pers. pl., Fut. Perf.*
3. Sasha had played (for several hours) [yesterday] *Third pers. sing., Past Perf.*
4. Have they moved (to Antioch?) *Third pers. pl., Pres. Perf.*
5. Had you finished (your) report (on time?) *Second pers. sing., Past Perf.*
6. [Really,] she hadn't decided [yet]. *Third pers. sing., Past Perf.*
7. He has [frequently] mowed (the) lawn (for Dad) *Third pers. sing., Pres. Perf.*
8. Have you boys finished [already]? *Second person pl., Pres. Perf.*
9. Dad will have arrived (in New York) (by now). *Third pers. sing., Fut. Perf.*
10. We had washed (Mom's car) (for her) *First pers. pl., Past Perf.*

CORRECT USAGE — REGULAR VERBS

Perfect Tenses

The **perfect tenses** express action completed at the time the sentence is spoken or written. Perfect tenses use the **past participle** of "doing" verbs. The past participle, you remember, is the -ed form of the verb *plus* forms of the verb *to have*.

Present Perfect:

You know that *have* and *has* are the present tense of *to have*. Therefore:

I have (Present) + talk*ed* = <u>Present</u> Perfect:

<u>I have talked</u>.   <u>He has talked</u>.

Past Perfect:

You know that *had* is the past tense of *to have*. Therefore:

I had (Past) + talk*ed* = <u>Past</u> Perfect:

<u>I had talked</u>.   <u>He had talked</u>.

Future Perfect:

You know that *will have* is the future tense of *to have*. Therefore:

I will have (Future) + talk*ed* = <u>Future</u> Perfect:

<u>I will have talked</u>.   <u>He will have talked</u>.

PRACTICE: Mark: <u>verbs</u>, <u>subjects</u>, (adjectives), [adverbs], (prep. phrases), label: **D.O., prep., O.P., appos.** In the space after each sentence, write the person and tense of the verb.

Example: [Yesterday] (the) principal had scheduled (the) assembly (for today)
Third pers. sing., Past Perf.

1. I have already played tennis today. _____

2. By lunch time, we will have played for two hours. _____

3. Sasha had played for several hours yesterday. _____

4. Have they moved to Antioch? _____

5. Had you finished your report on time? _____

6. Really, she hadn't decided yet. _____

7. He has frequently mowed the lawn for Dad. _____

8. Have you boys finished already? _____

9. Dad will have arrived in New York by now. _____

10. We had washed Mom's car for her. _____

© 1988, 1997 J. Weston Walch, Publisher

Steps to Good Grammar

FINAL DRILL

Write on the chalkboard the abbreviations listed in the Instructions for Practice, page 213, plus **Perf.** for *Perfect*, which students are to use for persons and tenses of each verb.

Review students' sentence analyses, and instruct students to change any errors they have made and write the correct form.

This page should be completed entirely in class. If necessary, finish the first twelve sentences one day, collect papers, check, and record a score for a representative number of sentences; next day, return papers and complete the page.

This is a perfect drill sheet for students to study to prepare for the test scheduled the next day.

1. You students had a good experience yesterday. *Second pers. pl., S. Past*

2. We will have more time tomorrow. *First pers. pl., S. Fut.*

3. John talks so fast! *Third pers. sing., S. Pres.*

4. Yesterday, they talked to the mayor. *Third pers. pl., S. Past*

5. Will you bring your raincoat? *Second pers. sing., S. Fut.*

6. The assembly has ended. *Third pers. sing., Pres. Perf.*

7. They will have returned by now. *Third pers. pl., Fut. Perf.*

8. Lin had stayed behind. *Third pers. sing., Past Perf.*

9. Have your neighbors moved to their new house? *Third pers. pl., Pres. Perf.*

10. Probably the teacher hasn't decided yet. *Third pers. sing., Pres. Perf.*

11. We will have finished our projects on time. *First pers. pl., Fut. Perf.*

12. I haven't cleaned my room for a week. *First pers. sing., Pres. Perf.*

13. Will you have finished packing in time? *Second pers. sing or pl., Fut. Perf.*

14. Yesterday we practiced for an hour. *First pers. pl., S. Past*

15. Have you received your grade yet? *Second pers. sing or pl., Pres. Perf.*

16. I will call you at noon tomorrow. *First pers. sing., S. Fut.*

17. We haven't decided about the gift. *First pers. pl., Pres. Perf.*

18. Had you boys listened to the instructions? *Second pers. pl., Past Perf.*

19. They will have landed in Paris by now. *Third pers. pl., Fut. Perf.*

20. We had climbed to the top of the mountain. *First pers. pl., Past Perf.*

CORRECT USAGE — REGULAR VERBS

FINAL DRILL: Simple and Perfect Tenses

Instructions: Underline verbs twice, subjects once. At the end of each sentence, write the person and tense of the verb:

- first, second, or third person, singular or plural;
- simple or perfect;
- present, past, or future.

Example: <u>I</u> <u>have</u> my pencil today! *First pers. sing., S. Pres.*

1. You students had a good experience yesterday._____

2. We will have more time tomorrow. _____

3. John talks so fast!_____

4. Yesterday, they talked to the mayor._____

5. Will you bring your raincoat? _____

6. The assembly has ended._____

7. They will have returned by now._____

8. Lin had stayed behind. _____

9. Have your neighbors moved to their new house? _____

10. Probably the teacher hasn't decided yet._____

11. We will have finished our projects on time._____

12. I haven't cleaned my room for a week. _____

13. Will you have finished packing in time?_____

14. Yesterday we practiced for an hour. _____

15. Have you received your grade yet? _____

16. I will call you at noon tomorrow. _____

17. We haven't decided about the gift. _____

18. Had you boys listened to the instructions? _____

19. They will have landed in Paris by now. _____

20. We had climbed to the top of the mountain._____

TEST

Write these abbreviations on the chalkboard for students to use:

pers. (person)   Pres. (Present)   Perf. (Perfect)
sing. (singular)   Fut. (Future)   S. (Simple)
pl. (plural)   Past

1 point, sing. or pl.
1 point, tense

Total points: 60

Use the grading scale for 62 points on page 184.

Verb and subject identification: 40 points

Use the grading scale on page 42.

Grading suggestions:

Person and tense identification:

1 point, 1st, 2nd, or 3rd pers.

1. <u>I</u> <u>had</u> a strange experience yesterday. _First pers. sing., S. Past_

2. <u>Dad</u> <u>will</u> not <u>work</u> tomorrow. _Third pers. sing., S. Fut._

3. Those <u>people</u> <u>have</u> a new car. _Third pers. pl., S. Pres._

4. Our <u>visitors</u> <u>arrived</u> yesterday. _Third pers. pl., S. Past_

5. <u>Will</u> <u>you</u> girls <u>volunteer</u> for the job? _Second pers. pl., S. Fut._

6. <u>Gram</u> <u>will</u> <u>have</u> <u>boarded</u> the plane by now. _Third pers. sing., Fut. Perf._

7. <u>Have</u> <u>you</u> boys <u>finished</u> lunch already? _Second pers. pl., Pres. Perf._

8. The <u>Joneses</u> <u>had</u> <u>returned</u> from their vacation. _Third pers. pl., Past Perf._

9. <u>I</u> <u>will</u> <u>have</u> <u>finished</u> that book by tomorrow. _First pers. sing. Fut. Perf._

10. <u>Had</u> <u>he</u> <u>informed</u> you about the test? _Third pers. sing., Past Perf._

11. <u>They</u> <u>have</u> <u>changed</u> the dates of their vacation. _Third pers. pl., Pres. Perf._

12. <u>Lew</u> <u>has</u> an expensive new watch. _Third pers. sing., S. Pres._

13. <u>We</u> <u>had</u> <u>waited</u> for a whole hour. _First pers. pl., Past Perf._

14. Soon <u>you</u> <u>will</u> <u>have</u> <u>practiced</u> for an hour. _Second pers. sing. or pl., Fut. Perf._

15. <u>We</u> <u>have</u> always <u>walked</u> to school. _First pers. pl., Pres. Perf._

16. <u>I</u> <u>will</u> <u>call</u> you at noon tomorrow. _First pers. sing., S. Fut._

17. <u>Haven't</u> <u>you</u> <u>finished</u> packing? _Second pers. sing. or pl., Pres. Perf._

18. Maria, <u>had</u> <u>you</u> <u>walked</u> home? _Second pers. sing., Past Perf._

19. Yes, <u>we</u> <u>mailed</u> the letter yesterday. _First pers. pl., S. Past._

20. The <u>test</u> <u>ends</u> here! _Third pers. sing., S. Pres._

CORRECT USAGE — REGULAR VERBS

TEST: Simple and Perfect Tenses

Instructions: Underline verbs twice, subjects once. At the end of each sentence, write the person and tense of the verb:

- first, second, or third person, singular or plural;
- simple or perfect;
- present, past, or future.

1. I had a strange experience yesterday. _____

2. Dad will not work tomorrow. _____

3. Those people have a new car. _____

4. Our visitors arrived yesterday. _____

5. Will you girls volunteer for the job? _____

6. Gram will have boarded the plane by now. _____

7. Have you boys finished lunch already? _____

8. The Joneses had returned from their vacation. _____

9. I will have finished that book by tomorrow. _____

10. Had he informed you about the test? _____

11. They have changed the dates of their vacation. _____

12. Lew has an expensive new watch. _____

13. We had waited for a whole hour. _____

14. Soon you will have practiced for an hour. _____

15. We have always walked to school. _____

16. I will call you at noon tomorrow. _____

17. Haven't you finished packing? _____

18. Maria, had you walked home? _____

19. Yes, we mailed the letter yesterday. _____

20. The test ends here! _____

Steps to Good Grammar

PRETEST: IRREGULAR VERBS, LIST I

Remind students that pretest grades have no effect on the report card grade.

There are 21 verbs to check. Subtract 5% for each incorrect verb choice.

Before you return the pretest, distribute and read aloud page 223.

Retain the pretest until you are ready to distribute page 225.

1. Our team has (beat, beaten) theirs.

2. Lance has surely (become, became) discouraged.

3. The game has already (begun, began).

4. The rabid squirrel might have (bit, bitten) our dog.

5. The wind (blew, blowed) hard yesterday, but it has (blown, blew) harder.

6. The baseball had (broke, busted, broken) the window.

7. Have you (brang, brought, brung) your lunch today?

8. Maddy must have (came, come) early.

9. Probably Dad has already (done, did) the dishes.

10. The boys (dragged, drug) the log to the campfire.

11. Sean had (drew, drawn) a prize-winning picture.

12. The mother cat had already (drunk, drank) her milk.

13. Could he have (drove, driven) faster safely?

14. My brother has already (ate, eaten) dinner.

15. That big rock must have (fell, fallen) on the highway last night.

16. Have you or your brother ever (flew, flown) to Hawaii?

17. The water in the pond was (froze, frozen).

18. The girls must have (gone, went) to the game by now.

19. Probably they had (grown, grew) tired of waiting.

20. The thief might have (hid, hidden) the money.

CORRECT USAGE — IRREGULAR VERBS

PRETEST: Irregular Verbs, List I

Instructions: Draw two lines under all "helping" verbs and under your choice of the words in parentheses; draw one line under the subjects.

1. Our team has (beat, beaten) theirs.

2. Lance has surely (become, became) discouraged.

3. The game has already (begun, began).

4. The rabid squirrel might have (bit, bitten) our dog.

5. The wind (blew, blowed) hard yesterday, but it has (blown, blew) harder.

6. The baseball had (broke, busted, broken) the window.

7. Have you (brang, brought, brung) your lunch today?

8. Maddy must have (came, come) early.

9. Probably Dad has already (done, did) the dishes.

10. The boys (dragged, drug) the log to the campfire.

11. Sean had (drew, drawn) a prize-winning picture.

12. The mother cat had already (drunk, drank) her milk.

13. Could he have (drove, driven) faster safely?

14. My brother has already (ate, eaten) dinner.

15. That big rock must have (fell, fallen) on the highway last night.

16. Have you or your brother ever (flew, flown) to Hawaii?

17. The water in the pond was (froze, frozen).

18. The girls must have (gone, went) to the game by now.

19. Probably they had (grown, grew) tired of waiting.

20. The thief might have (hid, hidden) the money.

Steps to Good Grammar

IRREGULAR VERBS

This page is self-explanatory.

Write the definitions:

Regular verbs *add -d or -ed to the present to form the past and past participle.*

Irregular verbs *change their spelling to form the past and past participle.*

CORRECT USAGE — IRREGULAR VERBS

Irregular Verbs

Regular verbs, as you know, are verbs that add *-d* or *-ed* to the present to form the past and past participle.

Irregular verbs are verbs that change their spelling to form the past and past participle.

If you have any confusion about using irregular verbs, you can clear it up right now.

A student once said, "What difference does it make if I say, 'I have already went to the library'? People understand what I mean!" The student was right! People do understand the meaning. But many people also understand that the student, for whatever reason, has not used correct grammar. Suppose this student were to use irregular verbs incorrectly a few years later during an interview with a prospective employer. His error could plant a question in the interviewer's mind about giving him the job.

A good reply to the student's remark is that people also understand when someone says, "I have already gone to the library." What's more, no question forms in the listener's mind!

For those of you who already use irregular verbs correctly, the next few days of study can give you complete confidence in your error-free use of them.

To be is the most irregular of the irregular verbs. You already know all its changes in spelling, since you know the first eight "helping" verbs. Fortunately, you don't have to memorize that many forms for any of the other irregular verbs.

Memorize the statements that define regular and irregular verbs.

Write the definitions:

Regular verbs _____

_____

_____

Irregular verbs _____

_____

_____

To be sure that you use irregular verbs correctly, you should memorize them, being sure to say "have" with each past participle. Recognizing sound differences is helpful.

Steps to Good Grammar

IRREGULAR VERBS — LIST I

After you have distributed the list, return the students' pretests. Instruct students to compare the errors they made on the pretest with the verbs in the list.

For many students, pointing out the sound differences below is very helpful. The fact that they should use helping verbs with the soft-sounding or the *n*-ending form of the verb is easy to remember.

When you read the example words, or cite other examples in the list, make the sound differences very clear.

Simply to memorize the forms of each verb is easy for other students. In doing so, they should emphasize the sound differences:

beat	beat	*have* beaten
become	became	*have* become

Each student should *keep* his or her list!

Inform students that they will have only two drill sheets to practice with before the test. They would be wise to read this list orally several times each night to establish in their minds the correct forms.

Sound Differences

1. In using irregular verbs, if you have a choice between a word with a sharp sound and one with a soft sound, almost always:

    No helper is used with the sharp sound:

became	began	drank

    Helping verbs *are* used with the soft sound:

have become	have begun	have drunk

2. If your choice is between a word that ends with an *n* sound and one that doesn't, use a helping verb with the word that ends with the *n* sound:

beat	have beaten
blew	have blown
did	have done

CORRECT USAGE — IRREGULAR VERBS

Irregular Verbs — List I

Present (Say, "Today I...")	Past (Say, "Yesterday I...")	Past Participle (Say, "Often I have...")
beat	beat	have beaten
become	became	have become
begin	began	have begun
bite	bit	have bitten
blow	blew	have blown
break	broke (never *busted*!)	have broken
bring	brought (never *brang*!)	have brought (never *brung*!)
choose	chose	have chosen
come	came	have come
do	did	have done
**drag	dragged (never *drug*!)	have dragged
draw	drew	have drawn
drink	drank	have drunk
drive	drove	have driven
eat	ate	have eaten
fall	fell	have fallen
fly	flew	have flown
freeze	froze	have frozen
get	got (never *gots*!)	have gotten
give	gave	have given
go	went	have gone
grow	grew	have grown
hide	hid	have hidden
know	knew	have known

** *Drag,* as you can see, is not an irregular verb. However, it is often incorrectly used; therefore, it is included in this list.

Lay and *lie* seem to cause special problems. They will be studied separately.

© 1988, 1997 J. Weston Walch, Publisher

Steps to Good Grammar

DRILL 1: IRREGULAR VERBS, LIST I

Students are instructed to underline the subjects and helping verbs as well as their choices in parentheses. Underlining helping verbs is essential, since the past participle form requires their use. Recognizing the subject by underlining it gives meaning to the sentence.

**Part II introduces the form that will be used on the next page of drill.

1. The whistle (blowed, blew)! The game (began, begun)! Would our team be (beat, beaten)?

2. This storm (come, came) up so suddenly. Branches have been (broke, broken, busted) off trees, and a huge tree has (fell, fallen).

3. Aunt Edna has (became, become) upset because her garden flowers have (froze, frozen).

4. After Jennifer had (done, did) the yardwork, she had (drug, dragged) herself to the table, had (ate, eaten) a huge dinner, and had (drunk, drank) several glasses of milk.

5. Ron just (brang, brought, brung) Joe's bat home and has (gave, given) it to him.

6. The police have already (drove, driven) to the place where the money had been (hid, hidden), and have (gone, went) back to the station.

7. Mom hadn't (knew, known) that Nathan would be (given, gave) an award for the portrait he (drawed, drew).

8. The pilot must have (gotten, got) the signal to take off; she has (flew, flown) completely out of sight.

9. Because a dog had once (bit, bitten) him, the child had (grown, grew) fearful of all animals.

10. For your book report, why did you (chose, choose) the book I had (chose, chosen)?

---

1. Our team has ___*beaten*___ theirs several times. (beat)

2. Dolly must have ___*become*___ very frightened. (become)

3. I have ___*begun*___ my homework. (begin)

4. The wind has ___*blown*___ really hard today. (blow)

5. The noise could have ___*come*___ from there. (come)

CORRECT USAGE — IRREGULAR VERBS

DRILL 1: Irregular Verbs — List I

Part I. Instructions: Draw two lines under helping verbs and under your choice of the words in parentheses: draw one line under the subjects.

1. The whistle (blowed, blew)! The game (began, begun)! Would our team be (beat, beaten)?

2. This storm (come, came) up so suddenly. Branches have been (broke, broken, busted) off trees, and a huge tree has (fell, fallen).

3. Aunt Edna has (became, become) upset because her garden flowers have (froze, frozen).

4. After Jennifer had (done, did) the yardwork, she had (drug, dragged) herself to the table, had (ate, eaten) a huge dinner, and had (drunk, drank) several glasses of milk.

5. Ron just (brang, brought, brung) Joe's bat home and has (gave, given) it to him.

6. The police have already (drove, driven) to the place where the money had been (hid, hidden) and have (gone, went) back to the station.

7. Mom hadn't (knew, known) that Nathan would be (given, gave) an award for the portrait he (drawed, drew).

8. The pilot must have (gotten, got) the signal to take off; she has (flew, flown) completely out of sight.

9. Because a dog had once (bit, bitten) him, the child had (grown, grew) fearful of all animals.

10. For your book report, why did you (chose, choose) the book I had (chose, chosen)?

Part II. Instructions: Draw two lines under helping verbs, one under the subjects. In the blank, write the correct form of the verb in parentheses.

1. Our team has _____ theirs several times. (beat)

2. Dolly must have _____ very frightened. (become)

3. I have _____ my homework. (begin)

4. The wind has _____ really hard today. (blow)

5. The noise could have _____ from there. (come)

Steps to Good Grammar

DRILL 2: IRREGULAR VERBS, LIST I

The test will be in this form. Students will be expected to know the three principal parts of each verb. They should memorize them and know how to spell them.

Students frequently make errors in spelling the past participle. To help them learn the correct spelling, instruct students to analyze aloud each sentence, as in this example:

Sentence 1: The principal parts of *become* are:

'Today I' *become.* 'Yesterday I' *became.*

'Often I' *have become.*

Draw one line under *I,* draw two lines under *had,* write *b-e-c-o-m-e.*

Draw one line under Susie, write *b-e-c-a-m-e.*

This will take time, but every student should then hear, write, and spell the correct words.

This drill could be sent home with the students to use as a study sheet in preparation for the test scheduled the next day.

1. (become) When I had _____ *become* _____ frightened, Susie _____ *became* _____ frightened.

2. (begin) It had _____ *begun* _____ to snow soon after the wind _____ *began* _____ to blow.

3. (know) Hadn't you _____ *known* _____ about the accident? I _____ *knew* _____ about it.

4. (eat) The family had already _____ *eaten* _____, so I _____ *ate* _____ by myself.

5. (draw) I just _____ *drew* _____ my map; have you _____ *drawn* _____ yours?

6. (hide) Mom _____ *hid* _____ some of the eggs; Dad has _____ *hidden* _____ the rest.

7. (grow) My horse has certainly _____ *grown* _____ skittish.

8. (go) Sis has just _____ *gone* _____ to the mall; I _____ *went* _____ yesterday.

9. (give) I _____ *gave* _____ my report today; Pat had _____ *given* _____ hers yesterday.

10. (fly) Have you ever _____ *flown* _____ to L.A.? We _____ *flew* _____ there last week.

11. (fall, freeze) My dog had _____ *fallen* _____ into the lake and had nearly _____ *frozen* _____.

12. (drive) The man _____ *drove* _____ rather fast; he should have _____ *driven* _____ more slowly.

13. (drink) Kip had _____ *drunk* _____ his Coke, so I _____ *drank* _____ mine quickly.

14. (drag) The bicycle was _____ *dragged* _____ a long distance.

15. (draw) Kai has _____ *drawn* _____ a picture like the one you _____ *drew* _____ yesterday.

16. (do) Al didn't _____ *do* _____ his homework yesterday; has he _____ *done* _____ it today?

17. (come) Tony _____ *came* _____ in late last night; he has _____ *come* _____ in late again.

18. (break) Lara certainly has not _____ *broken* _____ her promise.

19. (bring) Celie _____ *brought* _____ cheese; Roy has _____ *brought* _____ crackers.

20. (get, blow) I had _____ *gotten* _____ chilly when the wind had _____ *blown* _____ so hard.

CORRECT USAGE — IRREGULAR VERBS

DRILL 2: Irregular Verbs — List I

Instructions: Draw two lines under helping verbs, one under the subjects. In the blank, write the correct form of the verb in parentheses.

1. (become) When I had _____ frightened, Susie _____ frightened.

2. (begin) It had _____ to snow soon after the wind _____ to blow.

3. (know) Hadn't you _____ about the accident? I _____ about it.

4. (eat) The family had already _____, so I _____ by myself.

5. (draw) I just _____ my map; have you _____ yours?

6. (hide) Mom _____ some of the eggs; Dad has _____ the rest.

7. (grow) My horse has certainly _____ skittish.

8. (go) Sis has just _____ to the mall; I _____ yesterday.

9. (give) I _____ my report today; Pat had _____ hers yesterday.

10. (fly) Have you ever _____ to L.A.? We _____ there last week.

11. (fall, freeze) My dog had _____ into the lake and had nearly _____ .

12. (drive) The man _____ rather fast; he should have _____ more slowly.

13. (drink) Kip had _____ his Coke, so I _____ mine quickly.

14. (drag) The bicycle was _____ a long distance.

15. (draw) Kai has _____ a picture like the one you _____ yesterday.

16. (do) Al didn't _____ his homework yesterday; has he _____ it today?

17. (come) Tony _____ in late last night; he has _____ in late again.

18. (break) Lara certainly has not _____ her promise.

19. (bring) Celie _____ cheese; Roy has _____ crackers.

20. (get, blow) I had _____ chilly when the wind had _____ so hard.

Steps to Good Grammar

TEST: IRREGULAR VERBS, LIST I

Suggested grading:

33 written verbs
   -2 points each error   66% of grade

23 helping verbs underlined
   -1 point each error   23%

33 subjects underlined
   -¼ point each error   8%
                                ──────
                             97 % total

-½ point each spelling error

1. Aunt Maggie had ___*begun*___ (begin) to worry just before we ___*came*___ (come) in.

2. The wind had certainly ___*blown*___ (blow) hard; not only had branches ___*broken*___ (break) off trees, but also whole trees had ___*fallen*___ (fall).

3. The family had already ___*eaten*___ (eat) when I had finally ___*gotten*___ (get) home. Dad had ___*done*___ (do) the dishes and Mom had ___*gone*___ (go) out.

4. I ___*brought*___ my tennis racket. Why haven't you ___*brought*___ yours? (bring)

5. Someone has ___*bitten*___ (bite) a chunk out of this cookie. Probably my little brother ___*did*___ (do) it!

6. Dad ___*became*___ (become) rather upset when we ___*broke*___ (break) the news to him.

7. The little boys had ___*grown*___ (grow) very tired by the time they ___*dragged*___ (drag) themselves into camp. They were ___*given*___ (give) some hot chocolate which they ___*drank*___ (drink) slowly.

8. The team had certainly ___*become*___ (become) discouraged when they were ___*beaten*___ (beat) by the other team.

9. Arnie had not been ___*chosen*___ (choose) for the team.

10. Dad ___*drove*___ faster than he had ever ___*driven*___ before. (drive)

11. After I had ___*drawn*___ (draw) my map I had ___*gone*___ (go) back to the classroom.

12. Had you ___*known*___ (know) that someone had ___*hidden*___ (hide) my book?

13. Why haven't you ___*done*___ (do) your homework? You should have ___*begun*___ (begin) right after dinner.

14. The mouse ___*froze*___ (freeze) in terror when the owl ___*flew*___ (fly) overhead.

15. You haven't ___*drunk*___ (drink) your orange juice!

CORRECT USAGE — IRREGULAR VERBS

TEST: Irregular Verbs — List I

Instructions: Draw two lines under helping verbs, one under the subjects. In the blank, write the correct form of the verb in parentheses.

1. Aunt Maggie had _____ (begin) to worry just before we _____ (come) in.

2. The wind had certainly _____ (blow) hard; not only had branches _____ (break) off trees, but also whole trees had _____ (fall).

3. The family had already _____ (eat) when I had finally _____ (get) home. Dad had _____ (do) the dishes and Mom had _____ (go) out.

4. I _____ my tennis racket. Why haven't you _____ yours? (bring)

5. Someone has _____ (bite) a chunk out of this cookie. Probably my little brother _____ (do) it!

6. Dad _____ (become) rather upset when we _____ (break) the news to him.

7. The little boys had _____ (grow) very tired by the time they _____ (drag) themselves into camp. They were _____ (give) some hot chocolate which they _____ (drink) slowly.

8. The team had certainly _____ (become) discouraged when they were _____ (beat) by the other team.

9. Arnie had not been _____ (choose) for the team.

10. Dad _____ faster than he had ever _____ before. (drive)

11. After I had _____ (draw) my map I had _____ (go) back to the classroom.

12. Had you _____ (know) that someone had _____ (hide) my book?

13. Why haven't you _____ (do) your homework? You should have _____ (begin) right after dinner.

14. The mouse _____ (freeze) in terror when the owl _____ (fly) overhead.

15. You haven't _____ (drink) your orange juice!

Steps to Good Grammar

TO LAY AND *TO LIE*

The only way for students to clarify the confusion they all seem to have about these two verbs is for them to memorize, firmly and finally, the two complete sets.

Lay isn't really difficult, since all forms have the long-*a* sound. Students need to have this pointed out.

Students' resistance to using *lay* and *have lain* is difficult to overcome. Point out the long-*i* in *lie, lies, lying* and the long-*a* sound in *lay* and *have lain*.

After the correct forms have been established, instruct students to take turns reading the sentences aloud. Repeatedly hearing the correct sound should help.

1. Yesterday, <u>Dad</u> __*laid*__ the plank across the stream.
2. <u>Tom</u> always __*lays*__ his trumpet in the case carefully.
3. <u>Oscar</u> <u>had</u> carelessly __*laid*__ his wallet there.
4. <u>Mom</u> <u>was</u> __*laying*__ the baby in his crib.
5. Usually <u>Mary</u> __*lays*__ her books on the table.
6. Yesterday, <u>Joe</u> __*laid*__ the injured puppy in its basket.
7. <u>Had</u> your <u>brother</u> __*laid*__ his billfold there?
8. Why <u>are</u> <u>you</u> __*laying*__ your coat there?

1. <u>I</u> <u>will</u> __*lie*__ on our patio to get a tan.
2. <u>Randy</u> __*lay*__ in bed too long and missed the bus.
3. The <u>baby</u> <u>was</u> __*lying*__ peacefully in her crib.
4. How long <u>had</u> the old <u>letter</u> __*lain*__ on the attic floor?
5. <u>Dad</u> often __*lies*__ down after work.

CORRECT USAGE — IRREGULAR VERBS

Distinguishing Between *To Lay* and *To Lie*

To lay **means** *"to put."*

MEMORIZE THE PRINCIPAL PARTS:

    lay — simple present

    lays — *-s* is added for third person singular, simple present

    laying — *-ing* is added for present participle

    laid — *-y* is changed to *i* in spelling simple past

    have laid — past participle

REMEMBER: Present and past participles use helping verbs.

PRACTICE: Draw two lines under helping verbs, one line under subjects. In the blanks, write the correct form of *lay* (thinking the correct form of *put*).

1. Yesterday, Dad _____ the plank across the stream.

2. Tom always _____ his trumpet in the case carefully.

3. Oscar had carelessly _____ his wallet there.

4. Mom was _____ the baby in his crib.

5. Usually Mary _____ her books on the table.

6. Yesterday, Joe _____ the injured puppy in its basket.

7. Had your brother _____ his billfold there?

8. Why are you _____ your coat there?

To lie **means** *"to rest."*

MEMORIZE THE PRINCIPAL PARTS:

    lie — simple present

    lies — *-s* is added for third person singular, simple present

    lying — change *-ie* to *-y* in spelling present participle

    lay — thoroughly memorize simple past

    have lain — thoroughly memorize past participle

REMEMBER: Present and past participles use helping verbs.

PRACTICE: Draw two lines under helping verbs, one line under subjects. In the blanks, write the correct form of *lie* (thinking the correct form of *rest*).

1. I will _____ on our patio to get a tan.

2. Randy _____ in bed too long and missed the bus.

3. The baby was _____ peacefully in her crib.

4. How long had the old letter _____ on the attic floor?

5. Dad often _____ down after work.

Steps to Good Grammar

TO LAY AND *TO LIE* (continued)

Read, or call on students to read slowly, the sample sentences.

In the practice, sentences 1-5, use forms of *lie*; sentences 6-10 use forms of *lay*.

Sentence 14: Students may question "Our farm lies (rests) just over the hill." Point out that "Our farm lays (puts) just over the hill" doesn't make sense.

Sentence 15: The first verb is a form of *lie;* the second, a form of *lay.* The same is true of sentence 24.

Sentence 16: *Missed* requires *lay*, the past tense of *lie.*

If reading sentences that use forms of *lie* seems helpful, instruct students to circle the following sentence numbers and take turns reading the sentences: 1-5, 11, 13, 14, 16, 18, 21, 22, 23, 25. You may wish to point out to students that *lie* takes no D.O., while *lay* does take a D.O. Students may take this page home to study in preparation for the test scheduled the next day.

1. Soon I will _____ *lie* _____ down.
2. My coat is _____ *lying* _____ on the chair.
3. Every day Dad _____ *lies* _____ down after work.
4. Yesterday I _____ *lay* _____ in the sun too long.
5. Our dog has often _____ *lain* _____ on the front porch.
6. Dad will _____ *lay* _____ the baby in her crib.
7. Yesterday, Ron _____ *laid* _____ his bike there.
8. Tina always _____ *lays* _____ her purse there.
9. Ken was _____ *laying* _____ the puppy in its basket.
10. Had you _____ *laid* _____ your report on my desk?
11. You must have _____ *lain* _____ in the sun too long.
12. Please don't _____ *(you) lay* _____ your wet coat there.
13. When the phone rang, Pete was _____ *lying* _____ down.
14. Our farm _____ *lies* _____ just over the hill.
15. Your book has _____ *lain* _____ there ever since you _____ *laid* _____ it there.
16. At camp I often _____ *lay* _____ in bed too long and missed breakfast.
17. Don must have _____ *laid* _____ his racket on the bench.
18. *(you)* Don't just _____ *lie* _____ there and watch! Help me!
19. Why are you _____ *laying* _____ your keys in the refrigerator?
20. Jill had _____ *laid* _____ her homework on the teacher's desk.
21. The baby is _____ *lying* _____ there so peacefully.
22. Grandma is _____ *lying* _____ down; she often _____ *lies* _____ down after lunch.
23. Frightened, I _____ *lay* _____ there without moving.
24. Amy's coat was _____ *lying* _____ right where she had _____ *laid* _____ it.
25. How long has that money _____ *lain* _____ there?

CORRECT USAGE — IRREGULAR VERBS

Distinguishing Between *To Lay* and *To Lie* (continued)

Principal Parts: *TO LIE*
(say "rest")

I **lie** down to rest.
Dad **lies** down after work.
Mom **is lying** down.
Yesterday I **lay** on the beach.
Often I **have lain** on the beach.

Principal Parts: *TO LAY*
(say "put")

I **lay** my books here every day.
Dad **lays** his wallet there usually.
Mom **is laying** her keys there.
Yesterday I **laid** my book there.
Often I **have laid** my book there.

PRACTICE: In the blanks, write the correct form of *lie* or *lay*. Draw two lines under helping verbs that "help" *lie* or *lay*. Draw one line under the subjects.

1. Soon I will _____ down.

2. My coat is _____ on the chair.

3. Every day Dad _____ down after work.

4. Yesterday I _____ in the sun too long.

5. Our dog has often _____ on the front porch.

6. Dad will _____ the baby in her crib.

7. Yesterday, Ron _____ his bike there.

8. Tina always _____ her purse there.

9. Ken was _____ the puppy in its basket.

10. Had you _____ your report on my desk?

11. You must have _____ in the sun too long.

12. Please don't _____ your wet coat there.

13. When the phone rang, Pete was _____ down.

14. Our farm _____ just over the hill.

15. Your book has _____ there ever since you _____ it there.

16. At camp I often _____ in bed too long and missed breakfast.

17. Don must have _____ his racket on the bench.

18. Don't just _____ there and watch! Help me!

19. Why are you _____ your keys in the refrigerator?

20. Jill had _____ her homework on the teacher's desk.

21. The baby is _____ there so peacefully.

22. Grandma is _____ down; she often _____ down after lunch.

23. Frightened, I _____ there without moving.

24. Amy's coat was _____ right where she had _____ it.

25. How long has that money _____ there?

Steps to Good Grammar

TEST: *LIE* AND *LAY*

This reproducible page contains two copies of one half-page drill/test. Cut each duplicated page in half; give each student one half-page.

Suggested grading:

	Percentage of Grade:
5 points each written verb (15)	75 %
-½ point each spelling error	
2 points each underlined helping verb (10)	20 %
½ point each underlined subject (13)	6½%
	101½%

1. Many more <u>leaves</u> <u>were</u> *lying* on the ground this morning than <u>had</u> *lain* there yesterday.

2. <u>Dad</u> <u>is</u> *laying* the rest of the patio bricks; <u>he</u> *laid* most of them yesterday.

3. <u>Meg and I</u> *lay* in the sun too long yesterday.

4. We're nearly there; our <u>farm</u> *lies* just around this curve.

5. Yesterday, <u>Granddad</u> *lay* down for a nap; <u>he</u> hasn't *lain* down at all today.

6. <u>I</u> <u>have</u> *laid* the towel on the beach; now <u>I</u> <u>shall</u> *lie* on it.

7. <u>Dan</u> <u>was</u> *laying* the puppy in its box.

8. <u>Mom</u> always *lays* her briefcase there when she comes in.

9. <u>Great-Grandmother</u> <u>must have</u> *laid* the diary there; <u>it</u> <u>has</u> *lain* there ever since.

10. (you) Don't *lay* your wet raincoat there.

CORRECT USAGE — IRREGULAR VERBS

TEST: Use of *Lie* and *Lay*

Instructions: In the blanks, write the correct forms of *lie* and *lay*. Draw two lines under verbs that "help" *lie* or *lay;* draw one line under subjects.

1. Many more leaves were _____ on the ground this morning than had _____ there yesterday.

2. Dad is _____ the rest of the patio bricks; he _____ most of them yesterday.

3. Meg and I _____ in the sun too long yesterday.

4. We're nearly there; our farm _____ just around this curve.

5. Yesterday, Granddad _____ down for a nap; he hasn't _____ down at all today.

6. I have _____ the towel on the beach; now I shall _____ on it.

7. Dan was _____ the puppy in its box.

8. Mom always _____ her briefcase there when she comes in.

9. Great-Grandmother must have _____ the diary there; it has _____ there ever since.

10. Don't _____ your wet raincoat there.

NAME _____ DATE _____ 237

CORRECT USAGE — IRREGULAR VERBS

TEST: Use of *Lie* and *Lay*

Instructions: In the blanks, write the correct forms of *lie* and *lay*. Draw two lines under verbs that "help" *lie* or *lay;* draw one line under subjects.

1. Many more leaves were _____ on the ground this morning than had _____ there yesterday.

2. Dad is _____ the rest of the patio bricks; he _____ most of them yesterday.

3. Meg and I _____ in the sun too long yesterday.

4. We're nearly there; our farm _____ just around this curve.

5. Yesterday, Granddad _____ down for a nap; he hasn't _____ down at all today.

6. I have _____ the towel on the beach; now I shall _____ on it.

7. Dan was _____ the puppy in its box.

8. Mom always _____ her briefcase there when she comes in.

9. Great-Grandmother must have _____ the diary there; it has _____ there ever since.

10. Don't _____ _____ your wet raincoat there.

Steps to Good Grammar

PRETEST: IRREGULAR VERBS, LIST II

Grading suggestions:

Remind students that the purpose of this pretest is for them to find out which of the irregular verbs they should be sure to study. Their score has nothing to do with their report card grade.

Sentence 3: had yelled has nothing to do with the irregular verbs; give it no point value. However, We is the subject of had run, so it is counted.

Return the pretests after you have distributed Irregular Verbs — List II.

	Percentage of grade:
33 verb choices — 2 points each	66 %
23 helping verbs — 1 point each	23 %
29 subjects — ¼ point each	7¼%
	96¼%

1. I had (rode, ridden) my bike to school and arrived just after the bell had (rang, rung).

2. I (seen, saw) Brad when he (sneaked, snuck) out of the shop.

3. We had yelled at the man and had (run, ran) toward him, or he might (of, have) (stole, stealed, stolen) the car.

4. Glenn has (swore, sworn) that another student had (took, taken) his paper, had (tore, torn) it in two, and had (throwed, thrown, threw) it into the wastebasket.

5. Today Mark (swum, swam) faster than he has ever (swum, swam) before.

6. Ellen must have (set, sat) there for an hour and hadn't (spoke, spoken) to anyone.

7. Had your dad (saw, seen) the boat when it (sunk, sank), or had it (sunk, sank) before he got there?

8. Have you (set, sat) the casserole on the table yet?

9. I had (sprung, sprang) to one side just in time when Judd carelessly (swung, swang) the bat.

10. Ty hadn't (took, taken) the money; the thief (stole, stealed) it.

11. I had (written, writen, wrote) my sister a note telling her that I had (wore, worn) her coat.

12. Has the chorus ever before (sung, sang) the song they (sung, sang) today?

13. The little girl had (shrank, shrunk) back when the huge dog had (rose, risen) to its feet.

14. Dad had been noticeably (shook, shaken) when Shawn had (showed, shown) him his report card.

15. After my sweater (shrunk, shrank), I (took, tooked) it back.

CORRECT USAGE — IRREGULAR VERBS

PRETEST: Irregular Verbs, List II

Instructions: Draw two lines under all "helping" verbs and under your choice of the words in parentheses; draw one line under the subjects.

1. I had (rode, ridden) my bike to school and arrived just after the bell had (rang, rung).

2. I (seen, saw) Brad when he (sneaked, snuck) out of the shop.

3. We had yelled at the man and had (run, ran) toward him, or he might (of, have) (stole, stealed, stolen) the car.

4. Glenn has (swore, sworn) that another student had (took, taken) his paper, had (tore, torn) it in two, and had (throwed, thrown, threw) it into the wastebasket.

5. Today Mark (swum, swam) faster than he has ever (swum, swam) before.

6. Ellen must have (set, sat) there for an hour and hadn't (spoke, spoken) to anyone.

7. Had your dad (saw, seen) the boat when it (sunk, sank), or had it (sunk, sank) before he got there?

8. Have you (set, sat) the casserole on the table yet?

9. I had (sprung, sprang) to one side just in time when Judd carelessly (swung, swang) the bat.

10. Ty hadn't (took, taken) the money; the thief (stole, stealed) it.

11. I had (written, writen, wrote) my sister a note telling her that I had (wore, worn) her coat.

12. Has the chorus ever before (sung, sang) the song they (sung, sang) today?

13. The little girl had (shrank, shrunk) back when the huge dog had (rose, risen) to its feet.

14. Dad had been noticeably (shook, shaken) when Shawn had (showed, shown) him his report card.

15. After my sweater (shrunk, shrank), I (took, tooked) it back.

Steps to Good Grammar

IRREGULAR VERBS — LIST II

After you have distributed this list, return the students' pretests so they can compare the errors they made with the verbs in the list.

Emphasize to the students:

1. Hearing the sound differences (see page 224):

   Soft and sharp sounds:

   > sang, sank, swam
   > have sung, have sunk, have swum

   Non-*n* and *n* endings:

   > saw, spoke wrote
   > have seen, have spoken, had written

2. Saying "Today I...," "Yesterday I...," "Often I have..." as they read or memorize the words.

3. Spelling correctly.

4. Not losing the list!

5. Learning these usage **Reminders**:

   (a) *learn* means "to acquire information":
   > We had **learned.**

   teach means "to give instruction":
   > The teacher had **taught** us.

   (b) *bring* means motion toward the speaker:
   > "**Bring** your book to class."

   take means motion away from the speaker:
   > "**Take** them when you leave."

   (c) *have* is a helping verb, *of* is a preposition:
   > You should (~~of~~, **have**) come with us.

CORRECT USAGE — IRREGULAR VERBS

Irregular Verbs — List II

Present	Past	Past Participle
(Say, "Today I...")	(Say, "Yesterday I...")	(Say, "Often I have...")
ride	rode	have ridden
ring	rang	have rung
rise	rose	have risen
run	ran	have run
see	saw	have seen
set (put)	set	have set
shake	shook	have shaken
show	showed	have shown
shrink	shrank	have shrunk
sing	sang	have sung
sink	sank	have sunk
sit (rest)	sat	have sat
**sneak	sneaked	have sneaked
	(not *snuck*!)	
speak	spoke	have spoken
spring	sprang	have sprung
steal	stole	have stolen
swear	swore	have sworn
swim	swam	have swum
swing	*swung*	have swung
take	took	have taken
tear	tore	have torn
throw	threw	have thrown
wear	wore	have worn
write	wrote	have written

** *Sneak* is an often incorrectly used *regular* verb.

© 1988, 1997 J. Weston Walch, Publisher

Steps to Good Grammar

DRILL 1: IRREGULAR VERBS, LIST II

This page of drill includes only half of the words on List II — from *ride* through *sneak*.

Convince students that "snuck" really is *not* correct.

After you check students' choices, instruct the students to read aloud each complete sentence.

This formula is really helpful to many students who have spelling problems:

Sentence 1: Last week my friend had r-i-d-d-e-n her bike to my house; yesterday I r-o-d-e mine to her house.

1. Last week my friend had (rode, ridden) her bike to my house; yesterday I (rode, ridden) mine to her house.

2. The bell (rung, rang) late last period; it had never (rung, rang) late before.

3. Has the river ever (rose, risen) this high before? It (rised, rose) higher last year.

4. Tom (ran, run) a good race yesterday, but he had (ran, run) better.

5. Have you (seen, saw) a UFO? I thought I (seen, saw) one once.

6. The dog had (set, sat) on the pad which we had (set, sat) out for him.

7. Everyone had (shaken, shook) the speaker's hand. I (shaked, shook) her hand first.

8. Have you (showed, shown) him your ring? I (showed, shown) him mine.

9. The chorus (sung, sang) the song they had (sung, sang) at the assembly.

10. Has your sweater (shrank, shrunk)? Mine (shrank, shrunk) a little.

11. The boat (sank, sunk) this morning, but Dad thought it had (sank, sunk) last night.

12. We had (sneaked, snuck) out as they (sneaked, snuck) in.

13. Bella could have (rode, ridden) with us, but she (rode, ridden) with them.

14. His voice (sunk, sank) to a whisper.

15. I was somewhat (shook, shaken) when the telephone (rung, rang).

16. I had (shrank, shrunk) back into the shadows as the strange man (snuck, sneaked) in.

17. Geraldo had (rode, ridden) his horse that day, but we hadn't (saw, seen) him.

18. Has Dad (showed, shown) the inspector how high the river had (risen, rose)?

19. Doria had (ran, run) in and (set, sat) down.

20. I hadn't (sang, sung) because they hadn't (sang, sung).

CORRECT USAGE — IRREGULAR VERBS

DRILL 1: Irregular Verbs, List II

Instructions: Draw two lines under all helping verbs and under your choice of words in parentheses; draw one line under the subjects.

1. Last week my friend had (rode, ridden) her bike to my house; yesterday I (rode, ridden) mine to her house.

2. The bell (rung, rang) late last period; it had never (rung, rang) late before.

3. Has the river ever (rose, risen) this high before? It (rised, rose) higher last year.

4. Tom (ran, run) a good race yesterday, but he had (ran, run) better.

5. Have you (seen, saw) a UFO? I thought I (seen, saw) one once.

6. The dog had (set, sat) on the pad which we had (set, sat) out for him.

7. Everyone had (shaken, shook) the speaker's hand. I (shaked, shook) her hand first.

8. Have you (showed, shown) him your ring? I (showed, shown) him mine.

9. The chorus (sung, sang) the song they had (sung, sang) at the assembly.

10. Has your sweater (shrank, shrunk)? Mine (shrank, shrunk) a little.

11. The boat (sank, sunk) this morning, but Dad thought it had (sank, sunk) last night.

12. We had (sneaked, snuck) out as they (sneaked, snuck) in.

13. Bella could have (rode, ridden) with us, but she (rode, ridden) with them.

14. His voice (sunk, sank) to a whisper.

15. I was somewhat (shook, shaken) when the telephone (rung, rang).

16. I had (shrank, shrunk) back into the shadows as the strange man (snuck, sneaked) in.

17. Geraldo had (rode, ridden) his horse that day, but we hadn't (saw, seen) him.

18. Has Dad (showed, shown) the inspector how high the river had (risen, rose)?

19. Doria had (ran, run) in and (set, sat) down.

20. I hadn't (sang, sung) because they hadn't (sang, sung).

© 1988, 1997 J. Weston Walch, Publisher

Steps to Good Grammar

DRILL 2: IRREGULAR VERBS, LIST II

This drill includes verbs from the last half of List II — from *speak* through *write*.

Use the spelling and sound-reinforcing second reading of the sentences after you check verb forms.

Continue to check a representative section of all the drill and practice pages. When students know that they're earning grades on their daily work, they tend to concentrate more and really learn.

1. Ally has not (spoke, spoken) to me today, although she (spoke, speaked) to you.

2. He hadn't (stole, stoled, stolen) the money; he never (stole, stealed, stoled) anything.

3. Derek has never (took, taken) anything from anyone.

4. Huck (swore, sworn) not to tell the secret because Tom had (swore, sworn) not to tell.

5. Yesterday I (swung, swang) across the creek on that rope. Have you (swung, swang) on it?

6. I must have (tore, tored, torn) the page.

7. My sister (wore, worn) the coat, so I could not (of, have) (wore, worn) it.

8. Was the trap *sprung* ? A fox just *sprang* away from it. (sprung, sprang)

9. The paper carrier *threw* the paper carefully today; yesterday he had *thrown* it on the roof. (throwed, threw, thrown)

10. I *wrote* my report early because I have usually *written* it late. (wrote, written)

11. I *swam* in their pool yesterday; have you ever *swum* in it? (swum, swam)

12. I have *taken* to the library the book that I *took* to school with me. (took, taken, taked)

13. Mom thought she *tore* the page, but Dad said he had *torn* it. (tore, tored, torn)

14. Samantha *swam* twenty laps today; yesterday she had *swum* twenty-two. (swum, swam)

15. Why have you *worn* the same costume you *wore* last year? (wore, worn)

CORRECT USAGE — IRREGULAR VERBS

DRILL 2: Irregular Verbs, List II

Instructions: Draw two lines under all helping verbs and under your choice of words in parentheses, 1–8; in the blanks, write the correct word in parentheses at the end of the sentences; underline the subjects of your verb choices once.

1. Ally has not (spoke, spoken) to me today, although she (spoke, speaked) to you.

2. He hadn't (stole, stoled, stolen) the money; he never (stole, stealed, stoled) anything.

3. Derek has never (took, taken) anything from anyone.

4. Huck (swore, sworn) not to tell the secret because Tom had (swore, sworn) not to tell.

5. Yesterday I (swung, swang) across the creek on that rope. Have you (swung, swang) on it?

6. I must have (tore, tored, torn) the page.

7. My sister (wore, worn) the coat, so I could not (of, have) (wore, worn) it.

8. Was the trap _____? A fox just _____ away from it. (sprung, sprang)

9, The paper carrier _____ the paper carefully today; yesterday he had _____ it on the roof. (throwed, threw, thrown)

10. I _____ my report early because I have usually _____ it late. (wrote, written)

11. I _____ in their pool yesterday; have you ever _____ in it? (swum, swam)

12. I have _____ to the library the book that I _____ to school with me. (took, taken, taked)

13. Mom thought she _____ the page, but Dad said he had _____ it. (tore, tored, torn)

14. Samantha _____ twenty laps today; yesterday she had _____ twenty-two. (swum, swam)

15. Why have you _____ the same costume you _____ last year? (wore, worn)

Steps to Good Grammar

FINAL DRILL: IRREGULAR VERBS, LIST II

Students should be sure they have shown the correct forms on this page so they can use it to study for the test scheduled the next day.

1. Have you ever _ridden_ Mike's motorcycle? I _rode_ it once. (ride)

2. The telephone had _rung_ at the exact moment the doorbell _rang_. (ring)

3. We _saw_ a UFO yesterday. Have you ever _seen_ one? (see)

4. Jean has often _sat_ there; she _sat_ there yesterday. (set, sat)

5. Paolo had _shown_ Denny how to throw a lasso, and yesterday Denny _showed_ me. (show)

6. Has the river ever _risen_ as high as it _rose_ today? (rise)

7. I _shook_ my brother to wake him up after Dad had _shaken_ me to wake me up. (shake)

8. Garfield could (of, have) (run, ran) much faster.

9. Kelsey has (swore, sworn) that my sweater hadn't (shrunken, shrank, shrunk) when she (wore, worn) it last week.

10. The girl (set, sat) down with relief after she had (sung, sang).

11. Alex had (spoke, spoken) softly to me as he (snuck, sneaked) out.

12. If we had (took, taken) the other road, we would (of, have) (throwed, thrown, threw) him off our trail.

13. The boys had (wrote, written) me a note saying that they had (swum, swam) in our pool.

14. The thief must have (sunk, sank) the boat right after he had (stoled, stole, stolen) it.

15. Mom (took, taked) me to the doctor to see if I had (tore, torn) a ligament.

CORRECT USAGE — IRREGULAR VERBS

FINAL DRILL: Irregular Verbs, List II

Part I. Instructions: Draw two lines under helping verbs, one under the subjects. Using the verb in parentheses, write the correct form in the blanks.

1. Have you ever _____ Mike's motorcycle? I _____ it once. (ride)

2. The telephone had _____ at the exact moment the doorbell _____ . (ring)

3. We _____ a UFO yesterday. Have you ever _____ one? (see)

4. Jean has often _____ there; she _____ there yesterday. (set, sat)

5. Paolo had _____ Denny how to throw a lasso, and yesterday Denny _____ me. (show)

6. Has the river ever _____ as high as it _____ today? (rise)

7. I _____ my brother to wake him up after Dad had _____ me to wake me up. (shake)

Part II. Instructions: Draw two lines under helping verbs and your choice in parentheses. Draw one line under the subjects.

8. Garfield could (of, have) (run, ran) much faster.

9. Kelsey has (swore, sworn) that my sweater hadn't (shrunken, shrank, shrunk) when she (wore, worn) it last week.

10. The girl (set, sat) down with relief after she had (sung, sang).

11. Alex had (spoke, spoken) softly to me as he (snuck, sneaked) out.

12. If we had (took, taken) the other road, we would (of, have) (throwed, thrown, threw) him off our trail.

13. The boys had (wrote, written) me a note saying that they had (swum, swam) in our pool.

14. The thief must have (sunk, sank) the boat right after he had (stoled, stole, stolen) it.

15. Mom (took, taked) me to the doctor to see if I had (tore, torn) a ligament.

Steps to Good Grammar

TEST: IRREGULAR VERBS, LIST II

Sentence 4: Point out that he didn't know does not need to be underlined.

Sentence 15: Point out that I told does not need to be underlined.

Grading suggestions:

		% of test
31 written verbs — 2½ points each		77½
18 helping verbs underlined — 1 point each		18
26 subject words underlined — ¼ point each		6½
(-½ point each spelling error)		102

or 31 written verbs — 3 points each: 99%

¼ point extra credit for each helping verb and subject underlined

1. My <u>dog</u> <u>had</u> *sprung* out of the bushes just before the <u>fox</u> *sprang* out. (spring)

2. In the accident, <u>Don</u> <u>was</u> really *shaken* up. (shake)

3. <u>Lee</u> <u>must have</u> *run* faster today than <u>he</u> *ran* yesterday. (run)

4. <u>Becky</u> *saw* him do it; he didn't know <u>she</u> <u>had</u> *seen* him. (see)

5. The <u>teacher</u> <u>had</u> *shown* Ted the solution; then <u>he</u> *showed* us. (show)

6. <u>Mike</u> *threw* the newspaper carefully today; <u>he</u> <u>had</u> *thrown* it carelessly yesterday. (throw)

7. <u>Lynn</u> *wrote* a letter last night; <u>she</u> <u>has</u> just *written* another. (write)

8. The <u>phone</u> *rang* ten times this morning; <u>it</u> <u>has</u> just *rung* again. (ring)

9. The <u>boys' chorus</u> just *sang*; the <u>girls' chorus</u> <u>had</u> *sung* earlier. (sing)

10. The "ghost" <u>ship</u> *sank* right where other <u>ships</u> <u>have</u> *sunk*. (sink)

11. The strange <u>man</u> *shrank* (shrank, shrunk) back into the shadows and *sneaked* away. (snuck, sneaked)

12. <u>Dad</u> <u>had</u> *swung* (swung, swang) into the slow lane and <u>had</u> *taken* (took, taken) the off-ramp.

13. <u>I</u> <u>would</u> *have* (of, have) *sworn* (swore, sworn) Lex <u>couldn't</u> *have* (have, of) *swum* (swum, swam) so far.

14. The <u>teacher</u> <u>had</u> *risen* (rose, risen) from his chair and <u>had</u> *spoken* (spoke, spoken) softly.

15. Why <u>have</u> <u>you</u> *worn* (wore, worn) that blouse? I told you <u>it</u> <u>was</u> *torn*. (torn, tore)

CORRECT USAGE — IRREGULAR VERBS

TEST: Irregular Verbs, List II

Part I. Instructions: Draw two lines under helping verbs, one under the subjects of the verbs in the blanks. Using the verb in parentheses, write the correct form in the blanks.

1. My dog had _____ out of the bushes just before the fox _____ out. (spring)

2. In the accident, Don was really _____ up. (shake)

3. Lee must have _____ faster today than he _____ yesterday. (run)

4. Becky _____ him do it; he didn't know she had _____ him. (see)

5. The teacher had _____ Ted the solution; then he _____ us. (show)

6. Mike _____ the newspaper carefully today; he had _____ it carelessly yesterday. (throw)

7. Lynn _____ a letter last night; she has just _____ another. (write)

8. The phone _____ ten times this morning; it has just _____ again. (ring)

9. The boys' chorus just _____; the girls' chorus had _____ earlier. (sing)

10. The "ghost" ship _____ right where other ships have _____. (sink)

Part II. Instructions: In each blank, write your choice of the correct verb from the parentheses. Draw two lines under helping verbs, one line under the subjects.

11. The strange man _____ (shrank, shrunk) back into the shadows and _____ away. (snuck, sneaked)

12. Dad had _____ (swung, swang) into the slow lane and had _____ (took, taken) the off-ramp.

13. I would _____ (of, have) _____ (swore, sworn) Lex couldn't _____ (have, of) _____ (swum, swam) so far.

14. The teacher had _____ (rose, risen) from his chair and had _____ (spoke, spoken) softly.

15. Why have you _____ (wore, worn) that blouse? I told you it was _____. (torn, tore)

© 1988, 1997 J. Weston Walch, Publisher

Steps to Good Grammar

USING ADJECTIVES TO COMPARE NOUNS

This page presents several rules governing correct usage of adjectives and important related information. Practice in applying the rules is on page 253.

Remind students that adjectives modify or describe nouns and tell *which one, what kind, how many,* or *whose* about the nouns they modify.

Read the rules and simultaneously quiz students to establish their understanding.

Rule 2, sample sentence: "Of the three, this is the funniest."

The article *the* is used before a noun. In this sentence, although no noun is used, the reader understands that, in context, the noun is understood to be *cartoon*.

This is an example of an ellipsis, where a word necessary for the syntactical construction of a sentence but not necessary for understanding it has been omitted.

Emphasize the *Reminder* items:

-er and mo*re* to compare two nouns;

-est and mo*st* to compare three or more nouns.

These are obvious visual associations which the students easily remember.

You may wish to introduce your students to the terms for degrees of adjective comparison.

Positive: describes one noun
Comparative: compares two nouns
Superlative: compares three or more nouns

Students often encounter the Latin abbreviations *e.g.* and *i.e.* They should understand the meanings of these terms:

e.g. is the abbreviation for *exempli gratia,* meaning "for example."

i.e. is the abbreviation for *id est,* meaning "that is."

CORRECT USAGE — ADJECTIVES

Using Adjectives to Compare Nouns

You have learned to recognize and have studied the use of all types of adjectives. Now it is important for you to understand certain basic points of correct usage of adjectives.

Forming Adjectives for Comparison of Nouns

RULE 1: To one-syllable adjectives (e.g., *small*):
- add *-er* to compare two nouns;
- add *-est* to compare three or more nouns.

That is a small house.
Of the *two,* this is the small**er** house.
Of the *three,* this is the small**est** house.

> **Reminder:** two letters, **-er,** for two; three letters, **-est,** for three!

RULE 2: To two-syllable adjectives ending in *-y* (e.g., *funny*) or *-le* (e.g., *simple*):
- change the *-y* to *-i* or the *-le* to *-l*;
- add *-er* to compare two nouns;
- add *-est* to compare three or more nouns.

That is a funny cartoon.
Of the *two,* this is the funn**ier** cartoon.
Of the *three,* this is the funn**iest**.

That is a simple plan.
Of the *two,* this is the simpl**er**.
Of the *three,* this is the simpl**est**.

RULE 3: With other two-syllable adjectives (e.g., *hopeful*) and all adjectives with three or more syllables (e.g., *reliable*):
- use **more** before the adjective to compare *two;*
- use **most** before the adjective to compare *three*.

Michele has a hopeful attitude.
Of the *two,* Michele has a **more** hopeful attitude.
Of the *three,* Michele has the **most** hopeful attitude.

John is a reliable person.
Of the *two* boys, John is **more** reliable.
Of the *three,* John is the **most** reliable.

> **Reminder:** Similarity:
> *-er* and mo**re** for two;
> *-est* and mo**st** for three

RULE 4: A few adjectives are irregular (change their spelling) in forming their comparatives:

bad, ill	good, well	much, many	little	(in amount:	far
worse	better	more	less	e.g., little rain)	farther-further
worst	best	most	least		farthest-furthest

REMEMBER: Do not use double comparisons; i.e., if you use an adjective ending in *-er,* do not use *more* before it, and if you use an adjective ending in *-est,* do not use *most* before it.

Sal is m~~ore~~ busier than Pat.   (Using *more* doesn't make Sal busier!)
This road is the m~~ost~~ shortest.   (The road is already the shortest!)

Steps to Good Grammar

PRACTICE IN USING
ADJECTIVES TO COMPARE NOUNS

It may help if students verbalize their reasoning as they choose the correct form. For example, in Part I:

Sentence 1: *attractive* is a three-syllable word; two dresses are being compared; the correct form is *more attractive*.

Sentence 2: *short* is a one-syllable word; several boys are being compared; the correct form is *shortest*.

1. Of the two, this dress is the ___*more attractive*___ . (attractive)
2. Who is the ___*shortest*___ of all the boys? (short)
3. I am ___*hungrier*___ at breakfast than I am at lunch. (hungry)
4. Of my two sisters, Marcie is the ___*happier*___ (happy) and ___*more helpful*___. (helpful)
5. That girl has the ___*littlest*___ feet I've ever seen. (little)
6. The ___*cutest*___ (cute) of the four puppies is also the ___*clumsiest*___. (clumsy)
7. Ethan is the ___*taller*___ of the two boys. (tall)
8. Mallory's drawing is the ___*prettiest*___ picture in the class. (pretty)
9. Of the two, Tony is the ___*taller*___ (tall) and the ___*better*___ (good) athlete.
10. All the students' answers were silly, but Jason's was the ___*silliest*___. (silly)

1. When we compare the two teachers, Mr. Zilch's methods are the ~~most~~ *more* progressive.
2. Both Betty and Vera are good workers, but Vera is the ~~best~~ *better*.
3. Of all the boys on our team, Dale is the ~~more~~ *most* popular.
4. Toby's bike is new, but mine is ~~newest~~ *newer*.
5. It was much ~~more~~ hotter today than it was yesterday.
6. Win's horse is the ~~friskiest~~ *friskier* of the two.
7. I think your book report was the ~~better~~ *best* of the four.
8. Both plans are good, but this one seems to be the ~~most~~ *more* practical.
9. Nikki is much ~~more~~ shorter than Greta.
10. Becky thought Tom was the ~~most~~ noblest person alive.
11. Both families covered many miles on vacation, but one's destination had been ~~farthest~~ *farther* away.
12. Randy is an able student, but Jared is ~~most able~~ *abler*.
13. Is this road the ~~most~~ shortest of all?
14. Sal is ~~more~~ busier than Pam.
15. My mother is undoubtedly the most ~~patientest~~ *patient* person I know.

CORRECT USAGE — ADJECTIVES

Practice in Using Adjectives to Compare Nouns

Part I. Instruction: In the blanks, write the correct form of the adjective given in parentheses at the end of each sentence.

1. Of the two, this dress is the _____ . (attractive)

2. Who is the _____ of all the boys? (short)

3. I am _____ at breakfast than I am at lunch. (hungry)

4. Of my two sisters, Marcie is the _____ (happy) and _____. (helpful)

5. That girl has the _____ feet I've ever seen. (little)

6. The _____ (cute) of the four puppies is also the _____. (clumsy)

7. Ethan is the _____ of the two boys. (tall)

8. Mallory's drawing is the _____ picture in the class. (pretty)

9. Of the two, Tony is the _____ (tall) and the _____ (good) athlete.

10. All the students' answers were silly, but Jason's was the _____. (silly)

Part II. Instructions: Above each error, write the correct form; then cross out the errors.

1. When we compare the two teachers, Mr. Zilch's methods are the most progressive.

2. Both Betty and Vera are good workers, but Vera is the best.

3. Of all the boys on our team, Dale is the more popular.

4. Toby's bike is new, but mine is newest.

5. It was much more hotter today than it was yesterday.

6. Win's horse is the friskiest of the two.

7. I think your book report was the better of the four.

8. Both plans are good, but this one seems to be the most practical.

9. Nikki is much more shorter than Greta.

10. Becky thought Tom was the most noblest person alive.

11. Both families covered many miles on vacation, but one's destination had been farthest away.

12. Randy is an able student, but Jared is most able.

13. Is this road the most shortest of all?

14. Sal is more busier than Pam.

15. My mother is undoubtedly the most patientest person I know.

Steps to Good Grammar

MORE RULES FOR CORRECT ADJECTIVE USE

Rule 5 in the introductory material has been covered previously. Reinforce it.

Emphasize Rules 6 and 7.

Also remind students about correct usage of *a* and *an*:

Use *an* before words that begin with a vowel (*a, e, i, o,* short *u*) and silent *h: an* opportunity; *an* hour.

Use *a* before words that begin with a consonant or long *u: a* house; *a* union member.

About the sample sentences:

This type of stories is my favorite.

The use of the plural *of stories* is correct in that it implies *of all stories.* Some students prefer *of story,* which is also correct.

I like this kind of shoes.

Of shoes is preferred to *of shoe,* since shoes are referred to in pairs.

In the Practice sentences, make it clear that students should correct *adjectives.* For example, in sentence 2:

~~Those~~ *That* kind of apples ripens early.

Change the adjectives *those* to *that;* do not change the noun *kind.* Point out that the verb *ripens* requires the adjective change.

1. Each boy is responsible for ~~their~~ *his* uniform.
2. ~~Those~~ *That* kind of apples ripens early.
3. Neither dog has eaten ~~their~~ *its* food.
4. I felt ~~badly a~~ *bad an* hour ago, but I will feel ~~good~~ *well* soon.
5. ~~Them~~ *Those/These* nectarines aren't ripe.
6. ~~These~~ *This* sort of desserts is too rich for me.
7. Every tool has been put in ~~their~~ *its* proper place.
8. Any student may submit ~~their~~ *his/her* plan.
9. Some girl has forgotten ~~their~~ *her* gym suit.
10. No child was out of ~~their~~ *his/her* assigned seat.

CORRECT USAGE — ADJECTIVES

More Rules for Correct Adjective Use

RULE 5: Use *well* or *bad* in referring to health or appearance:

Mary feels (well, good) today; she felt (bad, badly) yesterday.

RULE 6: To use demonstrative pronouns (*this, that, these, those*) as adjectives:

Singular pronouns modify *singular nouns:*

this, that ——→ kind, sort, type

I like (this) kind (of shoes)

Plural pronouns modify *plural nouns:*

these, those ——→ kinds, sorts, types
(never *them!*)

Pat likes (these, them) kinds (of shoes)

> **Reminder:**
> *These* is the plural of *this* — refers to things close at hand.
> *Those* is the plural of *that* — refers to things further away.

REMEMBER: The object of a preposition is never the subject of a sentence. Be sure the verb agrees with the true subject.

(This) type (of stories) is my favorite.

(Them, These) sorts (of desserts) are very rich.

RULE 7: These singular words often modify a subject; as you read each one, think **one:**

> **each** (ONE) **every   any   either   neither   no**
> **some** (meaning no definite one)

Possessive pronouns that refer to these words should be singular:

(Each) girl has (their, her) key.

Does (either) boy have (their, his) pen?

(Some) student always forgets (their, his/her) book.

PRACTICE: Above each incorrectly used *adjective,* write the correct form; then cross out the errors.

1. Each boy is responsible for their uniform.

2. Those kind of apples ripens early.

3. Neither dog has eaten their food.

4. I felt badly a hour ago, but I will feel good soon.

5. Them nectarines aren't ripe.

6. These sort of desserts is too rich for me.

7. Every tool has been put in their proper place.

8. Any student may submit their plan.

9. Some girl has forgotten their gym suit.

10. No child was out of their assigned seat.

© 1988, 1997 J. Weston Walch, Publisher

Steps to Good Grammar

DRILL 1

Introduce the term "editing." The process of editing is the process of correcting written material to make it suitable or acceptable. Students are to edit these sentences.

Emphasize that students are to change *adjectives* only.

1. Each person is responsible for ~~their~~ *his* paper deliveries.

2. ~~These~~ *That* kind of jokes doesn't amuse me.

3. Has either girl volunteered ~~their~~ *her* help?

4. The ~~cheapest~~ *cheaper* of ~~them~~ *these/those* two rings isn't a good buy.

5. My uncle has been awarded ~~a~~ *an* unusual prize.

6. Every dog in the shelter was wagging ~~their~~ *its* tail.

7. Grandmother hasn't felt very ~~good~~ *well* all day.

8. Every boy has ~~their~~ *his* own ideas.

9. Of ~~them~~ *these* two plans, this one is the simpler and ~~most~~ *more* workable.

10. That book certainly has ~~a~~ *an* original plot.

11. No one could be ~~more lazy~~ *lazier* than I.

12. Sue felt really ~~badly~~ *bad* about the mistake.

13. Has Peg ever worn ~~these~~ *this* kind of shoes?

14. Neither Raul nor Hank ever remembers to bring ~~their~~ *his* pencils.

15. Every day, at least one student forgets ~~their~~ *his/her* book.

16. Lenore is the ~~shortest~~ *shorter* and ~~oldest~~ *older* of my two daughters.

17. My older brother thought that was the ~~greater~~ *greatest* of all his successes.

18. The wind blew every sailboat from ~~their~~ *its* berth at the wharf.

19. Yesterday was the ~~most hot~~ *hottest* of the last three days.

20. What would ~~a~~ *an* honest person do in a situation like that?

21. We should take the ~~shortest~~ *shorter* of the two roads.

22. I'm always ~~more~~ hungrier at dinnertime than Dad is.

23. How does ~~these~~ *this* sort of glasses look on me?

24. I hope that every student will remember to bring ~~their~~ *his/her* book.

25. This one seems the ~~most~~ simplest of all the plans.

CORRECT USAGE — ADJECTIVES

DRILL 1

Instructions: Above each error in *adjective* usage, write the correct form; then cross out the errors. Several sentences have more than one error.

1. Each person is responsible for their paper deliveries.

2. Those kind of jokes doesn't amuse me.

3. Has either girl volunteered their help?

4. The cheapest of them two rings isn't a good buy.

5. My uncle has been awarded a unusual prize.

6. Every dog in the shelter was wagging their tail.

7. Grandmother hasn't felt very good all day.

8. Every boy has their own ideas.

9. Of them two plans, this one is the simpler and most workable.

10. That book certainly has a original plot.

11. No one could be more lazy than I.

12. Sue felt really badly about the mistake.

13. Has Peg ever worn these kind of shoes?

14. Neither Raul nor Hank ever remembers to bring their pencils.

15. Every day, at least one student forgets their book.

16. Lenore is the shortest and oldest of my two daughters.

17. My older brother thought that was the greater of all his successes.

18. The wind blew every sailboat from their berth at the wharf.

19. Yesterday was the most hot of the last three days.

20. What would a honest person do in a situation like that?

21. We should take the shortest of the two roads.

22. I'm always more hungrier at dinnertime than Dad is.

23. How does these sort of glasses look on me?

24. I hope that every student will remember to bring their book.

25. This one seems the most simplest of all the plans.

Steps to Good Grammar

DRILL 2

The four sentences with no errors are 8, 13, 19, and 22.

Remind students to change adjective errors only.

1. Using ~~a~~ *an* index in a textbook can be ~~an~~ *a* help to students.
2. The roads were the ~~most muddy~~ *muddiest* I had ever seen.
3. Has the store put ~~them~~ *these/those* coats on sale?
4. We drove the ~~most~~ farthest we had ever driven in one day.
5. Has either boy finished ~~their~~ *his* homework?
6. The library has some of ~~those~~ *that* kind of computers.
7. Some student always leaves ~~their~~ *his/her* book in my room.
8. My little brother is the most mischievous kid I know.
9. Dad doesn't like ~~those~~ *that* type of tools.
10. Grandfather felt ~~badly~~ *bad* yesterday and doesn't feel too ~~good~~ *well* today.
11. Every rock collection has ~~their~~ *its* special place.
12. The sailor saw ~~a~~ *an* unidentified flying object.
13. Those kinds of scissors are quite expensive.
14. Of the three plans, Tim's is the ~~more simple~~ *simplest* and the ~~more~~ *most* practical.
15. Doesn't either girl have ~~their~~ *her* project completed?
16. Your house has the ~~most shiny~~ *shiniest* windows in the neighborhood.
17. ~~Them~~ *This/That* kind of sneakers certainly isn't my favorite.
18. Both your and his reports were good, but yours was the ~~best~~ *better*.
19. Every girl has finished her woodworking project.
20. No boy had forgotten ~~their~~ *his* lunch.
21. ~~These~~ *This* kind of stories is interesting to most students.
22. That type of fish lives in fresh water.
23. Of the two horses, mine is the ~~gentlest~~ *gentler* and the ~~most easy~~ *easier* to manage.
24. The ~~shorter~~ *shortest* of those four girls is the ~~better~~ *best* basketball player.
25. Has every eligible student gotten ~~their~~ *his/her* pass to the Red Sox game?

CORRECT USAGE — ADJECTIVES

DRILL 2

Instructions: Above each error in *adjective* usage, write the correct form; then cross out the errors. Four sentences have no errors; several sentences have more than one.

1. Using a index in a textbook can be an help to students.

2. The roads were the most muddy I had ever seen.

3. Has the store put them coats on sale?

4. We drove the most farthest we had ever driven in one day.

5. Has either boy finished their homework?

6. The library has some of those kind of computers.

7. Some student always leaves their book in my room.

8. My little brother is the most mischievous kid I know.

9. Dad doesn't like those type of tools.

10. Grandfather felt badly yesterday and doesn't feel too good today.

11. Every rock collection has their special place.

12. The sailor saw a unidentified flying object.

13. Those kinds of scissors are quite expensive.

14. Of the three plans, Tim's is the more simple and the more practical.

15. Doesn't either girl have their project completed?

16. Your house has the most shiny windows in the neighborhood.

17. Them kind of sneakers certainly isn't my favorite.

18. Both your and his reports were good, but yours was the best.

19. Every girl has finished her woodworking project.

20. No boy had forgotten their lunch.

21. These kind of stories is interesting to most students.

22. That type of fish lives in fresh water.

23. Of the two horses, mine is the gentlest and the most easy to manage.

24. The shorter of those four girls is the better basketball player.

25. Has every eligible student gotten their pass to the Red Sox game?

Steps to Good Grammar

TEST

This reproducible page contains two copies of one half-page drill/test. Cut each duplicated page in half; give each student one half-page.

Students are to correct errors in *adjective* usage only.

Suggested grading:
16 points — subtract 6% for each error.

1. She has looked really ~~badly~~ *bad* all day; doesn't she feel ~~good~~ *well*?

2. Of the twins, Leah is the ~~tallest~~ *taller* and the ~~best~~ *better* athlete.

3. For once, every student had done ~~their~~ *his/her* homework.

4. Although Bud is the ~~heavier~~ *heaviest* of the three boys, he is the ~~faster~~ *fastest* runner.

5. Jennifer and I saw ~~a~~ *an* unidentified flying object ~~a~~ *an* hour ago!

6. Tod's is the ~~more simpler~~ *simplest* and the ~~more~~ *most* practical of all the plans.

7. Doesn't either girl have ~~their~~ *her* project completed?

8. ~~Those~~ *That* kind of jeans certainly isn't my favorite.

9. Each person must have delivered all ~~their~~ *his/her* papers.

10. I feel ~~badly~~ *bad* about not raking ~~them~~ *these/those* leaves.

CORRECT USAGE — ADJECTIVES

TEST

Instructions: Above each error in *adjective* usage, write the correct form; then cross out the errors.

1. She has looked really badly all day; doesn't she feel good?

2. Of the twins, Leah is the tallest and the best athlete.

3. For once, every student had done their homework.

4. Although Bud is the heavier of the three boys, he is the faster runner.

5. Jennifer and I saw a unidentified flying object a hour ago!

6. Tod's is the more simpler and the more practical of all the plans.

7. Doesn't either girl have their project completed?

8. Those kind of jeans certainly isn't my favorite.

9. Each person must have delivered all their papers.

10. I feel badly about not raking them leaves.

CORRECT USAGE — ADJECTIVES

TEST

Instructions: Above each error in *adjective* usage, write the correct form; then cross out the errors.

1. She has looked really badly all day; doesn't she feel good?

2. Of the twins, Leah is the tallest and the best athlete.

3. For once, every student had done their homework.

4. Although Bud is the heavier of the three boys, he is the faster runner.

5. Jennifer and I saw a unidentified flying object a hour ago!

6. Tod's is the more simpler and the more practical of all the plans.

7. Doesn't either girl have their project completed?

8. Those kind of jeans certainly isn't my favorite.

9. Each boy must have delivered all their papers.

10. I feel badly about not raking them leaves.

Steps to Good Grammar

FACTS ABOUT ADVERBS

Students will remember that adverbs tell *how,* *when,* and *where* about verbs and *how much* about adjectives and other adverbs.

Read the Facts and quiz students about the information to help them remember it.

Point out that forming the comparisons of adverbs is similar to forming the comparisons of adjectives:

— *er* or mo*re* to compare two actions.

— *est* or mo*st* to compare three or more actions.

1. (soft) Ella walks ___*softly*___, but Cynthia walks ___*more softly*___; Lydia walks ___*most softly*___ of all.
2. (regular) I practice ___*regularly*___, Jerome practices ___*more regularly*___ than I, and Darlene practices ___*most regularly*___.
3. (wise) This twin buys ___*wisely*___, but the other twin buys ___*more wisely*___.
4. (gentle) You spoke to him ___*gently*___, Jane spoke ___*more gently*___ than you, and June spoke ___*most gently*___ of the three of you.
5. (heavy) Zane stomped ___*heavily*___; Susie stomped ___*more heavily*___ than he.

CORRECT USAGE — ADVERBS

Facts About Adverbs

As you know, adverbs modify (affect the meaning of) verbs, adjectives, and other adverbs; they tell *how, when, where,* and *how much* about the words they modify:

[Here,] [yesterday,] we [very] quickly finished a really challenging job.
(where?) (when?) (how   (how?)   (how much?)
              much?)

FACT 1: Most adverbs are formed simply by adding *-ly* to adjectives:

sure - surely   invisible - invisibly
bold - boldly.   hopeful - hopefully
sudden - suddenly   extravagant - extravagantly

Spelling changes may be made: simp*le* - simp*ly,* heav*y* - heav*ily*

FACT 2: Some words often used as adverbs do not end in *-ly,* such as:

not	often	too	now	where	anyway
never	almost	rather	how	here	nowhere
ever	always	very	when	why	sometimes

FACT 3: *Use adverbs to describe actions* of one person or thing, to compare actions of two or of three or more.

    a. Some adverbs add *-er* to compare two, *-est* to compare three:

        soon - sooner - soonest   hard - harder - hardest
        slow - slower - slowest   close - closer - closest

    b. Adverbs formed from adjectives use **more** before the adverb to compare two, **most** before the adverb to compare three or more:

        softly - more softly - most softly
        feebly - more feebly - most feebly
        easily - more easily - most easily

    c. Some adverbs have irregular comparisons:

        well - better - best   badly - worse - worst
        much - more - most   little - less - least

PRACTICE: In the blanks, write the adverb forms of the adjective in parentheses at the beginning of each sentence.

1. (soft) Ella walks _____, but Cynthia walks _____;

    Lydia walks _____ of all.

2. (regular) I practice _____, Jerome practices _____

    than I, and Darlene practices _____.

3. (wise) This twin buys _____, but the other twin buys _____.

4. (gentle) You spoke to him _____, Jane spoke _____

    than you, and June spoke _____ of the three of you.

5. (heavy) Zane stomped _____; Susie stomped _____

    than he.

Steps to Good Grammar

ADVERB RULES TO REMEMBER — 1

Students often use the incorrect forms listed in Common Errors.

Emphasize the definitions of *sure* and *real,* and the fact that the adverbs *well* and *badly* are used to describe how something is done.

1. Joe ~~is~~ always ~~real~~ *really* late.
   <small>LV · LVC-A</small>

2. The trail ~~sure~~ *surely* looks steep.
   <small>LV · LVC-A</small>

3. Molly ~~sure~~ *surely* feels ~~badly~~ *bad*; she did ~~bad~~ *badly* on the test.
   <small>LV · LVC-A</small>

4. I hadn't done ~~to good~~ *too well* on it myself.

5. Grandmother's house was damaged ~~real bad~~ *really badly* in the storm.

6. Dad talked ~~real serious~~ *really seriously* to me.

7. Dave ~~sure~~ *surely* dresses ~~neat~~ *neatly*.

8. Mark played ~~real good~~ *really well*, but Bob played ~~bad~~ *badly*.

9. That teacher speaks ~~real distinct~~ *really distinctly*.

10. The chorus ~~sure~~ *surely* sang ~~good~~ *well* at the concert.

CORRECT USAGE — ADVERBS

Adverb Rules to Remember—1

RULE 1: Do not use an adjective to modify a verb.

Common errors:	**Correct form:**
1. Cathy sure ran slow.	Cathy surely ran slowly.

    (*sure* is an adjective that means "certain" or "positive")

2. My pony was real skittish.   My pony was really skittish.

    (*real* is an adjective that means "genuine")

3. Oscar answered to quick.   Oscar answered too quickly.

    (*to* is a preposition; *quick* is an adjective)

4. Our team played good, but   Our team played well, but
their team played bad.   their team played badly.

    Note: *Well* may be used either as an adverb *or* as an adjective.

        a. After linking verbs, use the adjectives ***good*** and ***bad:***
            Yesterday the weather was bad; today it has been good.

           Exception: Use the adjective ***well*** to refer to good health or feeling:
            Today I feel well; yesterday I felt bad.

        b. *To describe how something is done,* use adverbs ***well*** and ***badly,*** as in
           sentence 4 above.

PRACTICE: Above an error in adverb or adjective usage in the sentences below, write the correct form; then cross out the errors. Underline verbs twice. Label: **LV, LVC-A.**

    Example: This cake ~~sure~~ *surely* is good.

1. James is always real late.

2. The trail sure looks steep.

3. Molly sure feels badly; she did bad on the test.

4. I hadn't done to good on it myself.

5. Grandmother's house was damaged real bad in the storm.

6. Dad talked real serious to me.

7. Dave sure dresses neat.

8. Mack played real good, but Bob played bad.

9. That teacher speaks real distinct.

10. The chorus sure sang good at the concert.

Steps to Good Grammar

PRACTICE USING ADVERB FACTS AND RULE 1

Part I, correct adverbs:

1. promptly
2. thoroughly
3. hastily
4. really
5. surely
6. gently but firmly
7. smoothly
8. slowly and
   thoughtfully

In Part II, remind students:

Sentence 2: *too* is an adverb.

Sentence 15: which (implies *which one*) (of the men) has lived . . .

Sentence 18: I is the subject of the elliptical verb *finished.*

1. Of the two boys, Tyrone ran ~~fastest.~~ *faster*
2. The chorus hadn't sung ~~to good~~ *too well* at the concert.
3. Your papers are always written so ~~neat.~~ *neatly*
4. Carmen spoke ~~soft~~ *softly* but ~~real distinct.~~ *really distinctly*
5. Davy behaved ~~bad~~ *badly* yesterday.
6. Of the three students, which one worked ~~better~~ *best*?
7. Fred came early; Derek came ~~more early~~ *earlier* than Fred; Phil came ~~most early~~ *earliest* of all.
8. Practice ~~sure~~ *surely* helped; we didn't play ~~to bad~~ *too badly* yesterday.
9. That teacher is ~~real~~ *really* nice.
10. *(You)* Walk ~~careful~~ *carefully* around that spilled oil.
11. Tomás ~~sure~~ *surely* does his homework ~~thorough.~~ *thoroughly*
12. Of the two pairs of sneakers, this one fits ~~most comfortable.~~ *more comfortably*
13. Frank dances ~~real smooth.~~ *really smoothly*
14. It snowed a little yesterday, but it snowed ~~most~~ *more* today.
15. Which of the two men has lived here ~~longest~~ *longer*?
16. Aunt Mary ~~sure~~ *surely* walks ~~slow.~~ *slowly*
17. Jennifer hadn't printed ~~to clear~~ *too clearly* on her map.
18. I answered all the questions ~~easy,~~ *easily* but Janek finished ~~quicker~~ *more quickly* than I.
19. Of the three of us, Huey finished ~~more~~ *most* quickly.
20. I didn't serve ~~to good~~ *too well* in our tennis match; Robin served much ~~more good~~ *better* than I.

CORRECT USAGE — ADVERBS

Practice Using Adverb Facts and Rule 1

Part I. Instructions: Using the adjective in parentheses, write the adverb form in the blank.

1.   Margie always arrives _____ (prompt).

2.   Curt usually studies _____ (thorough).

3.   The man looked around _____ (hasty).

4.   Addie entertains herself _____ (real) well.

5.   Mom _____ (sure) feels better.

6.   The teacher spoke _____ (gentle) but _____ (firm) to the students.

7.   The truck's motor is idling _____ (smooth).

8.   Karla answered _____ (slow) and _____ (thoughtful).

Part II. Instructions: Above errors in adverb or adjective usage, write the correct form; then cross out the errors.

1.   Of the two boys, Tyrone ran fastest.

2.   The chorus hadn't sung to good at the concert.

3.   Your papers are always written so neat.

4.   Carmen spoke soft but real distinct.

5.   Davy behaved bad yesterday.

6.   Of the three students, which one worked better?

7.   Fred came early; Derek came more early than Fred; Phil came most early of all.

8.   Practice sure helped; we didn't play to bad yesterday.

9.   That teacher is real nice.

10.   Walk careful around that spilled oil.

11.   Tomás sure does his homework thorough.

12.   Of the two pairs of sneakers, this one fits most comfortable.

13.   Frank dances real smooth.

14.   It snowed a little yesterday, but it snowed most today.

15.   Which of the two men has lived here longest?

16.   Aunt Mary sure walks slow.

17.   Jennifer hadn't printed to clear on her map.

18.   I answered all the questions easy, but Janek finished quicker than I.

19.   Of the three of us, Huey finished more quickly.

20.   I didn't serve to good in our tennis match; Robin served much more good than I.

Steps to Good Grammar

ADVERB RULES TO REMEMBER — 2, 3, & 4

In some Practice sentences, either of two forms would be correct. Both forms are shown on the Answer Key.

In sentences 4, 8, and 9, *somewhat, rather,* or *quite* could replace *pretty* and *sort of.*

1. During my school years, I worked ~~most~~ hardest in sixth grade.
2. {*none/any*} Not ~~none~~ of the students failed the test.
3. {*Don't*} ~~Don't~~ you have no *any* lunch money?
4. Sara's report was written ~~pretty good~~ *rather well*.
5. Why couldn't you have come ~~more~~ sooner?
6. I{*can't ever*} can'~~t~~ never repay you.
7. Matt couldn't find his baseball ~~nowhere~~ *anywhere*.
8. I did ~~sort of bad~~ *rather badly* on the test.
9. The band marched ~~pretty good~~ *quite well* yesterday.
10. How much ~~more~~ farther must we walk?

CORRECT USAGE — ADVERBS

Adverb Rules to Remember — 2, 3, & 4

RULE 2: Do not use *more* before adverbs ending in *-er* or *most* before adverbs ending in *-est:*

Can't you run ~~more~~ faster? (*More* doesn't make *faster* faster!)

Of the three, Tom runs ~~most~~ fastest. (*Most* doesn't increase *fastest!*)

RULE 3: Use only one negative word to express a negative idea:

I have no time. ⎫ (The meaning is the same in both sentences.)

I haven't any time. ⎬ Each sentence has one negative word.)

I haven't no time. (Two negative words to express one negative idea — a double negative. The negative words cancel one another; the actual meaning of the sentence is: "I have time.")

Some negative words: **no, not, no one, nobody, never, scarcely, hardly, none**

Incorrect Double Negative:
Nobody can't enter.
Scarcely no one came.
I can't hardly see you.

Correct Single Negative:
Nobody can enter. Not anyone can enter.
Scarcely anyone came. Almost no one came.
I can hardly see you. I almost can't see you.

RULE 4: In formal expression, avoid using *pretty, sort of,* and *kind of* when you mean *somewhat, rather,* or *quite:*

I tried ~~pretty~~ hard . . . . I tried rather/quite hard.

Dad spoke ~~sort of~~ angrily . . . . Dad spoke rather/somewhat angrily.

Pete was yelling ~~kind of~~ loudly . . . . Pete was yelling quite loudly.

PRACTICE: Above each incorrect or substandard form, write the acceptable form; cross out the errors.

1. During my school years, I worked most hardest in sixth grade.

2. Not none of the students failed the test.

3. Don't you have no lunch money?

4. Sara's report was written pretty good.

5. Why couldn't you have come more sooner?

6. I can't never repay you.

7. Matt couldn't find his baseball nowhere.

8. I did sort of bad on the test.

9. The band marched pretty good yesterday.

10. How much more farther must we walk?

Steps to Good Grammar

FINAL DRILL

Either of two forms could be used to correct the double negatives in sentences 4, 7, 14, 18, and 20.

One of several words could replace *pretty* and *kind of* in sentences 15, 18, and 19.

1. Two [really] good movies have been shown [here] [recently].

2. My watch [usually] keeps [quite] good time.

3. I put my glasses [down] [somewhere] but do [not] remember the place [now].

4. Your grades are improving [slowly] but [steadily].

5. The child eyed me [timidly] and [then] smiled [nervously].

1. At chess, Hope can outplay me ~~easy.~~ *easily*

2. Dad ~~sure~~ *surely* surprised us.

3. The outfield played ~~bad,~~ *badly* but the infield played ~~real good.~~ *really well*

4. Andy can'~~t~~ hardly read such fine print.

5. Probably we should have come ~~more~~ sooner.

6. Which of the two roads was repaired ~~most recent~~? *more recently*

7. Carlos has~~n't~~ never attended a major league game.

8. Of the three T-shirts, Carrie likes this one ~~better.~~ *best*

9. Do you feel ~~real good~~ *really well* now? I know you felt ~~badly~~ *bad* last night.

10. Which girl studies ~~most careful~~, *more carefully* Trish or Janet?

11. I feel ~~real badly~~ *really bad* about the mistake. I could have avoided it ~~easy.~~ *easily*

12. Alan could have run much ~~more~~ faster.

13. Each of the girls did ~~real good~~ *really well* with her project.

14. I can't ~~never~~ *ever* remember the name of that song.

15. Dad spoke ~~pretty loud~~ *rather loudly* and ~~real stern.~~ *quite sternly*

16. (*You*) Come in ~~quick~~ *quickly* and close the door ~~quiet.~~ *quietly*

17. After attending obedience school, our new puppy is behaving ~~real good.~~ *really well*

18. The applause ~~kind of~~ *quite* pleased all of us; we had~~n't~~ never performed in a play before.

19. We'll be finished with dinner ~~pretty~~ *quite* soon, we'll load the dishwasher ~~quick,~~ *quickly* and then we'll leave.

20. Haven't you gotten ~~no~~ *any* answers to your advertisement?

CORRECT USAGE — ADVERBS

FINAL DRILL

Part I. Instructions: Draw brackets around each adverb in these sentences.

1. Two really good movies have been shown here recently.

2. My watch usually keeps quite good time.

3. I put my glasses down somewhere but do not remember the place now.

4. Your grades are improving slowly but steadily.

5. The child eyed me timidly and then smiled nervously.

Part II. Instructions: Above each substandard or incorrect use of adverbs or adjectives, write the standard or correct form; cross out the errors.

1. At chess, Hope can outplay me easy.

2. Dad sure surprised us.

3. The outfield played bad, but the infield played real good.

4. Andy can't hardly read such fine print.

5. Probably we should have come more sooner.

6. Which of the two roads was repaired most recent?

7. Carlos hasn't never attended a major league game.

8. Of the three T-shirts, Carrie likes this one better.

9. Do you feel real good now? I know you felt badly last night.

10. Which girl studies most careful, Trish or Janet?

11. I feel real badly about the mistake. I could have avoided it easy.

12. Alan could have run much more faster.

13. Each of the girls did real good with her project.

14. I can't never remember the name of that song.

15. Dad spoke pretty loud and real stern.

16. Come in quick and close the door quiet.

17. After attending obedience school, our new puppy is behaving real good.

18. The applause kind of pleased all of us; we hadn't never performed in a play before.

19. We'll be finished with dinner pretty soon, we'll load the dishwasher quick, and then we'll leave.

20. Haven't you gotten no answers to your advertisement?

Steps to Good Grammar

TEST

This reproducible page contains two copies of one half-page drill/test. Cut each duplicated page in half; give each student one half-page.

Either of two forms, as shown in the Answer Key, could be used to correct the double negative in sentence 1.

One of several words could replace *pretty* in sentence 5, *sort of* in sentence 6, and *kind of* in sentence 7.

Suggested grading:

There are 18 forms to be corrected; use the grading scale for choice of pronouns on page 116.

1. { ~~Didn't nobody~~ tell you about the test? *(Didn't anybody)*

2. How much ~~more~~ farther must we walk?

3. A voice called out ~~loud~~ and ~~clear~~. *loudly   clearly*

4. Mack played ~~pretty good~~, but Bob ~~sure~~ played ~~bad~~. *rather well   surely   badly*

5. I ~~sort of~~ like that teacher. *rather*

6. The wind blew ~~wild~~, and the rain pounded ~~steady~~. *wildly   steadily*

7. I had done ~~kind of good~~ on the test. *quite well*

8. Of the three roads, we'll take the one that was resurfaced ~~more recent~~. *most recently*

9. Jane finished the test ~~quicker~~ than I. *more quickly*

10. The chorus hadn't sung ~~to good~~ at the assembly. *too well*

CORRECT USAGE — ADVERBS

TEST

Instructions: Above each incorrect or substandard use of adverbs or adjectives, write the correct or standard form; cross out the errors.

1. Didn't nobody tell you about the test?

2. How much more farther must we walk?

3. A voice called out loud and clear.

4. Mack played pretty good, but Bob sure played bad.

5. I sort of like that teacher.

6. The wind blew wild, and the rain pounded steady.

7. I had done kind of good on the test.

8. Of the three roads, we'll take the one that was resurfaced more recent.

9. Jane finished the test quicker than I.

10. The chorus hadn't sung to good at the assembly.

NAME _____ DATE _____ 273

CORRECT USAGE — ADVERBS

TEST

Instructions: Above each incorrect or substandard use of adverbs or adjectives, write the correct or standard form; cross out the errors.

1. Didn't nobody tell you about the test?

2. How much more farther must we walk?

3. A voice called out loud and clear.

4. Mack played pretty good, but Bob sure played bad.

5. I sort of like that teacher.

6. The wind blew wild, and the rain pounded steady.

7. I had done kind of good on the test.

8. Of the three roads, we'll take the one that was resurfaced more recent.

9. Jane finished the test quicker than I.

10. The chorus hadn't sung to good at the assembly.

Steps to Good Grammar

CAPITALIZING PROPER NOUNS

Students should understand that all "given names," just like theirs, are proper nouns and should be capitalized. The name Oak Street was given to a special street; *Street* should be capitalized, not just *Oak*. An oak is a kind of tree. The special street is Oak Street.

Emphasize the exception (4b).

1. I told granddad that I was working for dr. e. l. lewis.

2. superintendent farley said he knows your aunt carole and my aunt stella.

3. captain schmidt was pilot of a ferry boat across carquinez strait.

4. The teacher, ms. north, reminded mr. gray that his son jeremy should write his report.

5. pat told mom that sis and I would meet at dad's office.

CORRECT USAGE — CAPITAL LETTERS

Capitalizing Proper Nouns

UNDERSTAND: The **first letter** of many words is **capitalized** to tell the reader that the word is "special." The word is special because it is a **"given name"** or because it is in a special **"first" position**.

DEFINITION: A **proper noun** is a "given" name, a name given to *one special* person, place, or thing, the *name* everyone uses in writing or speaking about it.

RULE 1: *Capitalize proper nouns.*

A. *Special persons*

   1. **Given name:** Jerome Gray

   2. **Initials** with names: L. T. Bray

   3. **Titles** with names: Captain John Smith; Dr. Eric Snyder; Mr. and Mrs. J. N. Gilbert; Ms. Janice Shaw; Mayor Doris Drew; Superintendent Alice Grafton; Uncle Pete

   4. **Family members,** when used instead of a given name: Mom, Grandfather, Sis, Son.

     a. Do not capitalize *mother, aunt*, etc., if an article (*a, an, the*) or a possessive noun or pronoun precedes it:

       All *the m*others, except *Ted's m*other and *my m*other, left early.

     b. *Exception:* If the given name is used, capitalize the title: Tom's *U*ncle Pete left. My *A*unt Sue arrived.

   5. Always capitalize the pronoun *I*:

     I'm thinking about it. *I*'ve not decided. *I* may go.

B. *Common nouns used as part of a proper noun* (a given name)

Common	Proper	Common	Proper
street/	Elm Street	mountain	Cheyenne Mountain
road	Polson Road	strait	Bering Strait
city	New York City	ocean	Indian Ocean
county	El Paso County	school	John Muir School
river	American River	company	Ford Motor Company
lake	Lake Okeechobee	building	Chrysler Building

PRACTICE: Using Rule I, change lower-case letters to capital letters in these sentences.

1. i told granddad that i was working for dr. e. r. lewis.

2. superintendent farley said he knows your aunt carole and my aunt stella.

3. captain schmidt was pilot of a ferry boat across carquinez strait.

4. The teacher, ms. north, reminded mr. gray that his son jeremy should write his report.

5. pat told mom that sis and i would meet at dad's office.

       Steps to Good Grammar

CAPITALIZING PROPER NOUNS (continued)

Call attention to the Reminders. Write more examples on the chalkboard for any uses students are not clear about.

CORRECT USAGE — CAPITAL LETTERS

Capitalizing Proper Nouns (continued)

RULE 1: *Capitalize proper nouns* (continued).

C. *Given names* in the following groups:

    1. Cities, states, countries, sections within a country, races, nationalities, languages, continents, geographic features:

Concord	Midwest, South	Swedish	Antarctica
Alabama	Caucasian, Oriental	French	Arabian Peninsula
Canada	Indian	Europe	Continental Divide

> **Reminder:** Do not capitalize *south, west,* etc. when used to show direction: We drove *west* on Main Street.

    2. The Deity, religions, religious books and their parts:

       Allah, God, Methodist, Buddhist, Bible, Old Testament, Koran

    3. Parks, monuments, ships, airplanes, trains, artificial satellites:

       Yosemite National Park, Lincoln Memorial, the *Mayflower*, the *Spirit of St. Louis*, the *Starlight Limited, Telstar II*

    4. Calendar names, holidays; periods, events, documents in history:

       Monday, April, Memorial Day; Bronze Age, World War I, Declaration of Independence, Bill of Rights

> **Reminder:** Do not capitalize the seasons: summer, fall, winter, spring.

    5. Government branches, departments, agencies, political parties:

       House of Representatives, Congress, Department of the Interior; Democratic party, a Republican

> **Reminder:** Capitalize government officials' titles only when they are used immediately before the person's name: President Clinton; the president, secretary of labor, Secretary Christopher.

    6. Stars, planets, constellations:

       North Star, Mars, Big Dipper

> **Reminder:** Do not capitalize *sun* or *moon.*

    7. Organizations, clubs, business firms, newspapers, etc.:

       the Salvation Army, Denver Athletic Club, JCPenney Company, Inc., *The New York Times,* Boy Scouts of America

    8. In listing school subjects, capitalize the name only if it is a proper noun, if it uses a Roman numeral, or if it is an abbreviation:

       English, United States history, Art II, P.E.; shop, algebra, science, social studies

Remember that proper nouns are "given names." Capitalize them! Understand and apply the exceptions shown above in **Reminders.

Steps to Good Grammar

CAPITALIZING PROPER NOUNS AND PROPER ADJECTIVES

Proper Nouns — Practice

Sentence 1: *Northwest* is a location, not a given name.

Sentence 6: *Custodian* is just the name of an occupation, not a special name given to Mr. Dutton.

Rule 2 — Practice

Sentence 2: All fifty states share the common noun *state*, and all states have flags.

Sentence 3: Only the proper adjectives derived from the names of countries are capitalized (*Irish, Polish*), not the kinds of dances (jig, polka).

1. damone's house is on the northwest corner of pine street and shell avenue.
2. My father was born in tallahassee, florida; mother was born in york county, maine.
3. My best friend, amy, speaks french well because she lived for two years in paris, france.
4. The largest artificial lake in the world is lake mead, a reservoir formed by hoover dam in the colorado river.
5. The ural mountains in the u.s.s.r. form the boundary between the continents of europe and asia.
6. mr. dutton is the chief custodian at two schools, columbia elementary and the junior high.
7. The labor day parade began at the park across from the exchange national bank building and ended at the maryville city hall.
8. The sunday edition of valley news had an interesting article about shenandoah national park.
9. After we visited the lincoln memorial, we went to watch a session of the house of representatives.
10. I like american history, but p.e. and shop are my favorite subjects.

1. I rode my schwinn ten-speed to the store to buy some sunkist oranges, some ivory soap, and some windex window cleaner.
2. At all california public schools, two flags are displayed, the american flag and the california state flag.
3. In dance class, we learned the irish jig, the polish polka, and the italian tarantella.

CORRECT USAGE — CAPITAL LETTERS

Capitalizing Proper Nouns and Proper Adjectives

PRACTICE: Capitalizing Proper Nouns

Instructions: Using Rule 1, change small letters to capital letters where appropriate in the following sentences.

1. damone's house is on the northwest corner of pine street and shell avenue.

2. My father was born in tallahassee, florida; mother was born in york county, maine.

3. My best friend, amy, speaks french well because she lived for two years in paris, france.

4. The largest artificial lake in the world is lake mead, a reservoir formed by hoover dam in the colorado river.

5. The ural mountains in the u.s.s.r. form the boundary between the continents of europe and asia.

6. mr. dutton is the chief custodian at two schools, columbia elementary and the junior high.

7. The labor day parade began at the park across from the exchange national bank building and ended at the maryville city hall.

8. The sunday edition of *valley news* had an interesting article about shenandoah national park.

9. After we visited the lincoln memorial, we went to watch a session of the house of representatives.

10. i like american history, but p.e. and shop are my favorite subjects.

Capitalizing Proper Adjectives

RULE 2: *Capitalize proper adjectives* made from proper nouns; also capitalize trade names and other proper nouns used as proper adjectives. A proper adjective tells "what kind" about common nouns.

PRACTICE: Where appropriate in the following sentences, change lower-case letters to capital letters, using Rule 2.

1. I rode my schwinn ten-speed to the store to buy some sunkist oranges, some ivory soap, and some windex window cleaner.

2. At all california public schools, two flags are displayed, the american flag and the california state flag.

3. In dance class, we learned the irish jig, the polish polka, and the italian tarantella.

Steps to Good Grammar

CAPITALIZING FIRSTS

Review the Rule and examples orally with students, and answer any questions students may have about the Practice sentences.

1. "Brenda, I'm not at all sure," said Nancy, "that I can go ice-skating."
2. In the 1870's, a pioneer physician, Dr. Brewster M. Higley, wrote "A Home on the Range."
3. Aunt Helen remarked, "When I attended high school in the East, we were required to read The Mill on the Floss."
4. In January, I had the lead part in the one-act play, The Shock of His Life.
5. Jake said, "I'll probably go to college at U.C. Berkeley."

CORRECT USAGE — CAPITAL LETTERS

Capitalizing Firsts

RULE 3: *Capitalize these Firsts.*

A. *First word in a sentence:*

Turpentine comes from various pine trees.
Even the bark from pine trees can be used commercially.

B. *First word in a direct quotation:*

"I have found," said Abraham Lincoln, "that folks are just about as happy as they've made up their minds to be."
Louise asked, "Have you finished your homework, Mary?"

C. *First word in each line of traditional poetry:*

A bird came down the walk:
He did not know I saw;
He bit an angle-worm in halves
And ate the fellow, raw. — Emily Dickinson

D. *First word, only, in a letter closing:*

Very truly yours,   With love,

E. *First word and any nouns in a letter salutation:*

My dear Grandson,   Dear Sir:

F. *First and last and all important words within titles* of articles, themes, songs, short stories, poems, books, etc.:

The Little House on the Prairie
"The People Will Live On"
"A Home on the Range"
"How to Catch Fish — or Not!"

Reminder: Do not capitalize articles *(a, an, the)*, conjunctions *(but, and)*, or short prepositions *(in, on, at, for, to, by,* etc.) *within* a title.

PRACTICE: Using Rules 1, 2, and 3, change lower-case letters to capital letters where appropriate in the following sentences.

1. "brenda, i'm not at all sure," said nancy, "that i can go ice-skating."

2. in the 1870's, a pioneer physician, dr. brewster m. higley, wrote "a home on the range."

3. aunt helen remarked, "when i attended high school in the east, we were required to read *the mill on the floss.*"

4. in january, i had the lead part in the one-act play, *the shock of his life.*

5. jake said, "i'll probably go to college at u.c. berkeley."

Steps to Good Grammar

FINAL DRILL

Missionary (sentence 1), *national director* (sentence 9), and *scientist* (sentence 13) are not titles or designations given to just one person. They should not be capitalized.

Sentence 4: There are many kinds of oil and tires —Shell and Firestone are special kinds, used as proper adjectives in this sentence.

     G   *F*   *L*
1. "grandma," felicia asked, "did you say that your father was a lutheran missionary in the
   P   *I*
philippine islands?"

         K   *M*   *D*   *A*
2. In the koran, the sacred book of the moslems, the name of the deity is allah.

   I   *T H*   *N*   *I*
3. i am going to write a report on the book *the house with nobody in it.*

                S   *F*
4. My father always buys shell oil and firestone tires.

                S   *B*   *C*
5. I like this short story, "shortest boy in the class."

   M
6. my cousin says that his favorite school subjects are science, united states history, and spanish.

     G   *F*   *A*   *F*   *T*   *W*   *DCA*   *L*
7. On good friday, april 14, 1865, at ford's theatre in washington, d.c., abraham lincoln was

fatally wounded.

       K   *A*   *I*
8. Some of kareem's ancestors were apache indians.

   M
9. my aunt is a national director of the girl scouts of america.

               G   *J*   *H* *S*
10. On our way to garfield junior high school on the corner of elm avenue and willow street, we

drove east several blocks before turning north.

            T   *R*
11. In the book *tales to remember,* I read the short story, "ride fast from danger."

                   T   *D*
12. [lines of poetry]   "the sun that brief december day

                   R
                   rose cheerless over hills of gray."

—John Greenleaf Whittier

      I   *G*   *J*
13. The italian scientist galileo discovered that jupiter has moons traveling around it.

                          S   *C*   *C* *J*   *J* *M*
14. The prestige and power of the supreme court were raised by chief justice john marshall.

   M   *S*   *Y*
15. my dear sir: yours truly,

CORRECT USAGE — CAPITAL LETTERS

FINAL DRILL

Instructions: Where appropriate, change lower-case letters to capital letters.

1. "grandma," felicia asked, "did you say that your father was a lutheran missionary in the philippine islands?"

2. In the koran, the sacred book of the moslems, the name of the deity is allah.

3. i am going to write a report on the book *the house with nobody in it.*

4. My father always buys shell oil and firestone tires.

5. I like this short story, "shortest boy in the class."

6. my cousin says that his favorite school subjects are science, united states history, and spanish.

7. On good friday, april 14, 1865, at ford's theatre in washington, d.c., abraham lincoln was fatally wounded.

8. Some of kareem's ancestors were apache indians.

9. my aunt is a national director of the girl scouts of america.

10. On our way to garfield junior high school on the corner of elm avenue and willow street, we drove east several blocks before turning north.

11. In the book *tales to remember*, I read the short story, "ride fast from danger."

12. [lines of poetry]   "the sun that brief december day

    rose cheerless over hills of gray."

    —John Greenleaf Whittier

13. The italian scientist galileo discovered that jupiter has moons traveling around it.

14. The prestige and power of the supreme court were raised by chief justice john marshall.

15. my dear sir: yours truly,

© 1988, 1997 J. Weston Walch, Publisher

Steps to Good Grammar

TEST

Sentence 10: *Earth*, being referred to as a planet along with Venus, should be capitalized.

Grading suggestion: Deduct 1 point for each capital letter omitted or incorrectly inserted.

1. Jews revere the old testament in the bible; christians revere both the old and new testaments.

2. Both my dad and my uncle paul belonged to the boy scouts of america when they were young. they grew up in salt lake city, utah.

3. eighth-grade students at martinez junior high read the adventures of tom sawyer in their english classes.

4. Several stores in sun valley mall sell adidas shoes.

5. "hey, sis," called caitlin to her older sister, "do you have a copy of the call of the wild? I'm supposed to read it before we visit the jack london state park on friday."

6. my aunt brenda bought goodyear snow tires for her chevrolet pickup.

7. In 1981, the house of representatives and the senate ratified president reagan's appointment of the first woman, sandra d. o'connor, to the supreme court of the united states.

8. "When we're in the east," jimmy's mother said, "we'll definitely go to the top of the empire state building."

9. the ancient japanese art of self-defense, judo, was first included in formal competition at the 1964 olympics.

10. The planet venus is closer to the sun than earth is.

11. senator a. l. shelton will speak at the fourth of july celebration.

12. [lines of poetry] "before I built a wall I'd ask to know what I was walling in or walling out."

— Robert Frost

CORRECT USAGE — CAPITAL LETTERS

TEST

Instructions: Capitalize lower-case letters where appropriate.

1. jews revere the old testament in the bible; christians revere both the old and new testaments.

2. Both my dad and my uncle paul belonged to the boy scouts of america when they were young. they grew up in salt lake city, utah.

3. eighth-grade students at martinez junior high read *the adventures of tom sawyer* in their english classes.

4. Several stores in sun valley mall sell adidas shoes.

5. "hey, sis," called caitlin to her older sister, "do you have a copy of *the call of the wild*? i'm supposed to read it before we visit the jack london state park on friday."

6. my aunt brenda bought goodyear snow tires for her chevrolet pickup.

7. in 1981, the house of representatives and the senate ratified president reagan's appointment of the first woman, sandra d. o'connor, to the supreme court of the united states.

8. "When we're in the east," jimmy's mother said, "we'll definitely go to the top of the empire state building."

9. the ancient japanese art of self-defense, judo, was first included in formal competition at the 1964 olympics.

10. The planet venus is closer to the sun than earth is.

11. senator a. t. shelton will speak at the fourth of july celebration.

12. [lines of poetry]   "before i built a wall i'd ask to know

    what i was walling in or walling out."

— Robert Frost

Steps to Good Grammar

END PUNCTUATION

Emphasize the Understand paragraph.

Explain to students that around A.D. 600, writers began leaving spaces between their words to make it easier for their readers to understand their communications. In the sixteenth century, scholars finally succeeded in developing a system of punctuation that was generally accepted.

Students should be able to:

1. Describe or give examples of the three different types of sentences.

2. Distinguish between direct and indirect questions.

3. Recognize *what* and *how* used as introductory words in exclamations.

Gram says she used to scoff at the comic strip "Buck Rogers." She used to say, "What an imagination that author has! He lets it run away with him!"   Today, however, she doesn't scoff, since astronauts are using space equipment similar to what Buck used. She believes that someday there will be cities in space much like those pictured in the comic strip. Do you doubt this? "Don't scoff!" Gram will warn. "Progress often rides on the shoulders of an active imagination."

CORRECT USAGE — PUNCTUATION

End Punctuation

JUST IMAGINE! Earlywritinglookedlikethisbecausethewordswerewrittenwithnospacesbetween themandwithnopunctuationofanykind

UNDERSTAND: When you speak, your choice of words and the tone and pitch of your voice let your listener know your thoughts, moods, and feelings. When you write, you must depend upon punctuation marks to help your reader to understand your meaning.

Use of periods, question marks, and exclamation points to end sentences

PERIODS

A. To end a **declarative sentence** — a statement:

I really enjoy mystery stories. This one looks good.

B. To end an **imperative sentence** — a command or request:

Bring your books to class tomorrow. Don't forget.

(A strong imperative may end with an exclamation point, as explained below: Run!)

QUESTION MARKS

A. To end an **interrogative sentence** — a direct question:

Can you come with us? How soon can you be ready?

B. An indirect question, one that does not use a speaker's words, ends with a period:

Lori asked, "May I borrow that book?" (direct question)

Lori asked if she might borrow that book. (indirect question)

EXCLAMATION POINTS

A. To end an **exclamation** — an expression of strong feeling which may or may not be a complete sentence:

Run!   Such beautiful colors!   There's my ring!

B. Sentences that begin with *what* and *how* and do not ask questions are exclamations; end them with exclamation points:

What a lovely sunset!   How surprised I was!

PRACTICE: Read the following paragraph to get the meaning. Then read it a second time and insert appropriate end marks.

Gram says she used to scoff at the comic strip "Buck Rogers " She used to say, "What an imagination that author has   He lets it run away with him "   Today, however, she doesn't scoff, since astronauts are using space equipment similar to what Buck used   She believes that someday there will be cities in space much like those pictured in the comic strip   Do you doubt this   "Don't scoff "   Gram will warn   "Progress often rides on the shoulders of an active imagination "

Steps to Good Grammar

USING PERIODS IN ABBREVIATIONS AND NUMBERS

Emphasize the limited number of abbreviations used in formal writing.

Mention that the U.S. Postal Service has developed two-capital-letter abbreviations for the states, to use in addresses. Tell students they will be given a full list of ZIP Code state abbreviations on the next reproducible page.

Students frequently use the abbreviations listed in D. They should memorize the meanings. *Postscript* may be defined as a message or information added at the end of a letter, a book, an article, or the like.

Often *etc.* is incorrectly written as *ect.* Demonstrate the derivation of the abbreviation from the Latin original:

*et c*etera = etc.

Give special attention to *etc., vs., B.C., A.D.,* and *i.e.,* since they are used in the unit test. Point out the correct use of B.C. and A.D.:

- B.C. follows the date — 44 B.C.
- A.D. precedes the date — A.D. 982

1. Dr. and Mrs. L. P. Smith bought a rare book for $500.00. [five hundred]

2. The 5:00 P.M. plane from St. Louis is late.

3. Among the guests were Mr. John P. Souza and Ms. Mary L. Tune.

4. 5.5 is the decimal form of 5½.

5. Susie's address is 532 Ridgeway Ave., Alton, Ill.

6. Mr. and Mrs. Harold Sinton, Sr., met Mr. Harold Sinton, Jr., in St. Paul.

7. The U.S. Steel Co. has a branch office in St. Louis.

8. The abbreviation for *et cetera* is __etc.__ It means __and other things or and so forth.__

9. The abbreviation for *id est* is __i. e.__ It means __that is.__

10. The abbreviation for *versus* is __vs.__ It means __against.__

CORRECT USAGE — PUNCTUATION

Using Periods in Abbreviations and Numbers

A. **After an initial** that stands for a name:

R.O. Baldwin; J. Philip Gray; Louisa M. Bates

B. **After a title** used with a name:

Acceptable in formal writing before a name: Mr., Mrs., Ms., Dr., Prof., St. (Saint) (no period after Miss)
Acceptable in formal writing after a name: Sr., Jr.
Avoided in formal writing: Capt., Rev., Gov., Pres.

C. **Standard** but avoided in formal writing:

Streets: Ave., St., Blvd., Ct., Rd.   States: Calif., Mass.
Months, Days: Jan., Fri.   Firm names: Co., Inc., Ltd., Bros.

D. **Standard**, using only capital first letters; use a period after each letter, leave no space between:

U.S. — United States
U.S.N. — United States Navy
U.N. — United Nations
U.S.S.R. — Union of Soviet Socialist
        Republics
R.S.V.P. — (French) *Répondez s'il vous
        plait* — Please reply

B.C. — before the birth of Christ
A.D. — *anno Domini* — after Christ's birth
        ("in the year of the Lord")
A.M. — *ante meridiem* — before noon
P.M. — *post meridiem* — after noon
P.S. or p.s. — postscript

E. **After Latin words and phrases** written in lower-case letters:

i.e. — *id est* — that is
vs. — *versus* — against
etc. — *et cetera* — and so forth, and other things

e.g. — *exempli gratia* — for example
et al. — *et alii* — and others

F. **With numbers** to show decimals, and dollars and cents:

3.7 (three and seven tenths)
$5.50 (five dollars and fifty cents)

PRACTICE: Supply periods where they are needed in the following sentences.

1. Dr and Mrs L P Smith bought a rare book for $50000 [five hundred]

2. The 5:00 P M plane from St Louis is late

3. Among the guests were Mr John P Souza and Ms Mary L Tune

4. 5 5 is the decimal form of 5½

5. Susie's address is 532 Ridgeway Ave , Alton, Ill

6. Mr and Mrs Harold Sinton, Sr , met Mr Harold Sinton, Jr , in St Paul

7. The U S Steel Co has a branch office in St Louis

8. The abbreviation for *et cetera* is _____ It means _____

9. The abbreviation for *id est* is _____ It means _____

10. The abbreviation for *versus* is _____ It means _____

© 1988, 1997 J. Weston Walch, Publisher

Steps to Good Grammar

OMITTING PERIODS IN ABBREVIATIONS

This is mainly a resource page to which students may refer.

Point out that the U.S. Postal Service ZIP Code includes the two-letter state abbreviation and the ZIP Code number. No period is used after the state abbreviation, and no comma separates the state letters and the ZIP number: CT 06880.

Students often use the acronyms SADD, NASA, and ZIP. They should know what the letters stand for.

CORRECT USAGE — PUNCTUATION

Omitting Periods in Abbreviations

A.   It is becoming customary to write initial abbreviations of names of companies and organizations with no spaces or periods between them:

RFD — Rural Free Delivery
NFL — National Football League
PTA — Parent-Teacher Association
TWA — Trans World Airlines

B.   **Acronyms:** pronounceable words formed from the first letters of name words.

1.   Many organizations and agencies choose names that can become acronyms:

SADD — Students Against Drunk Driving
NASA — National Aeronautics and Space Administration
ZIP — Zone Improvement Plan
NATO — North Atlantic Treaty Organization

2.   Some acronyms have become regular words and do not use capital letters or periods:

scuba — *Self-contained Underwater Breathing Apparatus*
laser — *Light Amplification by Stimulated Emission of Radiation*
radar — *Radio Detecting and Ranging*
snafu — *Situation Normal, All Fouled Up*
awol — *Absent Without Leave*

C.   **U.S. Postal Service ZIP Code** state abbreviations; use no periods.

State	ZIP Code Abbrev.						
Alabama	AL	Louisiana	LA	Ohio	OH
Alaska	AK	Maine	ME	Oklahoma	OK
Arizona	AZ	Maryland	MD	Oregon	OR
Arkansas	AR	Massachusetts	MA	Pennyslvania	PA
California	CA	Michigan	MI	Rhode Island	RI
Colorado	CO	Minnesota	MN	South Carolina	SC
Connecticut	CT	Mississippi	MS	South Dakota	SD
Delaware	DE	Missouri	MO	Tennessee	TN
Florida	FL	Montana	MT	Texas	TX
Georgia	GA	Nebraska	NE	Utah	UT
Hawaii	HI	Nevada	NV	Vermont	VT
Idaho	ID	New Hampshire	NH	Virginia	VA
Illinois	IL	New Jersey	NJ	Washington	WA
Indiana	IN	New Mexico	NM	West Virginia	WV
Iowa	IA	New York	NY	Wisconsin	WI
Kansas	KS	North Carolina	NC	Wyoming	WY
Kentucky	KY	North Dakota	ND	District of Columbia	DC

© 1988, 1997 J. Weston Walch, Publisher

Steps to Good Grammar

QUESTION MARKS, EXCLAMATION POINTS, AND PERIODS — PRACTICE

Explain to students that the commas that have been used in the sentences are correct.

Sentences 3 and 4:

Exclamation points follow immediately the words that were exclaimed. Quotation marks are used *after* the exclamation point.

Question marks follow immediately the words that made up the question. Quotation marks are used *after* the question mark.

Announce test scheduled for the next day.

1. At 8:30 A.M. on Sat., Apr. 15, Mom went to a yard sale set up by Mrs. R. J. Duncan at 42 Elm Ave., Concord, Calif.

2. She bought a crystal bowl for $12.50 [twelve dollars and fifty cents] that she said was worth at least $50.00. [fifty dollars]

3. Suddenly she cried, "Look! The bowl is cracked!"

4. Dad said, "I noticed the crack. Didn't you?"

5. The abbreviation for *exempli gratia* is _e. g._ It means _for example._

6. The letters that are an abbreviation for "Please reply" are _R. S. V. P._

7. Write 12½ in decimals like this: _12.5_.

8. Most people know that *A.M.* means "before noon" and *P.M.* means "after noon."

9. D. M. Jones, Sr., is Ken's grandfather, and D. M. Jones, Jr., is Ken's father.

10. The acronym for Zone Improvement Plan is _ZIP._

11. The abbreviation for *et cetera* is not *ect.*; it is _etc._

12. The standard abbreviation for United States is _U.S._

13. Students at M. J. H. S. have recently organized a chapter of SADD, which means _Students Against Drunk Driving._

14. I learned recently that "Radio Detecting and Ranging" is the meaning of the acronym _radar_.

15. The head office of the Continental Baking Co., Inc., is Checkerboard Sq., St. Louis, MO 63164.

CORRECT USAGE — PUNCTUATION

Question Marks, Exclamation Points, and Periods — Practice

Instructions: Insert question marks, exclamation points, and periods where appropriate.

1. At 8:30 A M on Sat , Apr 15, Mom went to a yard sale set up by Mrs R J Duncan at 42 Elm Ave , Concord, Calif

2. She bought a crystal bowl for $1250 [twelve dollars and fifty cents] that she said was worth at least $5000 [fifty dollars]

3. Suddenly she cried, "Look   The bowl is cracked "

4. Dad said, "I noticed the crack   Didn't you "

5. The abbreviation for *exempli gratia* is _____ It means _____

6. The letters that are an abbreviation for "Please reply" are _____

7. Write 12½ in decimals like this: _____

8. Most people know that *A M* means "before noon" and *P M* means "after noon."

9. D M Jones, Sr , is Ken's grandfather, and D M Jones, Jr , is Ken's father.

10. The acronym for Zone Improvement Plan is _____

11. The abbreviation for *et cetera* is not *ect.*; it is _____

12. The standard abbreviation for United States is _____

13. Students at M J H S have recently organized a chapter of SADD, which means _____
    _____ _____ _____

14. I learned recently that "Radio Detecting and Ranging" is the meaning of the acronym _____

15. The head office of the Continental Baking Co , Inc , is Checkerboard Sq , St Louis, MO 63164

Steps to Good Grammar

TEST: PERIODS, QUESTION MARKS, AND EXCLAMATION POINTS

This reproducible page contains two copies of one half-page drill/test. Cut each duplicated page in half; give each student one half-page.

Grading suggestion:

1 point each written answer and each required mark of punctuation:

48 total points — deduct 2 points for each error.

1. "Stop that man**!** He took my purse**!**" shouted Miss Powell**.**

2. The correct abbreviation for *et cetera* is ___*etc.*___ , which means ___*{ and other things or and so forth }*___

3. I received this memorandum: Dr**.**C**.**D**.**Hughes will see you at 9:00 A**.**M**.**, in her office at 315 Main St**.**, on Fri**.**, Sept**.**8**.**

4. The last game of the season will be Miramonte ___*vs.*___ [Latin abbreviation for "against"] Alhambra **.**

5. Do most students know that *B.C.* means "___*Before the birth of Christ*___," and that *A.D.* means "___*after the birth of Christ*___"

6. Last month my sister earned $65**.**50 [sixty-five dollars and fifty cents] babysitting for Mr**.**J**.**C**.** Kelsey, Jr**.**

7. The head office of the Continental Baking Co**.**, Inc**.**, is Checkerboard Sq**.**, St**.**Louis, MO 63164**.**

8. Did you notice that Prof**.**Haines used *i.e.* very often in his lecture about the U**.**S**.**S**.**R**.?**

9. You may write 7½ as 7**.**5 in decimals**.**

10. Hurray**!** I've finished **!** *or* **.**

CORRECT USAGE — PUNCTUATION

TEST: Periods, Question Marks, and Exclamation Points

Instructions: Where appropriate, insert question marks, exclamation points, and periods; write words or abbreviations in the blanks to make a correct statement.

1. "Stop that man He took my purse " shouted Miss Powell

2. The correct abbreviation for *et cetera* is _____, which means _____

3. I received this memorandum: Dr C D Hughes will see you at 9:00 A M , in her office at 315 Main St , on Fri , Sept 8

4. The last game of the season will be Miramonte _____ [Latin abbreviation for "against"] Alhambra

5. Do most students know that *B.C.* means "_____ ," and that *A.D.* means " _____ "

6. Last month my sister earned $6550 [sixty-five dollars and fifty cents] babysitting for Mr J C Kelsey, Jr

7. The head office of the Continental Baking Co , Inc , is Checkerboard Sq , St Louis, MO 63164

8. Did you notice that Prof Haines used *i e* very often in his lecture about the U S S R

9. You may write 7½ as 75 in decimals

10. Hurray   I've finished

NAME _____ DATE _____ 295

CORRECT USAGE — PUNCTUATION

TEST: Periods, Question Marks, and Exclamation Points

Instructions: Where appropriate, insert question marks, exclamation points, and periods; write words or abbreviations in the blanks to make a correct statement.

1. "Stop that man He took my purse " shouted Miss Powell

2. The correct abbreviation for *et cetera* is _____, which means _____

3. I received this memorandum: Dr C D Hughes will see you at 9:00 A M , in her office at 315 Main St , on Fri , Sept 8

4. The last game of the season will be Miramonte _____ [Latin abbreviation for "against"] Alhambra

5. Do most students know that *B.C.* means "_____ ," and that *A.D.* means " _____ "

6. Last month my sister earned $6550 [sixty-five dollars and fifty cents] babysitting for Mr J C Kelsey, Jr

7. The head office of the Continental Baking Co , Inc , is Checkerboard Sq , St Louis, MO 63164

8. Did you notice that Prof Haines used *i e* very often in his lecture about the U S S R

9. You may write 7½ as 75 in decimals

10. Hurray   I've finished

© 1988, 1997 J. Weston Walch, Publisher

Steps to Good Grammar

COMMAS, RULES 1-4

In *Steps to Good Grammar,* students have not yet covered punctuation used with addresses or with dates.

Read and quiz students on their understanding of the items included in Rules 1 and 2.

Students should easily recognize nouns of direct address and appositives and remember the use of commas to set them off in a sentence. The review in Rules 3 and 4 should reinforce the students' understanding.

Remind students that they use a noun of address when writing a person's name as though they were speaking to the person.

Remind students that an appositive is a noun or pronoun that identifies or describes the word it follows.

1. At that time, Richard, we were living on a farm near Brush, Colorado. *(N.A.)*

2. Does Lisa now live at 2670 Platte Avenue, Lincoln, Nebraska?

3. The husky, an Eskimo dog used to pull sledges, looks rather like a wolf. *(appos.)*

4. Suzanne, please bring me my literature book, the one lying on my desk. *(N.A.)(appos.)*

5. That day, Easter Sunday, April 7 1996, it snowed. *(appos.)(appos.)*

6. I was born on _____ _____, _____ in _____, _____.
                    Month   Day Year   City   State

7. I try not to miss my favorite TV program, _____. *(appos.)*
                                                  Name it

8. I live here: _____ _____, _____, _____.
                 Number Street   City   State & ZIP

CORRECT USAGE — PUNCTUATION

Commas, Rules 1-4

Commas are used to indicate a slight separation in ideas, or in grammatical parts of a sentence. Follow these rules for using commas.

RULE 1: Separate **parts of an address** — number and street, city, state and ZIP:

Susie's address is 322 Toyon Way, Martinez, California 94553.
(or *Calif. 94553* or *CA 94553*).

RULE 2: Separate **parts of a date** — the month and day from the year; if a date is used in the middle of a sentence, a comma should follow the year (and precede the month and day if the date is an appositive):

On Thursday, *June 19, 1986,* I sent the information to her.

RULE 3: Separate a **noun in direct address (N.A.)** from the rest of the sentence:

N.A.
Please let me know, Alex, when you plan to arrive.
N.A.
Alex, please let me know when you plan to arrive.

RULE 4: Separate an **appositive (appos.)** from the rest of the sentence:

appos.
Do you know Eric O'Neill, the captain of our team?
appos.
The captain of our team, Eric O'Neill, is our leading scorer.

PRACTICE

Part I: Insert commas where needed; label **N.A.** and **appos.**; draw an arrow from an appositive back to the word it identifies.

1. At that time Richard we were living on a farm near Brush Colorado.

2. Does Lisa now live at 2670 Platte Avenue Lincoln Nebraska?

3. The husky an Eskimo dog used to pull sledges looks rather like a wolf.

4. Suzanne please bring me my literature book the one lying on my desk.

5. That day Easter Sunday April 7 1996 it snowed.

Part II: Fill the blanks in the following sentences; *use commas correctly.*

6. I was born on _____ _____ _____ in _____ _____.
                     Month   Day   Year   City   State

7. I try not to miss my favorite TV program _____.
                                         Name it

8. I live here: _____ _____ _____ _____.
            Number Street   City   State & ZIP

Steps to Good Grammar

COMMAS, RULES 5-7

The Practice sentences for Rule 5 graphically illustrate that correct use of punctuation helps a writer to communicate understandably.

1. Inside,
2. Far below,
3. Before,
4. The week before,
5. Soon after,

Rule 6 reinforces the students' understanding of material covered in Unit 8, Written Expression. Call attention to the Note items.

Rule 7 restates an idea presented in the previous study of adjectives.

1. We had baked beans, grilled steaks, and a tossed green salad for dinner.

2. Yes, I am sure Arturo is going.

3. No, I can't go.

4. Dad has friends living in Colorado, in Kansas, and in Oklahoma.

5. The cute little boy was hot, tired, and cranky.

CORRECT USAGE — PUNCTUATION

Commas, Rules 5-7

RULE 5:   Separate an **introductory** *yes, no, well, oh:*

Yes, they are planning to go.   Well, please think about it.

Note: Certain other introductory words and short phrases sometimes need commas to make the meaning clear to the reader:

By exercising, Ron built up his endurance.

PRACTICE: Add the necessary commas to the following sentences.

1.   Inside the Greek warriors were prepared to attack the Trojans.

2.   Far below the parachutists could see a tiny village.

3.   Before I could only do twelve push-ups.

4.   The week before Dad finished painting our house.

5.   Soon after the rain began.

RULE 6:   Separate three or more items used as **compound parts** of sentences:

John, Kyle, Loal, and Duncan went to the game.
Lief plays football, runs the quarter mile, and captains the basketball team.

Note: Use a comma before *and* in a series to show that the last item is as important as the earlier ones:

The colors of our flag are red, white, and blue.

Note: Use no commas where all items in a series are joined by *and* or *or*.

Three men, Mr. Wood *and* Mr. Davis *and* my dad, are being transferred. They will go to Georgia *or* Maryland *or* Pennsylvania.

RULE 7:   Separate **adjectives in a series** if *and* can be used sensibly between them; just two adjectives may make up a series:

I grew big, delicious tomatoes. (Here, "big *and* delicious" would be sensible.)
Tom jumped over the low picket fence (Here, "low *and* picket fence" would not be sensible.)
Does that frisky, playful, yipping little puppy belong to you?

PRACTICE: Insert necessary commas.

1.   We had baked beans grilled steaks and a tossed green salad for dinner.

2.   Yes I am sure Arturo is going.

3.   No I can't go.

4.   Dad has friends living in Colorado in Kansas and in Oklahoma.

5.   The cute little boy was hot tired and cranky.

© 1988, 1997 J. Weston Walch, Publisher

Steps to Good Grammar

DRILL: USING COMMAS

This reproducible page contains two copies of one half-page drill/test. Cut each duplicated page in half; give each student one half-page.

1. Our parakeet is a cheerful, friendly bird.

2. Oh, aren't you finished?

3. Alfred Nobel, the inventor of dynamite, *appos.* left five million dollars to finance prizes for achievements in physics, chemistry, medicine, literature, and the advancement of world peace.

4. Are you doing your homework, Lynn? *N.A.*

5. The sunburned, thirsty, hungry hikers came into view.

6. Jon, why aren't you eating your dinner? *N.A.*

7. Are Paul, Dennis, and Derek coming with us?

8. Yes, my brother is attending Tuskegee Institute.

9. Would you like chocolate cake or lemon pie or caramel pudding?

10. We had lemonade, ham and cheese sandwiches, cookies, and fruit for lunch.

CORRECT USAGE — PUNCTUATION

DRILL: Using Commas

Instructions: Apply rules for using commas; label **N.A.** and **appos.**; draw an arrow from the appositive to the word it identifies.

1. Our parakeet is a cheerful friendly bird.

2. Oh aren't you finished?

3. Alfred Nobel the inventor of dynamite left five million dollars to finance prizes for achievements in physics chemistry medicine literature and the advancement of world peace.

4. Are you doing your homework Lynn?

5. The sunburned thirsty hungry hikers came into view.

6. Jon why aren't you eating your dinner?

7. Are Paul Dennis and Derek coming with us?

8. Yes my brother is attending Tuskegee Institute.

9. Would you like chocolate cake or lemon pie or caramel pudding?

10. We had lemonade ham and cheese sandwiches cookies and fruit for lunch.

NAME _____ DATE _____ 301

CORRECT USAGE — PUNCTUATION

DRILL: Using Commas

Instructions: Apply rules for using commas; label **N.A.** and **appos.**; draw an arrow from the appositive to the word it identifies.

1. Our parakeet is a cheerful friendly bird.

2. Oh aren't you finished?

3. Alfred Nobel the inventor of dynamite left five million dollars to finance prizes for achievements in physics chemistry medicine literature and the advancement of world peace.

4. Are you doing your homework Lynn?

5. The sunburned thirsty hungry hikers came into view.

6. Jon why aren't you eating your dinner?

7. Are Paul Dennis and Derek coming with us?

8. Yes my brother is attending Tuskegee Institute.

9. Would you like chocolate cake or lemon pie or caramel pudding?

10. We had lemonade ham and cheese sandwiches cookies and fruit for lunch.

Steps to Good Grammar

COMMAS, RULES 8a & 8b

Rule 8a. **Introductory prepositional phrases**

1. Students should clearly understand that the prepositional phrases are introductory words that change the natural order of the sentence and, therefore, are set off by commas.

2. Emphasize using commas in the Practice sentences.

Sentence 5: Tell students that *huddled in our bunks* is a participial phrase used as an adverb that tells *how/where*. Participial phrases are covered in 8b.

Rule 8b. **Introductory participial phrases**

1. From their study of irregular verbs, students know that present participles end in *-ing* and that past participles end in *-d* or *-ed*.

2. Students should recognize the main sentence, the independent clause.

3. With instructions, students should realize that the participial phrases are, indeed, introductory words before each main sentence and, therefore, should be set off by a comma.

Sentence 4: Explain that *having* is a helping verb for *studied*, which is the past participle.

1. (Across the stream)(in a clump)(of aspen trees), we <u>saw</u> three deer.

2. (In the sunset's rosy-coral glow), the <u>countryside seemed</u> transformed.

3. (Among the branches)(of the willow trees), we <u>found</u> several nests.

4. (Down the narrow aisle)(between the trees), the stunt <u>pilot</u> <u>flew</u> her plane.

5. (During the lightning-flashing, thunder-rolling storm), we <u>sat</u> huddled in our bunks.

1. Entering the dark, dilapidated house, Joe walked cautiously. *Pres. Part.*

2. Annoyed by making so many errors, I resolved to work more carefully. *Past Part.*

3. Coming suddenly upon the strange man, we stopped dead in our tracks. *Pres. Part.*

4. Having studied regularly, Kara felt well-prepared for the test. *Past Part.*

5. While cleaning his room, Jacob found his "lost" report. *Pres. Part.*

CORRECT USAGE — PUNCTUATION

Commas, Rules 8a and 8b

RULE 8: Use a comma to separate **introductory words** that **change the natural order** of a sentence. (In *natural order,* the sentence begins with the subject and verb.)

a. **Prepositional phrases** of several words:

Early in the morning on Saturday, we started on our trip.

PRACTICE: Insert necessary commas. Then mark: verbs, subjects, prep. phrases. Label: **prep., O.P.**

1. Across the stream in a clump of aspen trees we saw three deer.

2. In the sunset's rosy-coral glow the countryside seemed transformed.

3. Among the branches of the willow trees we found several nests.

4. Down the narrow aisle between the trees the stunt pilot flew her plane.

5. During the lightning-flashing, thunder-rolling storm we sat huddled in our bunks.

b. **Participial phrases** — descriptive phrases that begin with the present participle (*walking*) or the past participle (*walked*) of a verb:

Standing beside the stream, I could see many trout.

Embarrassed by my little nephew's behavior, I decided not to take him shopping with me again.

PRACTICE: Insert necessary commas. On the blank at the end of each sentence, label the participle **Pres. Part.** or **Past Part.**

1. Entering the dark, dilapidated house Joe walked cautiously. _____

2. Annoyed by making so many errors I resolved to work more carefully. _____

3. Coming suddenly upon the strange man we stopped dead in our tracks. _____

4. Having studied regularly Kara felt well-prepared for the test. _____

5. While cleaning his room Jacob found his "lost" report. _____

Steps to Good Grammar

COMMAS, RULES 8c, 9, & 10

Rule 8c.   Introductory Dependent Clause

1. Point out that the word group introduced by the subordinate conjunction is not a complete sentence; it is a *dependent clause* that *depends* upon the *independent clause*, the complete sentence, for complete meaning.

2. In "Though she seemed calm," if *though* were left out, the remaining three words would be a complete sentence. The word *though* keeps the clause from being a complete sentence. Relate this fact to the five sentences in Practice.

3. Emphasize using a comma after an introductory dependent (subordinate) clause.

Rule 9.

Students have not previously received instruction regarding parenthetical words. However, the need to use commas to separate such words from the rest of the sentence should become obvious as they realize that the words are not necessary to express the meaning of the sentence.

Working through the Practice sentences should establish the principle.

Rule 10.

Students have previously studied the use of commas to separate parts of a compound sentence.

Emphasize the fact that the comma should be inserted *before* the conjunction. The first sentence actually ends before the conjunction. The comma replaces the period that would be used if the sentence were not compound.

Since the sentences contain only sentence parts the students have studied, you could have students analyze the complete sentences for review.

RULE 8:
1. [When] we left the house, we locked the door.
2. [Until] the rain stops, we really shouldn't leave.
3. [Because] Dad had warned us, we drove very carefully.
4. [As] the speaker droned on, I became sleepier and sleepier.
5. [If] we leave at once, we will probably arrive on time.

RULE 9:
1. By the way, your entry fee is due tomorrow.
2. Somehow, we all forgot our lunch money.
3. Just ahead, finally, we saw the cabin.
4. You are, I do believe, beginning to understand the concept.
5. Some students, on the other hand, still seem confused.

RULE 10:
1. Mom seemed angry, but she spoke quietly.
2. Most of the questions were easy, so I answered them quickly.
3. The early morning was fresh and clean, and drops of dew glistened in the sunlight.
4. Jennie and Alison prepared the report, and Jules typed the final copy.
5. Sarah arrived on time, but Michelle was late.

CORRECT USAGE — PUNCTUATION

Commas, Rules 8c, 9, & 10

RULE 8: Use a comma to separate **introductory words** that **change the natural order** of a sentence.

   c. **Dependent clauses** — word groups, introduced by subordinate conjunctions, that contain a subject and verb but are *not* complete sentences:

Though she seemed calm, Jill was really quite nervous.

Some subordinate conjunctions: **when, while, as, if, since, because, though, until, before.**

PRACTICE: Insert necessary commas. Mark: verbs, subjects; bracket subord. conjunctions.

1. When we left the house we locked the door.

2. Until the rain stops we really shouldn't leave.

3. Because Dad had warned us we drove very carefully.

4. As the speaker droned on I became sleepier and sleepier.

5. If we leave at once we will probably arrive on time.

RULE 9: Separate **parenthetical words** (words not really needed to express the complete meaning) from the rest of the sentence:

You remember, of course, that we leave at 8:00 A.M.

PRACTICE: Insert needed commas.

1. By the way your entry fee is due tomorrow.

2. Somehow we all forgot our lunch money.

3. Just ahead finally we saw the cabin.

4. You are I do believe beginning to understand the concept.

5. Some students on the other hand still seem confused.

RULE 10: Separate the **parts of a compound sentence** by using a comma *before* the conjunction.

Grandpa may be elderly, but he has plenty of energy.

PRACTICE: Insert needed commas. Mark: verbs, subjects.

1. Mom seemed angry but she spoke quietly.

2. Most of the questions were easy so I answered them quickly.

3. The early morning was fresh and clean and drops of dew glistened in the sunlight.

4. Jennie and Alison prepared the report and Jules typed the final copy.

5. Sarah arrived on time but Michelle was late.

COMMAS, RULES 11 & 12

Rule 11.

Students have studied the use of capital letters and end punctuation with sentences of conversation.

In the sentences in the sample paragraph, remind students of all the elements:

a. Use a comma after the speaker tag; capitalize the speaker's first word; place quotation marks outside the period ending the speaker's words.

b. Place quotation marks outside the comma; use a lower-case letter to begin the speaker tag; place a period after the tag.

c. Since the speaker tag interrupts the speaker's sentence, use one comma before the tag and one after the tag; use a lower-case letter on the first word that continues the speaker's sentence.

In the sentences in the Note:

a. Place the question mark and the exclamation point at the end of the speaker's words; place the final quotation marks outside the question mark and the exclamation point.

b. Use a period after the speaker tag.

Rule 12.

The use of a comma after the salutation and closing of a friendly letter is easy for students to remember.

Reminders:

1. Capitalize the first word and all nouns in a salutation.

2. Capitalize *only* the first word in a closing.

RULE 11:

1. "When you get home**,**" Mom said**,** "call me at the office."
   N.A.

2. "I hope you win**,** Heath**,** since I voted for you**,**" said June.

3. Art said**,** "Yes**,** I like fruit**,** apples**,** ⌒ *appos.* ⌒ peaches**,** plums**,** *appos* all kinds. "

4. "Hey**!**" shouted the policeman**.** "What's the rush**?**"
   N.A.

5. "Rosemary**,** " Ivy asked**,** "how did you like the science test**?**"

6. "I like your typing**,**" said Mr. Dean**.** "How is your spelling**?**" he then asked **.**

RULE 12:   My dear Cousin**,**

I will arrive at the train station on Friday**,** June 25**,** at 2 P**.**M**.**

Sincerely yours **,**

Balki

CORRECT USAGE — PUNCTUATION

Commas, Rules 11 & 12

RULE 11: In **conversation**, with a comma or commas, separate the words that tell who is speaking from the words the speaker says; start a new paragraph with each change of speaker:

    a. Jack said, "You may use this pencil."
    b. "That pencil looks very familiar," replied Bill.
    c. "Well," said Jack, chuckling, "it should. You lent it to me!"

Note: If the words spoken are a question or an exclamation, replace the comma with a question mark or an exclamation point:

"May I borrow a pencil?" asked Fred.
"What, again!" exclaimed the teacher.

PRACTICE: Insert commas and end punctuation where needed; label **N.A.** and **appos**. where appropriate.

1. "When you get home " Mom said "call me at the office."

2. "I hope you win Heath since I voted for you " said June.

3. Art said "Yes I like fruit apples peaches plums all kinds "

4. "Hey " shouted the policeman "What's the rush "

5. "Rosemary " Ivy asked "how did you like the science test "

6. "I like your typing " said Mr. Dean "How is your spelling " he then asked

RULE 12: Use commas after the **salutation and closing** of a friendly letter:

My dear Grandson,   Dear Marjorie,

Lovingly,   With love,

PRACTICE: Punctuate this short letter.

My dear Cousin

    I will arrive at the train station on Friday June 25 at 2 P M

                          Sincerely yours

                          Balki

Steps to Good Grammar

FINAL DRILL: COMMAS

As students proceed through the final practice, review with them the rules that apply to each sentence.

Remind students to review all the punctuation rules they have studied to prepare for the test the next day.

1. "Yes, Don, " said Todd, "Jason played in the first, second, and third quarters." *(N.A.)*

2. Adam grinned and blushed and cleared his throat, but he said nothing.

3. The salesman remarked, "Mrs. Scott, if you have a complaint about your order, you should write to Monarch Books, Inc., Clay St., San Francisco, CA 94210." *(N.A.)*

4. After the bell rang, three girls, Gayle, Lana, and Janis, left the room, but Donna stayed and finished her book report and, of course, talked with the teacher. *(appos.)*

5. Above, the U.S. Navy jets were flying in formation.

6. "Help!" Arnie screamed suddenly. "Call Dad!"

7. In the topmost branches of the maple tree, two frisky little squirrels seemed to be playing tag.

8. Are you, by any chance, planning to go with us to the dance?

9. We moved into this house three days before Christmas, Dec. 22, 1996. *(appos.)*

10. In writing a friendly letter, a person should always use a ___comma___ after the ___salutation___ and the ___closing___.

11. We'll go as soon as you are ready.

12. As soon as you are ready, we'll go.

13. Dad asked me, "Did you try out for the track team, Gwen?" *(N.A.)*

14. Dad asked me if I had tried out for the track team.

15. In my entire life, I had never seen a more bedraggled, thoroughly soaked, obviously exhausted group of children.

16. On our trip I sent Mom several postcards, and Dad called her on the phone several times.

17. The last performance, I thought, was the best of all.

18. Concerned over violating our curfew, we hurried as fast as we could.

19. The little girl was short, chubby, wide-eyed, and smiling.

20. When they finished the last sentence, the students sighed with relief!

CORRECT USAGE — PUNCTUATION

FINAL DRILL: Commas

Instructions: Insert all necessary commas, periods, question marks, and exclamation points; label **N.A.** and **appos.**

1. "Yes Don " said Todd "Jason played in the first second and third quarters."

2. Adam grinned and blushed and cleared his throat but he said nothing.

3. The salesman remarked "Mrs Scott if you have a complaint about your order you should write to Monarch Books Inc Clay St San Francisco CA 94210."

4. After the bell rang three girls Gayle, **Lana,** and **Janis** left the room but Donna stayed and finished her book report and of course talked with the teacher.

5. Above the U S Navy jets were flying in formation.

6. "Help " Arnie screamed suddenly "Call Dad "

7. In the topmost branches of the maple tree two frisky little squirrels seemed to be playing tag.

8. Are you by any chance planning to go with us to the dance

9. We moved into this house three days before Christmas Dec 22 1996.

10. In writing a friendly letter a person should always use a _____ after the

    _____ and the _____.

11. We'll go as soon as you are ready.

12. As soon as you are ready we'll go.

13. Dad asked me "Did you try out for the track team Gwen "

14. Dad asked me if I had tried out for the track team

15. In my entire life I had never seen a more bedraggled thoroughly soaked obviously exhausted group of children.

16. On our trip I sent Mom several postcards and Dad called her on the phone several times.

17. The last performance I thought was the best of all

18. Concerned over violating our curfew we hurried as fast as we could.

19. The little girl was short chubby wide-eyed and smiling.

20. When they finished the last sentence the students sighed with relief!

© 1988, 1997 J. Weston Walch, Publisher

Steps to Good Grammar

TEST: END PUNCTUATION AND COMMAS

Many of the sentences in the test have been adapted or taken exactly from sentences in the practice exercises.

Sentence 7: Students may insert a comma after the first prepositional phrase, "Across the stream." Using a comma there is optional. Do not count it.

Suggested grading — 75 points total:

-1, 99	-8, 89	-15, 80	-22, 71	-29, 61
-2, 97	-9, 88	-16, 79	-23, 70	-30, 60
-3, 96	-10, 87	-17, 77	-24, 68	-31, 59
-4, 95	-11, 85	-18, 76	-25, 67	-32, 57
-5, 93	-12, 84	-19, 75	-26, 65	-33, 56
-6, 92	-13, 83	-20, 73	-27, 64	-34, 55
-7, 91	-14, 81	-21, 72	-28, 63	-35, 53

1. We moved into this house three days before Christmas, Dec. 22, 1996. *(appos.)*

2. Lori asked, "May I borrow that book?" Then she asked if she might also borrow the bookmark.

3. You are, I do believe, beginning to understand.

4. "Dad, did you know that Mr. Dent, our coach, was born in Boise, Idaho?" Dan asked. *(N.A. / appos.)*

5. By stretching, Jerome managed to reach the top shelf.

6. Does that yipping, frisky, playful, little black pup belong to you?

7. Across the stream in a clump of aspen trees, we saw three deer.

8. Although she appeared very calm, Jill was really quite nervous.

9. I became sleepier and sleepier as the speaker droned on.

10. John, Kip, and Loal played baseball, ran a mile, and went swimming.

11. Mother seemed angry, but she spoke quietly.

12. "Mrs. Scott," remarked the salesman, "if you have a complaint about your order, you should write to Monarch Books, Inc., 481 Clay St., San Francisco, Calif. 94210." *(N.A.)*

13. Yes, I'm sure it was on Tues. Oct. 9, 1996 that my aunt and uncle and three cousins moved into their new house *(appos.)*

14. "Mom, I can't find my boots!" shouted Darrel. "I've looked in my closet, on the back porch, and in the garage." *(N.A.)*

15. Punctuate this friendly letter:

    Dear Kirsten,

    Mom, Dad, and I are driving up to the cabin on Tues. Aug. 12. I can hardly wait! See you soon.

    Love,
    Yvonne

CORRECT USAGE — PUNCTUATION

TEST: End Punctuation and Commas

Instructions: Insert all necessary commas, periods, question marks, and exclamation points; label **N.A.** and **appos.**

1. We moved into this house three days before Christmas Dec 22 1996.

2. Lori asked "May I borrow that book " Then she asked if she might also borrow the bookmark

3. You are I do believe beginning to understand

4. "Dad did you know that Mr Dent our coach was born in Boise Idaho " Dan asked

5. By stretching Jerome managed to reach the top shelf

6. Does that yipping frisky playful little black pup belong to you

7. Across the stream in a clump of aspen trees we saw three deer

8. Although she appeared very calm Jill was really quite nervous

9. I became sleepier and sleepier as the speaker droned on

10. John Kip and Loal played baseball ran a mile and went swimming

11. Mother seemed angry but she spoke quietly

12. "Mrs Scott " remarked the salesman "if you have a complaint about your order you should write to Monarch Books Inc 481 Clay St San Francisco Calif 94210 "

13. Yes I'm sure it was on Tues Oct 9 1996 that my aunt and uncle and three cousins moved into their new house

14. "Mom I can't find my boots" shouted Darrel "I've looked in my closet on the back porch and in the garage "

15. Punctuate this friendly letter:

    Dear Kirsten

    Mom Dad and I are driving up to the cabin on

    Tues Aug 12   I can hardly wait   See you soon

    Love
    Yvonne

Steps to Good Grammar

QUOTATION MARKS

Emphasize: Quotation marks used with conversation are placed around the speaker's words, *not* the speaker tag.

Rules 1, 2, and 3: Refer students to sentences in the introductory episode for examples of each rule and of the Reminders.

Practice the suggestion with students after reading and demonstrating Rules 1, 2, and 3.

To apply and check the students' understanding of these rules, dictate, one at a time, the sentences in the introductory paragraph. After students have written each sentence, read it again, including the marks of punctuation, so students can correct any errors they may have made.

Rule 5 — point out:

"Blunder" is set off with commas because it is an appositive.

A comma is not used before "Speed Adjustments" because the title is the LVC-A in the sentence.

CORRECT USAGE — PUNCTUATION

Quotation Marks

Mom said, "I'll be ready as soon as we've cleared the table."
"Take your time," Dad replied.
"I'm leaving!" shouted Erik.
"Wait!" called Heather. "Don't you want your lunch?" she asked.
Grabbing his lunch sack, Erik said teasingly, "You just saved my life, Sis."
"Son," Dad offered, "on our way to work, Mom and I can drop you off at school."
"Thanks just the same, Dad. I'm meeting Randy on the bus. We have to talk about our plans for the debate," Erik explained.

RULE 1: Use quotation marks to show the exact words of the speaker.

RULE 2: Separate the words that tell who is speaking, the speaker tag, from the spoken words:

    a. with a comma or commas: Mom said⬚"I'll be ready . . ."

                  "Take your time⬚" Dad replied.

                  "Son⬚" Dad offered⬚"on our way . . ."

    b. with a question mark or an exclamation point if the spoken words are a question or an exclamation:

             "Wait⬚" called Heather. "Don't you want your lunch⬚" she asked.

> **Reminders:** Place the quotation marks *outside* the other punctuation marks.
>
>   Use only one set of quotation marks to enclose several sentences spoken by the same speaker.

RULE 3: Begin a new paragraph with each change of speaker.

RULE 4: Use no quotation marks around an indirect quotation.

    Direct: Mary said, "I can't go."
    Indirect: Mary said that she can't go.

> **Suggestion:** In writing conversation, use a variety of verbs to show the speaker's exact meaning and tone of voice, in the paragraph above:
>
>   *said, replied, shouted, called, offered, explained*
>
>   *Said* used time after time is boring and not descriptive.

RULE 5: Use quotation marks around titles of short stories, paintings, poems, songs, themes, and published articles:

    This short story, "Blunder," is a good example of science fiction.
    The poem I memorized is "Speed Adjustments."

RULE 6: Use quotation marks

    around words purposely misused:

        It was truly a "fun" day.

    around unusual nicknames:

        Babe Ruth, "The Sultan of Swat," had arrived.

    (Quotation marks are not needed if *nicknamed* or *called* is used: Babe Ruth was called The Sultan of Swat.)

Steps to Good Grammar

QUOTATION MARKS — PRACTICE

Sentence 6: "How Superstitious Are You?" is the subject of the sentence. Point out to students that, because this title is the subject, no comma should follow it to separate it from the rest of the sentence.

On the Answer Key, the labels N.A., appos., and LVC-N are included for titles to substantiate the use, or nonuse, of commas.

Quiz students regarding these sentence parts and instruct the students to add the labels appropriately to the Practice sentences.

1. "Here I come! exclaimed Andre. Are you ready?"

2. "When school is out, suggested Gino, let's go swimming."

3. "You really did well on the test! exclaimed Clair.

4. Willa said that she would have to postpone her party.

5. This short story, "The Monkey's Paw, has been made into a play.   appos.

6. "How Superstitious Are You? is the title of an interesting article I read.

7. "Emily, have you seen my glasses? inquired Grandmother.

8. Jake's favorite short story is "The Ransom of Red Chief."   LVC-N

9. George Washington Carver said, "Ninety-nine percent of the failures come from people who have a habit of making excuses."

10. Ali promised, "I will go."

11. Ali promised he will go.

12. "Before you make up your mind, Mom advised, you should check with your father."

13. Lori memorized the short monologue, "The Punishment of Mary Louise."   appos.

14. "Know the location of the nearest fire alarm, said the fire chief.

15. "There goes my diet! exclaimed Dad as he dug into his chocolate sundae.

16. A United States senator once said, "Easy roads all seem to lead downhill."

17. "The game has begun! shouted David. "Both teams are playing hard."

18. Mom said, rather impatiently, "Alice, turn down the volume on the TV."   NA.

19. "I never think of the future, said Albert Einstein. "It comes soon enough.

20. My "easy" day at school included three tests and two pop quizzes.

CORRECT USAGE — PUNCTUATION

Quotation Marks — Practice

Instructions: Insert quotation marks, commas, periods, question marks, and exclamation points where appropriate.

1. Here I come exclaimed Andre Are you ready

2. When school is out suggested Gino let's go swimming

3. You really did well on the test exclaimed Clair

4. Willa said that she would have to postpone her party

5. This short story The Monkey's Paw has been made into a play

6. How Superstitious Are You is the title of an interesting article I read

7. Emily, have you seen my glasses inquired Grandmother

8. Jake's favorite short story is The Ransom of Red Chief

9. George Washington Carver said Ninety-nine percent of the failures come from people who have a habit of making excuses

10. Ali promised I will go

11. Ali promised he will go

12. Before you make up your mind Mom advised you should check with your father

13. Lori memorized the short monologue The Punishment of Mary Louise

14. Know the location of the nearest fire alarm said the fire chief

15. There goes my diet exclaimed Dad as he dug into his chocolate sundae

16. A United States senator once said Easy roads all seem to lead downhill

17. The game has begun shouted David Both teams are playing hard

18. Mom said, rather impatiently Alice turn down the volume on the TV

19. I never think of the future said Albert Einstein It comes soon enough

20. My easy day at school included three tests and two pop quizzes

© 1988, 1997 J. Weston Walch, Publisher

Steps to Good Grammar

UNDERLINING AND HYPHENS

Establish in students' minds the difference between the use of quotation marks to call attention to the titles of short stories, songs, poems, and so on, and of underlining for books, magazines, newspapers, and plays.

Read the rules and simultaneously quiz students about the use of hyphens to divide words from one line to the next. Instruct students to complete the Practice.

As you give correct divisions, students should correct any errors they may have made.

Read Hyphen Rules 2-4 and demonstrate on the chalkboard some of the hyphenated words.

A half-page of practice in using hyphens is on page 321.

1. _a_ murmur _mur-mur_
2. _b_ planned _planned_
3. _a_ teacher _teach-er_
4. _c_ enough _enough_
5. _a_ gorgeous _gor-geous_
6. _c_ cooky _cooky_
7. _a_ manuscript _man-u-script_
8. _b_ length _length_

CORRECT USAGE — PUNCTUATION

Underlining and Hyphens

Underlining:

In handwriting or typewriting, *underline* all words that are shown in italics in printing. These include:

RULE 1: **Titles** of books, magazines, newspapers, and plays:

<u>Jane Eyre</u>   <u>Time</u>   <u>Denver Post</u>   <u>Oliver</u>

RULE 2: **Names** given to special trains, ships or boats, and airplanes and spacecraft:

<u>Starlight Limited</u>   Robert Fulton's <u>Clermont</u>
<u>Sputnik I</u>   Charles Lindbergh's <u>Spirit of St. Louis</u>

RULE 3: **Words** referred to as words:

Try not to use *and* so often in your paragraphs.

Hyhens:

RULE 1: Use a hyphen to **divide a word** at the end of a line of writing.

    a. Divide a word only between syllables: *ac-com-mo-date*
    b. Do not divide a one-syllable word: *wrecked*
    c. Do not divide a word so that a single letter is placed at the end of the line, or at the beginning of the next line.

    PRACTICE: Divide each word below with hyphens; in the space before the word, write a, b, or c to show the rule that applies.

    Example: _*a*_ Columbus *Co-lum-bus* _*c*_ adopt _*adopt*_

    1. _____ murmur _____   5. _____ gorgeous _____
    2. _____ planned _____   6. _____ cooky _____
    3. _____ teacher _____   7. _____ manuscript _____
    4. _____ enough _____   8. _____ length _____

RULE 2: Use a hyphen to join the parts of a word with two or more parts:

Nouns: safe-conduct, by-line, self-control
Verbs: baby-sit, cross-question, double-date
Adjectives: color-blind, snow-capped, wind-blown
Made-up adjectives: a hard-to-please person, a six-year-old child
Adverbs: pell-mell, helter-skelter, self-confidently

RULE 3: Use a hyphen in writing certain number words:

    a. Compound numbers: sixty-seven, one hundred fifty-three
    b. A word beginning with a number:
        18-inch ruler or eighteen-inch ruler
        8-hour day or eight-hour day

RULE 4: Use a hyphen with a word beginning with a single capital letter:
X-ray, A-frame, T-shirt, U-turn

Steps to Good Grammar

APOSTROPHES

Rules 1 and 2:

Many possessive nouns have been used in sentences throughout *Steps to Good Grammar*. No specific rules have been stated. Instruct students to memorize the rules given here.

Call attention to the Reminder items.

As students insert the apostrophes appropriately in the Practice, have them explain their reasoning.

Rule 3:

Students should understand that when items need underlining — alphabet letters and words used as words—the apostrophe and *s* should not be underlined.

Rule 4:

Instruction has been given earlier about forming helping verb contractions with nominative pronouns. Remind students that the apostrophe is inserted where letters have been left out: *n't*.

A half-page of practice in using apostrophes is on page 321.

1. firemen _____firemen's_____
2. James _____James's_____
3. team _____team's_____
4. Indians _____Indians'_____
5. monkey _____monkey's_____
6. Danny _____Danny's_____
7. puppies _____puppies'_____
8. children _____children's_____
9. Joneses _____Joneses'_____
10. Frances _____Frances's_____

1. they are _____they're_____
2. does not _____doesn't_____
3. who has _____who's_____
4. cannot _____can't_____ (is)
5. it is _____it's_____
6. is not _____isn't_____
7. do not _____don't_____
8. did not _____didn't_____
9. have not _____haven't_____
10. will not _____won't_____
11. you are _____you're_____
12. there is _____there's_____

CORRECT USAGE — PUNCTUATION

Apostrophes

RULE 1: To form the **possessive of a singular noun,** write the noun and add *'s:*

Doris — Doris*'s* plan; boy — boy*'s* book

RULE 2: To form the **possessive of a plural noun,** write the plural noun:

a. if it ends in *s,* add only an apostrophe (*'*): girls*'* shoes; Kelleys*'* house

b. if the plural noun does not end in *s,* add apostrophe and *s* (*'s*), as with a singular noun: men*'s* suits; two deer*'s* tracks; women*'s* dresses

Reminder: *Never* use an apostrophe to write a simple plural noun: the boys' toys. *Never* use an apostrophe with a possessive pronoun: hers, ours.

PRACTICE: Beside each noun, write the possessive form to show ownership.

Example: friend *friend's house* the Smiths *the Smiths' house*

1. firemen _____
2. James _____
3. team _____
4. Indians _____
5. monkey _____

6. Danny _____
7. puppies _____
8. children _____
9. Joneses _____
10. Frances _____

RULE 3: Use an apostrophe and *s* (*'s*) to form **plurals of numbers, signs, alphabet letters, and words referred to as words;** for letters and words, underline the *item,* not the *'s.*

Numbers: Try to make your 9's look less like 7's.

Signs: Please don't use &'s; write *and* instead.

Letters: These may be *n*'s, but they look like *u*'s.

Words referred to as words: I counted a dozen *well*'s in his speech.

RULE 4: Use an apostrophe in **forming contractions;** a contraction combines two words by dropping some letters and inserting an apostrophe to take their place:

we have — we've   you are — you're   o'clock — of the clock
was not — wasn't   I am — I'm   let us — let's

PRACTICE: Write contractions of these words:

1. they are _____
2. does not _____
3. who has _____
4. cannot _____

5. it is _____
6. is not _____
7. do not _____
8. did not _____

   is

9. have not _____
10. will not _____
11. you are _____
12. there is _____

Steps to Good Grammar

UNDERLINING AND HYPHENATING PRACTICE

This reproducible page contains two different half-page drills. You may cut each duplicated page in half and give each student one-half page at a time, or you may distribute the entire duplicated page and work one drill at a time.

Underlining and Hyphenating Practice:

Work through this practice with students after going over page 317 on Underlining and Hyphens.

As students supply the necessary underlinings, instruct them to explain the reason — for example, "Underline the titles of plays and magazines to call them to the attention of the reader."

Instruct students to identify the part of speech of the hyphenated words:

Sentence 2: hyphenate the compound number, *seventy-three*, and the two-word adjective, *self-educated.*

Sentence 3: hyphenate the two-word adjective, *V-necked,* and the two-word noun, *T-shirts.*

Sentence 4: hyphenate the made-up adjective, good-to-the-last-page.

Apostrophe Practice:

Work though this practice with students after going over page 319 on Apostrophe usage.

┌─ Appos ─┐
1. I read a review of the play <u>The Diary of Anne Frank</u> in <u>Newsweek</u>.

2. Grandfather, who is seventy-three years old today, is a self-educated man.

3. Do you like V-necked T-shirts?

4. Matt says the story of the ship <u>Mary Jane</u> is really a good-to-the-last-page book.

5. In writing about an adventure, try not to use <u>well</u> and <u>well then</u> to connect your sentences.

Part II.   [strength]   military   carefully   waiting   borrow   [stretch]
                hospital   belief   disapprove   [awake]   hostess   [wrench]

1. Shouldn't there be four <u>s</u>'s, four <u>i</u>'s, and two <u>p</u>'s in *Mississippi?*

2. Don't many teachers use <u>+</u>'s instead of <u>C</u>'s to show a correct answer?

3. You're writing your <u>a</u>'s and <u>o</u>'s much more clearly now.

4. Aren't there supposed to be six <u>5</u>'s and five <u>6</u>'s in this column?

5. Haven't that child's <u>why</u>'s gotten on your nerves?

6. Wasn't that family's house destroyed in the fire?

7. The reason she couldn't go was that she hadn't been given permission.

8. I've found my book. Let's see if we can find yours.

9. Weren't all of those heroes' life stories printed in the newspaper?

10. The lion's roaring because it's gotten a thorn in its paw.

CORRECT USAGE — PUNCTUATION

Underlining and Hyphens — Practice

Part I. Instructions: Applying the rules, underline and hyphenate correctly the words in the following sentences.

1. I read a review of the play The Diary of Anne Frank in Newsweek.

2. Grandfather, who is seventy three years old today, is a self educated man.

3. Do you like V necked T shirts?

4. Matt says the story of the ship Mary Jane is really a good to the last page book.

5. In writing about an adventure, try not to use well and well then to connect your sentences.

Part II. Insert slashes in the following words where they may be divided between lines; put brackets around those that should not be divided.

| strength | military | carefully | waiting | borrow | stretch |
| hospital | belief | disapprove | awake | hostess | wrench |

CORRECT USAGE — PUNCTUATION

Apostrophes — Practice

Instructions: Insert apostrophes and underline where necessary.

1. Shouldnt there be four s s, four i s, and two p s in *Mississippi?*

2. Dont many teachers use + s instead of C s to show a correct answer?

3. Youre writing your a s and o s much more clearly now.

4. Arent there supposed to be six 5 s and five 6 s in this column?

5. Havent that childs whys gotten on your nerves?

6. Wasn't that familys house destroyed in the fire?

7. The reason she couldnt go was that she hadnt been given permission.

8. Ive found my book. Lets see if we can find yours.

9. Werent all of those heroes life stories printed in the newspaper?

10. The lions roaring because its gotten a thorn in its paw.

Steps to Good Grammar

FINAL DRILL: ALL PUNCTUATION

> This reproducible page contains two copies of one half-page drill/test. Cut each duplicated page in half; give each student one half-page.

Demonstrate to students the paragraph sign: ¶

Instruct students to label nouns in direct address, **N.A.**, and appositives, **appos.**, to explain the commas required to set them off.

1. "What a perfect day this is!" Wendy exclaimed. Then she asked, "Lenore, *N.A.* can you play tennis with Susie, Kim, and me?" ¶"Oh, Wendy, *N.A.* I'd really like to," Lenore replied, "but I have a dental appointment."

2. The lead article in the <u>Contra Costa Times</u> gave a by-line to the reporter.

3. Marjorie recited "Reverie," a fifty-line poem. *appos.*

4. Both boys' writing is improving, but their <u>n</u>'s still look like <u>u</u>'s.

5. All children's shoes are in the special sale.

6. In the Browns' garage we found all the <u>National Geographic</u> magazines published since 1944.

7. The thirty-one happy-go-lucky children finally settled down.

Part II.

[brought]   dis|arrange   [asleep]   be|tween   mis|take   care|less|ly   [grouchy]

CORRECT USAGE — PUNCTUATION

FINAL DRILL: All Punctuation

Part I. Instructions: Insert necessary commas, periods, question marks, exclamation points, quotation marks, ¶'s, hyphens, underlining, and apostrophes.

1. What a perfect day this is   Wendy exclaimed   Then she asked   Lenore can you play tennis with Susie Kim and me   Oh Wendy Id really like to Lenore replied but I have a dental appointment

2. The lead article in the Contra Costa Times gave a by line to the reporter.

3. Marjorie recited Reverie a fifty line poem

4. Both boys writing is improving but their n s still look like u s.

5. All childrens shoes are in the special sale.

6. In the Browns garage we found all the National Geographic magazines published since 1944.

7. The thirty one happy go lucky children finally settled down.

Part II. Mark the following words where they may be divided between lines; put brackets around the ones that should not be divided.

brought   disarrange   asleep   between   mistake   carelessly   grouchy

NAME _____ DATE _____ 323

CORRECT USAGE — PUNCTUATION

FINAL DRILL: All Punctuation

Part I. Instructions: Insert necessary commas, periods, question marks, exclamation points, quotation marks, ¶'s, hyphens, underlining, and apostrophes.

1. What a perfect day this is   Wendy exclaimed   Then she asked   Lenore can you play tennis with Susie Kim and me   Oh Wendy Id really like to Lenore replied but I have a dental appointment

2. The lead article in the Contra Costa Times gave a by line to the reporter.

3. Marjorie recited Reverie a fifty line poem

4. Both boys writing is improving but their n s still look like u s.

5. All childrens shoes are in the special sale.

6. In the Browns garage we found all the National Geographic magazines published since 1944.

7. The thirty one happy go lucky children finally settled down.

Part II. Mark the following words where they may be divided between lines; put brackets around the ones that should not be divided.

brought   disarrange   asleep   between   mistake   carelessly   grouchy

Steps to Good Grammar

FINAL TEST: ALL PUNCTUATION

This reproducible page contains two copies of
one half-page drill/test. Cut each duplicated
page in half; give each student one half-page.

Grading suggestions:

1 point: each pair of quotation marks
-½ point for one omitted
1 point: each word in syllabication
-½ point: comma or end punctuation outside
quotation marks

Total points: 62

Use the grading scale for 62 points on page 184.

1. When the teacher asked the question, Katie said, "I know the answer." "I do, too!" exclaimed
   Lisa. ¶ "All right, Katie," said the teacher, "let's hear yours first." ¶ "Oh," replied Katie, "why not
   have Lisa answer this one? I'll take the next one."
2. A suspense-filled play, The Pharmacist's Mate, is in our Projections in Literature book.
3. I've memorized a poem titled "Speed Adjustments."
4. My absent-minded brother doesn't care that his l's look like t's.
5. Did Joe say that the Smiths' car was wrecked last night?
6. All men's suits are on special sale.
7. Dad reads the Tribune and Time magazine regularly.
8. I couldn't believe I said twenty-one wells in my speech.
9. The lion's roaring because it's gotten a thorn in its paw.

Part II.   [strength]   mil|i|tary   [alone]   host|ess   dis|ap|prove   [creaky]   com|mu|ni|cate

CORRECT USAGE — PUNCTUATION

FINAL TEST: All Punctuation

Part I. Instructions: Insert necessary commas, periods, question marks, exclamation points, quotation marks, ℋ's, hyphens, underlining, and apostrophes.

1. When the teacher asked the question, Katie said   I know the answer   I do, too   exclaimed Lisa   All right, Katie   said the teacher   lets hear yours first   Oh replied Katie   why not have Lisa answer this one   Ill take the next one

2. A suspense filled play The Pharmacists Mate is in our Projections in Literature book

3. Ive memorized a poem titled Speed Adjustments

4. My absent minded brother doesnt care that his l s look like t s.

5. Did Joe say that the Smiths car was wrecked last night

6. All mens suits are on special sale.

7. Dad reads the Tribune and Time magazine regularly.

8. I couldnt believe I said twenty one wells in my speech.

9. The lions roaring because its gotten a thorn in its paw.

Part II. Mark the following words where they may be divided between lines; put brackets around those that should not be divided.

     strength   military   alone   hostess   disapprove   creaky   communicate

CORRECT USAGE — PUNCTUATION

FINAL TEST: All Punctuation

Part I. Instructions: Insert necessary commas, periods, question marks, exclamation points, quotation marks, ℋ's, hyphens, underlining, and apostrophes.

1. When the teacher asked the question, Katie said   I know the answer   I do, too   exclaimed Lisa   All right, Katie   said the teacher   lets hear yours first   Oh replied Katie   why not have Lisa answer this one   Ill take the next one

2. A suspense filled play The Pharmacists Mate is in our Projections in Literature book

3. Ive memorized a poem titled Speed Adjustments

4. My absent minded brother doesnt care that his l s looks like t s.

5. Did Joe say that the Smiths car was wrecked last night

6. All mens suits are on special sale.

7. Dad reads the Tribune and Time magazine regularly.

8. I couldnt believe I said twenty one wells in my speech.

9. The lions roaring because its gotten a thorn in its paw.

Part II. Mark the following words where they may be divided between lines; put brackets around those that should not be divided.

     strength   military   alone   hostess   disapprove   creaky   communicate

© 1988, 1997 J. Weston Walch, Publisher

Steps to Good Grammar